The Ethics (

MW00779455

In *The Ethics of Migration: An Introduction*, Adam Hosein systematically and comprehensively examines the ethical issues surrounding the concept of immigration. The book addresses important questions, such as:

- Can states claim a right to control their borders and, if so, to what extent?
- Is detention ever a justifiable means of border enforcement?
- Which criteria may states use to determine who should be admitted into their territory and how do these criteria interact with existing hierarchies of race and gender?
- Who should be considered a refugee?
- Which rights are migrants who are present in a territory entitled to?
- Is there an acceptable way to design a temporary worker program?
- When, if ever, are amnesties for unauthorized migrants appropriate?

Featuring case studies throughout, this textbook provides a philosophical introduction to an incredibly topical issue studied by students within the fields of political philosophy, applied ethics, global studies, politics, law, sociology, and public policy.

Adam Hosein is Associate Professor of Philosophy at Northeastern University, USA.

The Ethics of ...

When is it right to go to war? What are the causes of poverty? Are human intelligence and machine intelligence the same? What is cyber-terrorism? Do races exist? What makes a person a refugee?

Each engaging textbook from *The Ethics of...* series focuses on a significant ethical issue and provides a clear and stimulating explanation of the surrounding philosophical discussions. Focusing on moral debates at the forefront of contemporary society they have been designed for use by students studying philosophy, applied ethics, global ethics and related subjects such as politics, international relations and sociology. Features to aid study include chapter summaries, study questions, annotated further reading and glossaries.

The Ethics of War and Peace
An Introduction
Second Edition
Helen Frowe

The Ethics of Global Poverty
An Introduction
Scott Wisor

The Ethics of Surveillance
An Introduction
Kevin Macnish

The Ethics of Climate Change
An Introduction
Byron Williston

The Ethics of Development
An Introduction
David Ingram and Thomas Derdak

The Ethics of Migration
An Introduction
Adam Hosein

The Ethics of Migration

An Introduction

Adam Hosein

Routledge
Taylor & Francis Group

LONDON AND NEW YORK

First published 2019
by Routledge
2 Park Square, Milton Park, Abingdon, Oxon OX14 4RN

and by Routledge
52 Vanderbilt Avenue, New York, NY 10017

Routledge is an imprint of the Taylor & Francis Group, an informa business

© 2019 Adam Hosein

British Library Cataloguing-in-Publication Data
A catalogue record for this book is available from the British Library

Library of Congress Cataloging-in-Publication Data
Names: Hosein, Adam (Adam Omar), author.
Title: The ethics of migration : an introduction / Adam Hosein.
Description: Abingdon, Oxon ; New York, NY : Routledge, 2019. |
Series: The ethics of... | Includes bibliographical references and index.
Identifiers: LCCN 2018060402| ISBN 9781138659513 (hardback : alk. paper) |
ISBN 9781138659520 (pbk. : alk. paper) | ISBN 9780429029455 (ebk.)
Subjects: LCSH: Emigration and immigration--Moral and ethical aspects. |
Emigration and immigration--Social aspects. | Emigration and
immigration--Government policy.
Classification: LCC JV6035 .H67 2019 | DDC 172/.1--dc23
LC record available at https://lccn.loc.gov/2018060402

ISBN: 978-1-138-65951-3 (hbk)
ISBN: 978-1-138-65952-0 (pbk)
ISBN: 978-0-429-02945-5 (ebk)

Typeset in Times New Roman
by Taylor & Francis Books

To my immigrant family – Dorothy, Ian, Sarah, and Rory Hosein – with love.

Contents

Acknowledgments

I have been extremely fortunate to receive a lot of help over the years in this field and with this manuscript specifically. Michael Blake first convinced me that I might have something useful to contribute to immigration studies and gave me a lot support, intellectually and otherwise. I also owe a special thanks to Adam Cox, because a significant part of the book is drawn from work that we did together, and in many other places from conversations I was lucky to have with him. The project benefitted enormously from the expertise of José Jorge Mendoza. Shelley Wilcox shared her wisdom at multiple points in the process. I received very useful comments on parts of the manuscript from Serena Parekh and Caleb Yong. I am very grateful to Joseph Carens for generously reading earlier work of mine that has made it into the book. Large parts of the general discussion of global justice are drawn from work sagely overseen by Joshua Cohen and Rae Langton. And I owe a huge thanks to Sally Haslanger for many related discussions and for always being there for me.

I have also been very grateful for conversations with Crispino Akakpo, Mahrad Almotahari, Esma Baycan, Jan Brezger, Gillian Brock, Barbara Buckinx, Andreas Cassee, Amandine Catala, Joyce Chen, Helena de Bres, Candice Delmas, Helder De Schutter, Helen Frowe, Randall Hansen, Chris Heathwood, Mike Huemer, Eszter Kollar, Mitzi Lee, David Mapel, Laure Marest, Alastair Norcross, Martha Nussbaum, Kieran Oberman, Kristi Olson, David Owen, Alex Sager, Stephanie Silverman, Sarah Song, Christine Straehle, David Strauss, Philippe van Parijs, and Kit Wellman. I am also extremely indebted to Henry Shull for superb research assistance.

My greatest thanks are to my family, the fundamental basis for all of my ideas and motivation and to whom this book is dedicated.

The field of immigration ethics has exploded in the last 5–10 years, and I apologize to the many people doing important work that I was not able to include in this brief survey. I hope some readers will use the book as a launchpad into a growing literature with many exiting research projects. I would like to acknowledge that there are other major limitations of the book—largely because of the narrowness of my own abilities and learning; though sometimes because of the shape of the literature itself – including its skew toward the Anglophone world, its inclusion mainly of authors from the developed world, and the restricted range of topics discussed. May others do better.

Introduction

A. Immigration, ethics, and philosophy

A politician gives a TV interview on the topic of immigration, an issue of crucial importance to voters. The interviewer probes some of the politician's claims about why certain migrants are leaving their home countries: is it mainly political crisis, or is it the pull of jobs? They also discuss the impact of migration: will it buffer or burden the local welfare state? Each tries to cite some evidence in favor of their view, such as anecdotes about why certain people chose to migrate. Sociologists, economists, geographers, and so on try to answer these questions more rigorously and systematically: they compile larger quantities of data, and they attempt to build sophisticated theories to make sense of the data. We might call these "empirical" disciplines: those concerning what happens and why.

Suppose the TV interview now takes a slightly different turn. The politician says the government should deport all unauthorized migrants in the territory because those migrants have done wrong and deserve to be removed. The interviewer responds that some of those migrants have been present for decades. That doesn't matter, says the politician – if you choose to break the law, you have to bear the consequences. But, the interviewer responds, did they really have choices given what their country was like when they left? The politician replies, the interviewer responds, and so it continues....

This debate cannot be (fully) resolved by doing an economic or sociological study. The politician and interviewer are having a *moral* disagreement about which behaviors are wrong and what the correct response is to wrongdoing, and it is here that philosophers have something to contribute to the immigration debate. Notice that the politician and interviewer are engaged in the natural practice of making arguments for their perspectives: explaining their views and trying to support those views with *reasons*. Philosophers take that practice and try to carry it out more rigorously and systematically. Fundamentally, they look at whether the reasons people offer genuinely do support their views and whether there are alternative arguments that might support or tell against those views.

Now, sometimes the reasons people give for their preferred policy choices are in fact empirical, but other times they are not. This makes the study of immigration inherently interdisciplinary. In this book we'll try to separate out what can be resolved through purely philosophical reflection and what requires further empirical study. However, even where an issue needs to be turned over to, say, the sociologists, philosophers still have something important to contribute. They can help us work out which empirical questions we need to be asking and thus guide future research in the empirical disciplines. For example, after thinking philosophically about racial profiling in immigration, we might find that we need to know more about whether profiling makes people more fearful of the state.

This book examines arguments for different moral views about public policy, and some people are rather skeptical about the value of arguments in this area. We live in a world (actually the world has likely always been this way) where people do not always, or even frequently, make political decisions based on arguments. This may be especially true of political decision-making in the area of immigration. There are also philosophers (comparatively few, in fact, but some) who are skeptical about the value of moral arguments on more principled grounds. Nihilists, for instance, think that arguments are pointless because there are no moral constraints at all on human action or policy.

This is not the place to get deep into hard philosophical questions about the basic nature of morality,[1] but I hope you'll agree that on reflection, the practice of making and listening to arguments seems valuable. Even if in the abstract the existence of morality can seem puzzling, few people would disagree that at least some migration policies are clearly unjust. Just think of the forced migration that was the basis for slavery in the United Kingdom and its colonies. Or suppose you were stopped at a border and refused entry even though you held a passport for that country or a document explicitly granting you asylum there. Wouldn't you feel not just upset or angry but also *wronged, resentful* at your *mistreatment*? To feel these ways is not simply to be upset: it is to have a sense of being morally *wronged*. Likewise, some people in the modern world feel deeply mistreated by increases in immigration, which, they think, damage their wages and their culture. These people, too, are not merely unhappy about these effects: they think their state and their citizens are *letting them down* in some way, *wronging* them by ignoring their interests. If it is possible for people to be wronged by the immigration branches of the state, then it is important to know whether current policies do so or not. And to figure that out, we need to consider the extent to which current policies resemble, morally speaking, the ones we think are plainly unacceptable: we need arguments.

Now, offering and listening to arguments might not be the *only* acceptable way to collectively consider issues of migration. Perhaps, for instance, sharing personal narratives about migration, or being affected by migration, can help societies respectfully come to agreement on immigration policy. For our purposes, what matters is that arguments plausibly have *some* important role to play in finding such agreement. And even if debate over immigration sometimes falls well short of a quest for the moral truth, we can try to do better.

B. Methodological issues

Arguments require assumptions: in making them, we start from certain premises and try to use those to draw conclusions. The idea is that by starting with things that we feel fairly sure of, we can figure out what to think about matters we are less sure of. We need to decide, then, what our starting points will be. Hopefully the assumptions made in this book will seem at least somewhat plausible to most readers. They are drawn from sources that are often cited for their moral (sometimes legal but also moral) authority, such as the constitutions of various liberal democracies and major United Nations conventions, and also examples of policies that have been widely condemned or celebrated. But, of course, not everyone shares these values. In some places the book also explores where alternative values might lead someone to different conclusions. Where you find yourself in disagreement with the basic values assumed, you will have a good opportunity to either reevaluate your own perspective or gain a greater understanding of where other people might be going wrong. Even if you agree with a lot of the assumptions, there will almost certainly be something in here that you think is deeply wrong. There may even be views that you find offensive. In all of these cases, there is hopefully still something to be gained in terms of reflection on what you think. Even if you don't end up changing your own views much, you will at least hopefully have a better idea about how to respond to people with whom you disagree.

Another important question that comes up in moral thinking about immigration is how idealistic we should be. Should we spend our time trying to figure out what migration would look like in a perfect world? Or should we instead focus on what can be realistically achieved right now, given constraints of, for instance, bureaucratic capacity and political trends? There has been a lot of philosophical debate about this issue of whether it is better to do (so-called) ideal theory or non-ideal theory (Stemplowska and Swift 2012), and different theorists of migration have tended more in one direction or the other (Gibney 2004, 15–19).

One point to notice about this debate is that really there is no simply binary contrast between ideal and non-ideal approaches. It's more likely that there is a continuum of some kind between more and less ideal approaches. Almost all theories make some assumptions about what is possible, but they differ in how strict these assumptions are. At one end of the continuum, theories assume a relatively narrow range of options given the current political climate and balance of power between parties. At the other end of the continuum are theories that consider options involving significant changes in human motivation or a world with no states.

A second suggestion: maybe we don't have to choose which way is best? In this book, we'll look at both some relatively utopian proposals – such as a world with no borders at all, with unlimited freedom of movement – and also some proposals that could be more readily implemented – such as incremental changes intended to prevent domestic abuse of unauthorized migrants. Perhaps it is worth looking at each kind of proposal: the utopians challenge us to reconsider whether we have been taking for granted features of the world that are in fact deeply unjust and that we should try, at least in the long run, to change, while the more practical proposals challenge us to face difficult trade-offs that are forced on us by (say) political realities and connect theorizing more closely to present-day political advocacy, activism, and so on. In any case, hopefully by the end of the book you will be able to decide for yourself whether you find more value in some kinds of theorizing than in others – whether they are more or less idealized in their approach – and whether you think there is some value in all of the different approaches.

C. Scope and limitations

As alluded to earlier, migration is a vast topic in philosophy, even if we exclude all of the relevant work in other disciplines. This means that a book, especially an introductory book, can only touch on so much. Here are some ways in which the discussion will be circumscribed.

First, we will be mostly considering migration *policy* and looking at other moral questions – for instance, if and when it is wrong for an individual to cross a border without legal authorization – only insofar as they are relevant to policy questions. Some recent authors have criticized this "methodological nationalism": see Sager (2018) for further discussion.

Second, we will primarily look at migration that is at least somewhat voluntary. This means excluding many issues of forced migration. Historically, of course, huge numbers of people have been forced to cross borders, most obviously during the transatlantic slave trade. In the contemporary world there is substantial human trafficking. We will look at people – especially refugees – who leave their home countries because of unliveable conditions, but not people who are kidnapped or forced at gunpoint into moving.

Third, we will be looking primarily at *international* migration, across the political borders of nation-states. This leaves out a large amount of *internal* migration – within the boundaries of particular states – such as the large flows of people from more rural to more urban areas in countries such as China and Brazil.

Fourth, while there are some examples from around the world, we will mainly look at migration to more developed countries, such as Australia, Germany, and the United States. To some extent this can be justified by the fact that migration flows to these countries are especially strong: in 2010, more than 10 percent of the populations of more-developed countries was, on average, made up of migrants. The same figure for less-developed countries was under 3 percent. These numbers hide some crucial further variations, however. For instance, refugees are very much concentrated in certain less-developed countries. In the end, the focus on more-developed countries is simply a facet of much of the literature that we will survey – no doubt in part because the "major" journals largely accept papers written by people in those countries, often non-immigrants – and as we go through that literature it is worth asking whether this focus distorts those theories.

The book is divided into three main parts. Part I looks at debates about how "open" state borders should be: to what extent migrants should be able to enter a territory without impediment. We'll consider arguments for open and for "closed" borders, such as the fiscal impact of immigration on receiving countries and the place of immigration in addressing global inequality. Then we'll look at the enforcement mechanisms states use to close their borders, such as border guards and detention facilities.

Assuming that states are going to put some limits on immigration, they will have to come up with selection criteria for who gets to enter (as well as who gets to ultimately naturalize in the receiving country). For example, should they give special preference to people with family ties to existing members of society? Or people with ethnic ties to the society? Or refugees? Part II evaluates potential selection criteria, including ways of defining refugees. Part III looks at the rights and obligations of people who have migrated to a territory but are not citizens, including permanent residents, temporary workers, and unauthorized migrants. Can temporary workers be denied the ability to vote while they are present? Should unauthorized migrants ever be granted an "amnesty," giving them the right to stay in the state indefinitely?

The fact that the book is divided into these three parts should not make the reader think that the issues in each part are divorced from one another. In fact, the book finds many cases where they seem to be interrelated. For example, if we want to think about how many immigrants a state should admit, we need to think about how those immigrants are going to be selected and also what rights they will have when they enter.

Finally, some terminological notes are useful. Immigration laws sometimes distinguish between "immigrant" and "non-immigrant" "aliens." For our purposes, the term "alien" will be dropped, and "immigrant" and "migrant" will be used, interchangeably, to refer to anyone who has crossed a border or is attempting to do so. "Latinx" will be used in place of "Latino" for its gender inclusivity.[2] Countries to which people move will be called "receiving countries," and the places from which they move will be called "home" or "sending" countries. "Unauthorized" is used in place of "undocumented" or "illegal." Sometimes "native" will be used to refer to members of a society who are not part of an immigrant group, but I hope this will not give the impression that immigrant groups are not full members of a society or that there is no difference between indigenous groups (such as First Nations peoples in Canada) and the descendants of later settlers. Terminology is itself a matter of important moral debate in the politics of immigration, and you are very welcome to question the choices I have made—some will be controversial on the left and others on the right – I just flag them here to make the reader aware of them. (In Chapter 8, I discuss in greater detail the significance of some of these terms.)

Notes

1   For that you will need to look at a book on "metaethics" such as Van Roojen (2015).
2   For discussion, see Ramirez and Blay (2017).

References

Gibney, Matthew J. 2004. *The Ethics and Politics of Asylum: Liberal Democracy and the Response to Refugees.* Cambridge: Cambridge University Press.

Ramirez, Tanisha Love, and Zeba Blay. 2016. "Why People Are Using the Term 'Latinx.'" *Huffington Post*, July 5, 2016. https://www.huffingtonpost.com/entry/why-people-are-using-the-term-latinx_us_57753328e4b0cc0fa136a159.

Sager, Alex. 2018. *Toward a Cosmopolitan Ethics of Mobility: The Migrant's-Eye View of the World.* Cham, Switzerland: Palgrave Macmillan.

Stemplowska, Zofia, and Adam Swift. 2012. "Ideal and Nonideal Theory." In *The Oxford Handbook of Political Philosophy*, edited by David Estlund, 373–392. New York: Oxford University Press.

Van Roojen, Mark. 2015. *Metaethics: A Contemporary Introduction.* New York: Routledge.

Part I

The regulation of borders

In this part of the book, we will look at the "open borders debate": the debate over whether it is permissible at all for states to restrict people's movement into their territory. Along the way we'll also look at arguments for increasing (and restricting) immigration in a more incremental fashion.

1 Arguments for opening borders

States are territorially bounded: Just look at any standard map to see how current borders carve the world into distinct political units. And they generally regulate and guard those borders. Try to enter most countries, especially in the developed world, and you will be confronted with border security and immigration officers whose job is to ensure that only certain people – as determined by the states' policies – are able to enter. Many, probably most, people take for granted that at least some such border regulation is a normal and morally acceptable feature of a world with more than one state.

But some philosophers ask us to stand back from these assumptions. They point out that border regulation is not an inevitable feature of the world, even a world of multiple states. Distinct states could exercise control over distinct geographical areas, even while movement between these areas is completely unrestricted. For instance, the European Union is made up of distinct states – Italy, Finland, Slovakia, etc. – that make laws governing their territories, and this is compatible with the absence of restrictions on movement between, say, Italy and Finland (as is in fact the case, if we consider only EU citizens). This approach could be generalized so that Finland admits not just Italian immigrants but all who wish to enter its territory. In several parts of Africa, borders go virtually unguarded, enabling significant movement. And even the border between the United States and Mexico – currently monitored by more than 21,000 guards, plus drones and cameras, at an expense of about $18 billion (*Economist* 2013) – was more porous until the late nineteenth century, allowing most individuals to travel back and forth freely without documents or questions (Ngai 2014, 2–3). In this chapter, we will examine arguments for abandoning all restrictions on movement between territories: for open borders.

The open borders vision is clearly a very radical one. Is it even worth considering? The sheer fact that it challenges conventional understanding doesn't mean it should be dismissed out of hand: the idea that women should be allowed to vote was once radical.

A more practical concern is that individual policy makers are generally faced with a different choice than just whether to create a world of open borders or not. Current immigration levels are likely far lower than they would be in a world of fully open borders (at present, about 3 percent of people globally live in countries that they were not born in). The question for most policy makers (and voters, activists, and so on) is whether to aim to increase (or decrease) the number of migrants admitted, even if their state is not going to have completely open borders and even if their policies will not be part of a global trend (one that includes all states) toward more open borders. As we proceed, we'll consider how an ideal of open borders might bear on these more immediate policy choices and whether there are arguments for allowing greater (or lesser) migration that don't appeal directly to whether open borders would be the ideal.[1]

A. Efficiency and utility

One common argument for open borders focuses on the economic benefits of free movement of people (Clemens 2011). If borders are open, then companies can hire whichever workers will be most productive: able to produce greater output at a lower cost. The workers themselves will earn higher wages. Economists differ in their estimates of what exactly (more) open borders would achieve, but there is generally significant optimism about the net economic impact of substantially increased migration. According to a report by the World Bank (2018a, 2), a young unskilled worker moving to the United States gains about $14,000 a year. The report finds that "if we were to double the number of immigrants in high-income countries by moving 100 million young people from developing countries, the annual income gain would be $1.4 trillion" (World Bank 2018a, 1).

"Sending" countries can also benefit from emigration (though we'll look later at some potential costs of emigration in the form of "brain drain"). Emigration can reduce employment pressures in countries that have significant unemployment rates, and emigrants often send back "remittances" – payments to individuals, typically family members, in their countries of origin – which are sometimes relatively substantial inputs to the local economy: Remittances have exceeded 10 percent of the national budget in, for instance, El Salvador, Jamaica, and Jordan.

Now, maximizing wealth itself cannot be an imperative of morality: Money is important only because of its impact on more fundamental values. Amassing a large amount of money is not important in and of itself – imagine a large pile of dollar bills just sitting in someone's closet! It is a means of getting other things that matter, such as health care or a car. Utilitarians suggest that what matters ultimately is people's happiness: The money buys someone health care, the health care allows that person to live pain free, and this makes them happier. They buy a car, which allows them to see their friends more often, and this matters insofar as it brings them happiness. Utilitarians propose that what we ought to do, morally speaking, is maximize the amount of happiness in the world as a whole: Pick actions and policies that produce the greatest sum of happiness (or "utility") overall.

Utilitarianism is attractive (in part) because it seems to respect each person's equality as a human being (in fact, utilitarians are also able to include the happiness of other sentient beings). It takes into account the effects of policies on every person in the world, giving each person's interests equal weight. As J.S. Mill put it,

> Every man to count for one and no one to count for more than one.
>
> (Mill 1863)

Thus, while the sheer economic output produced by immigration doesn't matter in itself, it might be an important way to increase the total amount of happiness in the world. Immigration can also improve people's lives in ways that go beyond its economic impact. It allows them to see new and different practices and thereby stimulates them to think carefully about how best to live. "It is hardly possible to overrate the value ... of placing human beings in contact with persons dissimilar to themselves," Mill wrote (1848), because of its tendency to generate social progress.[2] Immigration creates just such contact.

Despite its initial attraction, there are some familiar reasons to question whether utilitarianism is the right moral theory. One standard concern about utilitarianism is that it prevents people from giving any special weight to their personal projects. It requires people to be wholly impartial – looking only at the total amount of happiness in the world and counting their own interests as just one input to that overall calculation. But this standard, objectors insist, is far too demanding. It might require someone to spend their whole life looking out for the interests of society at the expense of their personal projects (except, that is, insofar as pursuing their own projects is in fact a good way of promoting overall utility or provides them with the respite and motivation to keep maximizing utility elsewhere in their life). We do, of course, expect people to engage in some charitable work, look out for the good of their neighborhoods, and so on, but, the objection goes, surely morality permits people to take some time for themselves – writing their novels, playing their instruments, or enjoying television – even though it doesn't work for the good of the whole. Applied to the context of immigration, one might ask whether, just as individual people are permitted to show some partiality toward themselves, whole countries are also allowed to pursue their own projects, such as preserving a societal culture, at the expense of more open immigration and more overall happiness in the world.

A second common concern about utilitarianism is that in its overwhelming focus on the total happiness in the world, it gives no weight to fairness. Many of us care about not just how much wealth or happiness a policy produces overall but also how these are distributed. For example, it might matter whether the benefits of economic growth in a country are widely dispersed or, instead, as has been true in the United States over the last 50 years, captured mainly by people in the top 1 percent with little effect on the median wage.

Now, utilitarians can say that there is some reason to prefer more equal distributions of wealth and income, even on their view, because, generally speaking, people who start out with less money benefit more from having additional income than people who start out with more money. Just imagine the impact on Bill Gates's life of having an extra $2,000 a year, with the impact of that money on the life of a poor person who is now able to cover their rent more easily. This is a reason to favor a more equitable distribution of goods across the globe. But some people will insist that what really matters morally is how equitable the distribution of goods is *within* particular societies. They may complain that immigration would damage the wages of the least well off in a society, making it less equal overall. Let's now turn to some debates about fairness.

B. Fairness and equality

A second argument for open borders focuses on the relationship between migration and fairness in the distribution of global wealth, income, and advantage generally (Carens 2013, chap. 11). Consider first advantages in life that people have simply because they are, say, white or male. Defenders of the equality argument say that these forms of advantage are *unfair* because they constitute inherited privileges: benefits that people hold on to just because they happen to be born a particular race or gender. It is one thing to have less, they say, because you made some very reckless choices in life, and it is quite another to have less simply because of bad luck: inequalities of the latter kind are unfair. These unfair inequalities are unjust and ought to be corrected.

One's chances in life are also heavily affected by where one happens to be born: The likely lifetime income of a child born in Bangladesh is much lower than that of a child born in Switzerland. To be born in a poorer country is often plain bad luck with respect to certain economic metrics. So, the argument goes, this is another crucial form of inherited, and thus unfair, privilege. Border restrictions are one important mechanism that keeps this unfair privilege in place. Closed borders prevent the less well off from taking advantage of opportunities elsewhere by physically excluding them from the jobs and so on that would benefit them. Within individual societies, people born into poorer families are often stuck in disadvantaged neighborhoods – with fewer job opportunities, more pollution, worse sanitation – marked by, for instance, lack of public transportation. Border controls are even more obviously unjust than this, the equality argument says: They are like a fence erected directly to keep the poor away from the better-served parts of town. They arbitrarily exclude the poor from the advantages others are able to access.

Is this argument successful? It might be worth distinguishing here between two different ways of thinking about fairness and unfairness. On one conception of unfairness – what we might call "cosmic unfairness" – it is unfair in and of itself for someone to have more than someone else simply because of their better luck. It is this notion of fairness that we have in mind when we say that it is just not fair that, say, some people are simply born with sunnier dispositions than others and thus find it easier to walk around in gaiety. On a second conception of unfairness – "unfair treatment," let's call it – what matters fundamentally is how people are treated by other individuals or institutions. For instance, we might say that it is unfair if one employee gets a raise before another equally productive one: The company is treating the less-favored employee unfairly. What matters here is that they each have similar claims to get a raise and yet are being treated dissimilarly.

The equality argument trades on an appeal to cosmic fairness: It's just unfair in itself that some people came to life under worse conditions than others, and we ought to act in order to correct this unfairness. The situation is unfair even though no one (excepting, perhaps, a God) decided where each of us would be born.

In response to the equality argument, some theorists invoke requirements of fair treatment. They say that what matters is for people to be treated fairly, and especially that they be treated fairly by their own governments. There are various reasons why people might be owed fair treatment by their governments. One is that governments make a very special demand of their subjects: They make rules (laws) that constrain many aspects of subjects' lives and demand absolute obedience to those rules.[3] That demand, according to one important line of thought in political philosophy, means that governments must be able to justify their activities to each of their subjects, and thus must favor each equally. Another potential source of a demand of fairness is cooperative reciprocity: the requirement that people be fairly compensated for their contributions to cooperative schemes (Sangiovanni 2007). People contribute to their societies through working, paying taxes, and helping to maintain their institutions, and so governments may have to ensure that each individual is fairly compensated for their contributions.

Ordinary discussion invokes each of the two notions of fairness: People complain both about the unfairness of life – why am I stuck with a troublesome family?! – and also about the unfairness of their local city council – why are our parks less maintained than the people down the roads'?! And we might ask which of the two notions is the most relevant to justice: Does justice mainly require that we correct cosmic unfairness or that we prevent and redress instances of unfair treatment? This is a deep question that we can't fully address here, but we can provide a few pointers.

Against emphasizing cosmic fairness as the key requirement of justice, it might be said that even if there is always some reason to correct all inequalities caused by bad luck, still people must to some extent accept the sheer unfairness of life. Take again the person who happens to be born with a less sunny disposition than others (I don't mean clinical depression, which might bring with it special considerations, just quotidian being bummed out more than others). If we suddenly had some manna from heaven to give out, there would surely be some reason to give it to these people over others. But is there really a very strong duty – a requirement of justice – to compensate people for bad luck? If not, then we might ask whether the more fortunate must compensate the less fortunate when they would otherwise spend the money on their kids or on projects that they care deeply about.

It might be worth noting here how claims about cosmic fairness appear in political discourse and reflecting on what role those claims play. Here is an example. In 1977, US President Jimmy Carter was asked about a US Supreme Court decision that ruled that the federal government did not have to fund abortions for those who could not otherwise afford them. Carter said, "There are many things in life that are unfair, that wealthy people can afford and poor people can't. But I don't believe the federal government should take action to try to make these opportunities exactly equal" (Carter 1977, 1237).[4] President John F. Kennedy similarly said, fifteen years earlier, that certain inequalities are not unjust because "life is unfair," and many similar things have been said since.

Clearly the unfairness that Carter is speaking of is cosmic unfairness; he's trying to convince us that the differential access of rich and poor women to abortions is due to bad luck. And he is using that claim not to motivate political action to address these inequalities but rather to justify inaction with respect to those inequalities. Here, as elsewhere in familiar political discourse, the point of saying that an inequality is cosmically unfair, a feature of the "unfairness of life," is to deny that anyone has a responsibility to do anything about it. As an argument for greater global equality, then, an argument from cosmic unfairness is unlikely to generate much success.

Against emphasizing fair treatment over cosmic unfairness, it might be said even if only current members of a state are in fact subject to its laws, and make substantial contributions, still prospective immigrants would be happy to bear the same burdens if only they were allowed in (Carens 2013, 334n23). It is wrong to distinguish morally between current members and prospective immigrants, given that the prospective immigrants would be perfectly happy to do everything that current members do. Can we really say to someone that they don't get the same rights as insiders because they aren't (e.g.) major contributors, even though the only thing preventing them from contributing is their forcible exclusion from the territory? In reply, it might be said that even if there is significant luck involved in the fact that I am in a certain relationship, that relationship can still be morally important. For instance, perhaps I happened upon a really enjoyable club before some other people had heard of it. Now everyone wants in, but the existing members would prefer to keep current membership levels constant. Doesn't the fact that I pay my membership dues, accept various responsibilities of membership, and so on matter – entitle me to the special benefits of membership – even though plenty of other people would be happy to do the same if only they could gain admittance? It may be that membership itself matters even when there is some arbitrariness to who gets to be a member in the first place.

Now, one important line of argument, associated with Arash Abizadeh (2008) – in defense of a global equality principle – concedes that our focus should be on fair treatment rather than pure distributive fairness, but it questions the assumption that states need only aim to be fair among their own members. Rather, states have the same very strong responsibilities to each individual on the planet, and this means that they must be evenhanded in their treatment of these individuals, giving each person's interests equal weight. Thus, we might say that open borders are required for the state to treat all people fairly.

This argument asserts a very revisionary view of states' responsibilities. People ordinarily assume that the primary job of states is to serve their own citizens/ residents, even if they have other, weaker obligations to people elsewhere. They expect, say, the government of Chile to negotiate a trade deal with Brazil primarily with the interests of Chileans at heart, not the interests of Brazilians. Are they justified in this assumption? Why is it the job of the Chilean government to serve Chileans more than it serves citizens of other countries? The most influential answer, alluded to earlier, is that the Chilean government demands something of Chileans that it does not demand of others: It makes rules (laws) that it insists they must follow, and indeed threatens them with punishment should they disobey those rules. In return for making these special demands of Chileans, the government must in turn serve their interests, and it need not do the same for others (e.g., Brazilians) of whom it does not make such demands.

According to Abizadeh this last step involves a crucial mistake: The government of Chile does in fact make very serious demands of Brazilians. It does make rules that it demands they follow, namely rules about when and how they can cross its borders. And it backs up those rules with the threat of force. As Carens puts it, "Borders have guards, the guards have guns" (257). Moreover, as we'll explore later, border enforcement is often accompanied by detention rooms, and those rooms have locks.

Abizadeh and Carens are clearly right that the Chilean government does, to an extent, issue demands of Brazilians: It tells them to keep out, unless they have special permission. And it doesn't just recommend that they keep out, it says, "Keep out, or else." But does this really mean that the Chilean government makes equally weighty demands of Brazilians as of its own members? To its own members, the Chilean government says, "Here are a vast number of rules – about property, taxes, relationships, associations – that you must follow for the rest of your lives here." But to the Brazilians it excludes, it says only "Do as you please, just don't do it here." And this is arguably a very different, much weaker, demand that doesn't bring with it quite the same responsibility to serve their interests.[5]

C. Humanitarianism

The argument we just looked at is focused on equality: the *gap* between how some people are doing relative to how others are doing. And, as we saw, there are some philosophical controversies about when exactly it's *unjust* for there to be a gap. A less controversial argument for opening borders appeals directly to the fact that so many people in the world live in conditions of extreme poverty – are not just poorer than others, but very deprived in *absolute* terms – and suggests that allowing those people to move to wealthier countries is a useful way to alleviate their suffering. This includes all people who are denied the chance to lead a decent life, including the 767 million people who live on less than $1.90 a day, the World Bank's threshold for extreme poverty (World Bank 2018b). The fact that there is such a gap between these people and the better off might matter on this approach, not because it is inherently unfair but because it suggests that the better off should be able to do more to help the less well off, given all of their advantages (Scanlon 2003, 202–218).

One point to notice about this argument is that it doesn't really support open borders: The total removal of restrictions on immigration. Rather, what it supports is opening borders to allow immigration by a specific group of people, namely the world's poorest. This would still be a substantial change from the status quo, of course.

Second, we might ask whether simply opening borders, even to the least skilled, is likely to help the very poorest of the world, who in many cases will not be able to bear the costs of travel and resettlement (Lister 2013). You have to be able to get to the border to take advantage of the fact that no one will stop you from crossing it, which will often require that one have contacts, be able to pay a carrier, and so on. And finding a new home, looking for a job, and so on in the new country also requires resources. This is part of the explanation for why most migration from less-developed countries to more-developed countries is not migration of the very least well off: neither people from the poorest countries nor people from the poorest social classes (Castles, de Haas, and Miller 2014, 6).

In response, it might be said that an open borders policy could be combined with a broader set of policies aimed at helping the world's poor (Carens 2013, chap. 11). These could include forms of assistance aimed at enabling the least advantaged to travel as well as develop efforts aimed at benefiting those who are unable to travel through development aid and so on.

A third issue is the extent of developed countries' responsibilities for helping the needy. There is fairly widespread (though sadly not unanimous) agreement that people in developed countries have some form of duty to help the global poor. But the precise strength and nature of this duty is a matter of major philosophical dispute.

Peter Singer (1972, 2009) famously argues that these duties are extremely strong. Consider the following example. Suppose that you are out walking and notice that a child is drowning in a pond. You can relatively easily wade into the pond and reach down to save the child, but in doing so you will damage your expensive shoes. Surely you must save the child. Singer claims that the case supports the following principle:

> If it is in our power to prevent something bad from happening, without thereby sacrificing anything of comparable moral importance, we ought, morally, to do it.
>
> (Singer 1972, 233–234)

This principle requires more than just a potential sacrifice of one's shoes; One must continue to act to prevent bad things from happening right up to the point where doing so would result in a loss to yourself of something of "comparable moral importance." And when we are dealing with a preventable bad like the loss of a human life, only a very significant sacrifice seems to be of comparable moral importance, such as the loss of one's own life or one's home. What if, for instance, by wading into the pond you would destroy not just your shoes but also your very expensive iPhone (there's no time to take it out of your pocket)? Singer's principle again says that you must save the child.

That seems like the right result when we think about the child right in front of us. What happens when we consider children (and adults) whose lives are at stake but who are not before us, who live in other countries? Singer's principle again says that we must make sacrifices for those people, including significant sacrifices (up to the point where something of comparable moral importance would be lost). Applied to immigration, it would say that if a country can relieve extreme poverty by admitting people who suffer that poverty, then members of that country must support opening borders up to the point where doing so would so involve a sacrifice of something of comparable moral importance.

Are there really such strong duties to people who live in other countries? There are some obvious differences between the child right in front of some-one and people in other countries. But we need to ask whether these differ-ences are morally relevant: whether they make the two situations disanalogous, morally speaking. Singer points out that, for instance, the mere fact of their being further away from us – physically speaking – doesn't seem morally relevant. Another difference between the two cases is that any given member of the global poor can be helped by more than one person and more than one country. Only you can save the drowning child, but a poor person in sub-Saharan Africa could be admitted to various different developed nations. Is this a morally relevant difference? Singer points out that if other people were standing around the pond able to help the child, their sheer presence would be no excuse not to help. If you know that they aren't going to save the child – and most of the world's poor are unlikely to be helped by other people or countries – then you ought to do so.

Another difference between the drowning child example and assisting the global poor is that there are – as we saw earlier – a great many people among the global poor. If one poor individual is helped, there will still be many more others in need. The situation might be more properly analogized, Timmerman (2015) suggests, to one in which there are a great many children drowning nearby, so that every time you save one there are many others still dying. In this situation, perhaps there is a point at which you could refuse to save any extra children, even for the sake of something that is not of comparable moral importance, such as an afternoon with your friends. If so, then the duty to help the world's poor using immigration policy may also have limits, so that helping the needy can be traded off against various goods a country might be trying to pursue, such as equality within its borders or protection of its culture (see Chapter 2 for discussion of such goods). Still, any such trade-off should not be taken lightly. Even if in Timmerman's scenario you could take some time off from saving babies, though, that doesn't mean you can plug your ears and pretend that you are not living in the middle of a moral catastrophe. And Singer himself can also endorse the importance of self-care: Spending every last minute trying to save others is not sustainable in the long term.

D. A right to freedom of movement

According to this argument for open borders, restrictions on movement across borders are unjust because there is a basic individual right to freedom of movement. Liberal democracies generally protect a variety of basic liberties, such as freedoms of speech, religion, and association. These liberties protect various aspects of individual "autonomy"; they allow people to make funda-mental choices about what values and projects to adopt and to carry out plans based on those. For instance, they allow someone to hear about and reflect on the central tenets of Judaism and decide whether to take actions – such as building a synagogue – that reflect those tenets.

Carens suggests that freedom of movement should also be considered one of these fundamental rights, as do Kukathas (2005); Freiman and Hidalgo (2016); and Oberman (2016). People's decisions about where to live (can) also reflect their deepest values and aspirations. They might wish to immerse themselves in the landscape and historical architecture of a place that they deeply identify with. Or they might want to pursue a career – as a Qawwali singer, say – that requires training only available in a particular place. Free-dom of movement can also be a prerequisite for exercising other freedoms that are already considered to be basic liberties, such as religious freedom: To freely associate with members of one's religious group, one often needs to be physically in the same place as them. "Thus," Carens claims (2013, 227), "freedom of movement contributes to individual autonomy both directly and indirectly. Open borders would enhance this freedom."

Moreover, liberal democracies generally already recognize a right to free-dom of (let's call it) "intranational movement." They generally treat the right to move freely within the borders of a particular territory – from Sydney to Adelaide, or Ottawa to Vancouver – as a basic liberty. Carens argues that there is no reason to qualify the right in this way, limiting it to only internal movement because freedom of movement across borders serves exactly the same interest – in reflecting on, adopting, and acting on one's deepest values and aspirations – that free movement within a territory does. So we can formulate Carens's challenge as follows: Are there good reasons for thinking that there is only a right to freedom of intranational movement (within a particular territory) and not also a right to freedom of international movement (across territorial boundaries), especially given that each seems to serve the same fundamental interests?

i. The alternative grounds response

One response to Carens says that freedom of intranational movement has distinctive *grounds* that do not extend to justifying freedom of international movement. In other words, when we look at the reasons for adopting freedom of movement within a country, we find that those reasons do not support an unlimited right to move across political boundaries. We'll explore a few such grounds and consider whether they can support freedom of intranational movement without also supporting freedom of international movement.

First, though, it's worth looking at the structure of some other fundamental liberty rights – we'll focus on freedom of speech – since part of the argument for freedom of international movement is that it directly and indirectly serves the same functions as these other rights. Liberal democracies generally assert a strong right to freedom of speech for their membership. But these protections for the speech of members of a society are often not extended to people outside of that society. Consider the fact that – as is the case in the United States – foreign entities are often prohibited from purchasing advertisements that advocate for electoral candidates. Or consider the limits that the French government has often put on the distribution of foreign cultural media – Hollywood movies, for instance – within France. Thus, it often seems that places with strong commitments to freedom of internal speech do not have strong commitments to freedom of international speech.

Can this asymmetry between freedom of internal speech and freedom of international speech be justified? Let's go through some of the justifications for intranational speech and see whether they extend to international speech.

Liberal democracies often have especially stringent protections for political speech. One function political speech plays is providing a check on government abuse. Government misconduct can be more easily uncovered and those in power more easily held accountable. Newspapers might uncover substantial bribes being paid to officials, for instance. It also serves more positive functions in a democracy, fostering greater democratic deliberation. For instance, members of the society can become better informed about political candidates and the values that they represent, and they can also make their own contributions to the debate around these candidates and values. If we focus on political speech, it seems that protecting freedom of internal speech is more important. People need to be protected from abuse by their own government, which has the ability to make and enforce rules about their lives, and so it is more important for members of a particular society to be able to band together to criticize that government than it is for people of different countries to be able to talk politics together. Likewise, democracy requires that all members of a particular society come together as equals to make collective decisions about how that society is to be run. They thus need to be able to deliberate with one another to come to those decisions. But a non-member of that society has a much weaker claim to be able to contribute to deliberations about how it is to be run.

Parallel points can be made about freedom of movement and its role in political interactions. Freedom of intranational movement can help to provide a check on governmental abuse, because it limits the ability of governments to target particular disliked groups (Hosein 2013; Miller 2016, 55–56). For example, suppose that the government wishes to persecute Jewish people. This is made much easier if, as in fact happened historically in European cities, the state is able to concentrate Jewish people in ghettos, shut off from the rest of society. It can then direct resources away from those areas toward places with more favored communities. Freedom of movement, by contrast, makes it easier for groups that are stuck in less-favored areas of a city or country to move to other places, which in turn makes it harder for the state to target them. Like political speech, freedom of intranational movement can serve democracy in ways that go beyond just checking gross abuses of power (Hosein 2013). Although in the modern world, much communication can take place that isn't "face-to-face," there is still value in, for instance, people being able to travel around the country to hold rallies for their political campaign. And members of a country will be better able to make national decisions together if they are able to learn about life in different parts of the country, which often requires movement across the territory.

What about speech (and movement) that doesn't serve any particular political ends? For example, what about artistic expression and people who move in order to share their art in other parts of a country? People have an interest not only in contributing to the political institutions that they live under but also the broader social norms that are applied to their behavior and to others around them. For example, they might wish to have some impact on the sexual mores of the place in which they live, making them more hospitable to same-sex relationships. This justification also seems to provide significantly more support for freedom of internal speech than freedom of international speech. What matters most is the ability to shape the social norms that apply within one's own society, not those applied elsewhere.

Still, defenders of freedom of international movement might say, aren't there autonomy-related reasons for wanting freedom of movement both within and across borders that aren't just a matter of shaping one's social environment? For example, someone might wish to move in order to take a job in forestry that can't be found in their current (more urban) city or attend classes in flamenco dance that aren't offered in their village. This might require moving from one part of a particular territory to another, but it also might require moving across territories if the job or class isn't offered where they are.

Must governments ensure that a non-member can enter so they can take a job in that territory or attend a class there? To answer this, we might ask what responsibilities governments have to support any particular person's autonomy interests. We saw there are some theorists who think states have distinctive obligations to their own members to provide them with opportunities, for instance, because those members are subject to the state's authority or because they are members of a large cooperative enterprise. Those same reasons might lead us to think that the state has distinctive obligations to promote the autonomy of its own members. This means that states are required to make sure that their own members have access to jobs and other opportunities. But – according to this line of thought – states are not required to use their territory to enhance the autonomy of non-members (and nor are they required, or even permitted, to use the territory belonging to other states in order to enhance the autonomy of their own members).

One concern about this argument is the way it treats freedom of intranational movement as something like a benefit that states create for the sake of their members. Carens might object that freedom of movement should be thought of instead as a negative right – a right not to be interfered with (Carens 2013, 236). The right to freedom of movement has the same structure, he might say, as other rights we standardly think of as negative. Freedom of speech, for instance, is normally understood primarily as the right that the state not restrict you from speaking or impose special costs on your attempts to speak (such as a special tax on criticizing the government). It is not the right to be aided in speaking: People do not typically have constitutional rights to megaphones or other instruments that would increase their ability to get their message across. Likewise, the right to freedom of movement – as commonly understood – is infringed if the state decides to put clamps on your car to prevent you from crossing county lines, but not if the state fails to provide you with a car in the first place. It is a right to travel without inference, not a right to be enabled to travel however one pleases. Carens might continue: This negative right that one be able to travel without interference is infringed both when your car is stopped on the way from Moscow to St. Petersburg and when it is stopped on the way from Guyana to Suriname.

In fact, however, the analogy with freedom of speech may tell against Carens's position. The problem becomes apparent when we consider what counts as "interference" for purposes of recognizing rights violations. Suppose, for instance, that without my consent someone tries to set up a sound system in my garden to blare out their political message and begins spray-painting the same message on my car. I call the police, and when they arrive, they shut down the propagandist's operation. Could they reasonably complain that their right to freedom of expression was being violated? Not according to the ordinary understanding of that right. The right to freedom of expression is not the right to express yourself in any way you want without the government stopping you. It is the right to express yourself using whichever private and public resources you are entitled to without the government stopping you. Who gets to determine which resources you are entitled to use? There is generally disagreement about exactly what is mine, or thine, or public, and the state makes regulations that settle these matters. Or rather, the state makes regulations about who is entitled to what within its territory: Other states determine the rules within their territories. What if I want to use resources present in another country to further my expression? Here bilateral arrangements between our two countries are used to fix what I am entitled to. For instance, foreign corporations are not permitted to buy political advertisements in another country, but states often come to arrangements that allow foreign corporations to make certain investments within their territories.

ii. Targeted remedies

Suppose that defenders of freedom of international movement accept that states have special reasons to promote the autonomy of their own members. Still, they might insist, aren't there some interests so morally important that the state must take them into account, even in its dealings with non-members? Take, for instance, people's ability to live with their families. Carens and others might say that a non-member has such a strong interest in being able to live with their wife – and thus in being able to move to the country where their wife lives – that it would be unjust for a state to prevent them from doing so.

One possible response to this is to say that yes, there are such interests, but they can be satisfied without having fully open borders.[6] For example, states could grant a right to family reunification without allowing unlimited entry. But, the response goes, this doesn't mean giving significant weight to just any project someone might have. It is one thing to be denied the possibility of being near a person with whom one already has deep connections of intimacy and mutual concern. It is another to be denied the possibility of moving to a place where one thinks one might fall in love. In other cases, it may be possible to satisfy important interests without granting a full right to residency. For instance, suppose that there is a major international political meeting – such as World Trade Organization (WTO) negotiations – and people from poorer countries wish to protest various parts of the negotiations. These people may have strong interests in participating in the formulation of WTO regulations and other aspects of the global order. But this doesn't seem to require the ability to live in the country where the negotiations are taking place, merely the right to be in the country long enough to protest, agitate, and lobby during the negotiations.

What if there are such wide disparities of global power that to influence the global order people in the global South need to be able to involve themselves not only in specific international agreements but also more broadly in the foreign policies of countries in the North? Here we might ask whether there are alternative solutions than simply allowing mass migration. For example, it might be more desirable to find ways to enhance the power of *governments* in the global South to have their interests taken more seriously, for instance, by restructuring global institutions. The WTO, for example, might be rendered more democratic as a whole (Stiglitz and Charlton 2007).

So perhaps only certain specific interests of foreigners can ground a strict right to enter and reside in a state. But even if this is true it doesn't mean that weaker autonomy interests—interests in pursuing a different career in another country or in being exposed to other cultures—count for naught. States should still take them into account when setting immigration policy. And sometimes a state's immigration policies will affect the freedom of its *own* members to travel and live in other countries, as when participation in the European Union affects not only the ability of people in other countries to enter but also the ability of the state's own members to emigrate.

E. Freedom of contract

A related argument to the freedom of movement argument also says that open borders are required if we are to respect individual liberty. It relies ultimately on a particular kind of liberty, namely freedom of contract: The right to use your own property as you please, including by selling it, in whole or in part, to other people. If I own a house, then freedom of contract means I have the right to sell the house in its entirety or to rent out some part of it. The government may not interfere with these actions by, say, telling homeowners that they may only offer long-term rentals (we have seen prohibitions of the kind when governments have tried to prevent companies like Airbnb from affecting an area).

Many libertarians claim that not only do people have ownership rights over physical things, like houses, they are also self-owners, with full right of ownership over their own bodies (Nozick 1974). This means that they can also contract out their labor to other individuals and corporations. If a company offers to employ me in its factory, then my freedom of contract means that I should be able to sign on to whatever terms we negotiate, including the hours, wages, and work conditions. Likewise, the company's freedom of contract means that it ought to be able to bring into its factory whomever it pleases on whatever terms are negotiated. As the US Supreme Court put it in *Lochner v. New York* (1905, 45), an essential component of liberty is "the general right to make a contract ... and this includes the right to purchase and sell labor."

Restrictions on immigration prevent people from exercising their freedom of contract (Carens 1987, 253; Kukathas 2005, 210). Suppose that a hospital in Russia wishes to hire nurses from Malaysia, but government immigration quotas prevent this. Both the hospital's right to pay for their labor and the nurses' rights to sell their labor seems to be infringed. Thus, fully open borders seem to be required if we are to fully respect people's freedom of contract.

Do people really have a fundamental right to freedom of contract? Anti-libertarians will say that this right is simply not on par with the other freedoms that are given preeminence in liberal democracies, such as freedoms of conscience and speech. Compare a policy that says people are not allowed to put signs in their gardens that advocate for a political candidate with a policy that says employers may not hire workers to do more than 50 hours of labor per week. The former policy seems extremely problematic. It denies people the ability to express their political opinions, opinions that are, for many people, absolutely central to their identity and moral goals in life and also affect the nature of the rules that they will be required to follow. The latter policy denies employers the ability to run their factories exactly as they like, and perhaps to make as much money as they would hope. It also prevents those workers who would prefer to work the longer hours, perhaps for the sake of some additional pay, from doing so. Is that really, one might ask, as much of an assault on their liberty as the prohibition on political signs? If not, then a restriction that says a company may not hire foreign workers may not be as detrimental to individual freedom as the libertarian argument claims. If the state has good reasons to set these limits – maybe protecting workers from exploitation – then perhaps these restrictions can be justified, given that the restriction on liberty is not that severe.

Another objection to the libertarian argument is that it ignores all of the investments and decisions made by governments that affect how much property individual employers are able to accrue in the first place.[7] Suppose a company makes a large profit selling its products. This is generally only possible because the government has spent and done a huge amount to facilitate such enterprises. Companies often use technology that was developed with the help of government funds. Take the Advanced Research Projects Agency Network (ARPANET), an early form of computer network, which utilized technology that would ultimately become the foundation for the internet. Initial funding for ARPANET came mainly from the US Department of Defense, and later developments that helped expand the network came about through funding from the National Science Foundation. Thus, the many people and companies that have amassed enormous wealth and income through internet ventures owe their success in significant part to government investments and decisions. Mark Zuckerberg cannot say, "I did all of this alone."

Even where technologies were developed mainly through private funding, governments have still typically played an important role in enabling people to profit from those technologies. Take, for instance, intellectual property. When companies develop a new gadget, they seek to patent their product.

Governments provide the procedures that govern these applications, and they make rules about who is allowed to implement that technology. They then enforce those rules, fining people who use the technology without permission from the patent owner. Governments also determine how long the patent lasts: 14 or 15 years in the United States. All of these activities are funded with revenue raised through taxes on the general population and made possible more generally through the willingness of that population to uphold the government's decisions.[8]

In sum, when a company says, "We just made X amount of money selling our product," governments – and the populations who uphold and fund those governments – can reasonably point out that the money was made using an infrastructure put in place by the government (and ultimately propped up by individual members of society, through their support for the government and tax payments). So it seems fair for governments to insist on regulating the activities of these companies for the sake of the general good of that society. And this might include putting in place restrictions on immigration that are necessary to promote that good, even where those restrictions limit the ability of individuals to hire foreigners and so on.

F. Remedial justice: Responding to harm, exploitation, and colonialism

i. Trade, investment, and exploitation

The next set of arguments we will look at for (more) open borders is focused on relationships between more and less developed countries and the way the policies of more developed countries affect people in other places. One important argument for increased migration focuses on ways in which more developed countries (according to the argument) harm or exploit people in other countries. As an example, let's focus, as Wilcox (2014) does, on some ways that the Border Industrialization Project (BIP) and North American Free Trade Agreement (NAFTA) have affected Mexican workers and society.

First, a brief description of these policies and their outcomes (relying on Wilcox's characterization). The BIP created a special industrial zone just across the US-Mexico border, where US companies were freed to invest in factories, to ship components into the factories, and to ship the results back out while paying light taxes. The resulting automotive, clothing, and electronics assembly plants – known as *maquiladoras* – were attractive to the companies because they provided a source of cheap labor and attractive to the Mexican government because they provided jobs.

NAFTA created a freer flow of goods and capital across borders in North America. Barriers to trade such as tariffs and import quotas were substantially lowered: Tariffs, for instance, were eliminated entirely for more than one-half of American imports from Mexico and one-third of exports. As for financing, NAFTA enabled substantial foreign investment in areas such as banking, manufacturing, and information technology.

Wilcox points to several effects of these policies. The creation of the maquiladoras produced a large influx of workers from more rural areas into the new industrial zone. Women, especially, who had been inside the home with no direct remuneration were now taking these manufacturing jobs. Two effects of this were the heavy disruption of rural areas, making farming and other activities unsustainable, and the edging out of the labor market of men who had previously worked in industry either within Mexico or as temporary workers in the United States. NAFTA has had similar effects, again putting pressure on rural areas – for instance, because of the exportation to Mexico of subsidized U.S. corn – resulting in further exodus from those areas in search of industrial jobs, which were again offered at a higher rate to women, with male displaced farmers often left unemployed.

These effects, Wilcox argues, create a duty on the part of the United States to open its border with Mexico. Why? According to Wilcox, the structures put in place by the BIP and NAFTA constitute and cause exploitation. The agreements are one-sided, given that (a) they have disproportionate costs for Mexicans – given the burdens on people in rural areas and on male workers that have been pushed into unemployment – and (b) they have allowed the United States to benefit from extremely cheap labor without having to grant workers the kinds of employment regulations that would be insisted on for US workers. The long-term effects on the Mexican economy as a whole, Wilcox might add, do not seem to have been very positive, with Mexico seeing relatively sluggish growth for an economy at its stage of development (Rodrik 2014).

But didn't Mexico agree to these arrangements? And how would we know that they are exploitative? The sheer fact that an arrangement works more to the benefit of one part more than another, it might be said in response, is not enough to make it exploitative.[9] And even if the policy has had substantial costs for some Mexicans, others, such as women, have benefited, gaining the opportunity to leave the home and be paid a wage, or to be paid a higher wage than they were receiving in industries such as textiles (Aguayo-Téllez, Airola, and Juhn 2010). The Mexican economy as a whole has also some- times benefited from NAFTA, such as enabling a quick recovery from the December 1994 financial crisis (Stiglitz 2004).

Wilcox might respond that we do often insist on regulating even consensual interactions in order to ensure that they meet certain standards of fairness. (Although, of course, not everyone thinks that these regulations are accep- table: See the libertarian argument discussed earlier.) For example, liberal democracies often put limits on the hours per day that employees can be asked to work – eliminating 12-hour shifts as a cleaner, for instance – and make health and safety regulations that restrict the conditions of employ- ments. An employer who runs afoul of these requirements cannot escape fines

and other punishment simply by saying that the employees made a contractual agreement to work under those conditions. This suggests a commitment to ensuring that economic interactions are not excessively one-sided,
even where they are voluntary.

The objector to Wilcox could reply that the analogy with regulation of
agreements between members of a particular society is not helpful. Within a
society, people have heightened duties to one another, and this means that the
government ought to regulate their interactions, so that each member of that
society benefits somewhat equally from economic activities within the territory. No such duties are owed across borders, and so somewhat one-sided
agreements are acceptable.

Why exactly are there special duties between members of a particular
society, and not across territorial boundaries? We saw a key argument for this
view earlier, in our discussion of the egalitarian argument for open borders.
That argument rests on the idea that members of an individual society are all
subject to the same centralized *authority*, which exercises power over them by
requiring them to follow its rules. That authority must be justified to each if it
is to be acceptable, and this means ensuring that each person reaps fair benefits from living in that society. Members of the United States are all subject
to a unitary centralized authority, namely the federal government. But no
overarching entity – no regional or global government – exercises authority
over North America as a whole. So, the United States owes no special duties
to Mexicans: whichever arrangements both parties agree to are acceptable.[10]

This reply to Wilcox overlooks the background against which agreements
between the US and Mexico were made. Even though Mexico's government
signed off on the BIP and NAFTA, it did so from a much weaker bargaining
position, given that Mexico is a developing country with a much smaller
economy. Thus, it could be said, power is in fact exercised *internationally*. So
if it is the exercise of power that triggers heightened duties, then there is a
plausible case that the United States does have heightened duties to Mexico
and its members, especially duties to correct exercises of that power that make
Mexico an unequal partner in their relationship.

But even if the BIP and NAFTA genuinely created exploitative relations
between the two countries and their members, why would the right response be
to open borders? Why not attack the exploitation directly by trying to dismantle
the structures that constitute and enable it, such as one-sided trade agreements?
Let's look at two arguments Wilcox gives in response to these concerns.

a. The constitutive argument

One response Wilcox offers is to say that closed borders are a core *part* of the
background structures that enable exploitation. Opening the border is thus
itself an essential step in creating a more just set of structures. Why is the
closed border so tightly connected to exploitation? It creates, Wilcox says, "a

kind of apartheid, segregating ethnic groups and enforcing ... [a] caste system" (Wilcox 2014, 129). This claim becomes more and more plausible, according to Wilcox, "as a regional economy becomes progressively more integrated." In other words, the closer the U.S. and Mexican economies come to resemble the single economic system we see within an individual state, the more plausible it is to think that closed borders become an unjust form of segregation, one that enables exploitation.

To consider this claim, we can compare closed borders with the legally enforced racial segregation of the Jim Crow era, which we now see as plainly unjust. Can closed borders, especially under conditions of relatively strong transnational economic integration, create a similar form of injustice? Jim Crow segregation forced black people to live separately from white people in many different areas: Segregation was the rule for schools, neighborhoods, parks, railcars, restaurants, drinking fountains, and so on. What were the core moral problems with this? One was the sheer limitation on freedoms of movement and association: The fact that black people (as well as white people) were frequently able neither to use various different kinds of facilities nor to intermingle. Let's set that problem aside, since we've already considered arguments that borders are unacceptable because they restrict freedoms of movement and association. Two other moral concerns connect more closely with Wilcox's argument against the closed border. First, segregation created a message of black inferiority, one that stigmatized black people as lesser and degraded people. Why did it have this message? It was clear, in context, that the point of segregation was to protect white people from having to associate with black people and to enforce a moral code according to which it was inappropriate for white people to mix with black people as equals: A lord should not be educated alongside an underling, the low-born must not eat at the same table as their superiors, was the ideology of the time. Second, segregation created material inequalities between black people and white people. Since facilities designated for white people were generally of higher quality than facilities designated for black people (despite the ruling in *Plessy v. Ferguson* [1896] that separate facilities were acceptable only on the condition that they were "equal"), another problem with segregation was that it prevented black people from accessing important resources in society. These inequalities in turn enabled white people to exploit black people. Without access to the equal educational resources or social networks of white people, white people were able to keep black people in less skilled work, serving and taking orders from white people rather than occupying positions of economic or political advantage and power. Black people were thus perpetually subject to the control of white people and working in an economy that systematically served the interests of white people over the interests of black people.

Does the closed border with Mexico create unjust stigma and enable economic exploitation? To answer this we need to look, first, at the reasons behind the closed border. Plainly some amount of resistance to Mexican immigration is due to racist stereotypes about Mexicans. The clearest example of this is Donald Trump's famous claim that Mexican immigrants are in significant part drug dealers, criminals, and rapists ("and some, I assume, are good people"). And such statements stigmatize both potential Mexican immigrants and people of Mexican origin in the United States. But it is hard to estimate just how much resistance to immigration is based on racism. This seems especially difficult to know when we consider not just people's commitments to increasing or maintaining current levels of immigration, but also their support for some form of a closed border. Surely there are plenty of people who would not support a fully open border who are motivated by economic or political concerns of the kind we will look at in the following chapter, rather than simply racism. Given this complexity, the case for a fully open border does not seem as strong as the case for ending segregation was, although increasing immigration would be one way to demonstrate a strong commitment to anti-racism.

Would a more open border create less stigma and fewer opportunities for exploitation? Certainly an open border *alone* (as Wilcox would surely agree) would not end these problems. It's perfectly possible for there to be more significant movement of people across the Mexican border while immigrants remain stigmatized once they enter the United States. And while an open border would enable some Mexicans to enjoy the economic benefits of life in the United States, the open border would not directly address the background inequality between the *states* of Mexico and the United States. So it seems that an open border policy would have to be accompanied by both stricter anti-racism efforts within the United States and also efforts to correct background inequalities of power and advantage between the two states. And if these were achieved, would an open border still be necessary?

b. The "second-best" argument

Now for the second response that Wilcox gives to the claim that exploitation should be ended through the destruction of unjust global structures. Even if it were true, she says, that dismantling the structures is the *ideal* option, this does not provide us with much guidance in the world as we find it, where these structures are in place and entrenched. In this non-ideal situation, we should implement open borders as a second-best option (Wilcox 2014, 131), since the option of directly dismantling unjust global structures is not available.

Wilcox's argument seems to rest on one of two different interpretations of "available." First, she may be assuming that present economic and political structures can only be changed slowly, even with substantial political will to change them, because of the harms involved in transitioning away from those structures. Maquiladoras cannot simply be closed tomorrow. To abruptly shut the factories would be highly disruptive and would likely damage not just employers but also workers and Mexican society generally. There is also a difficult problem of deciding what to put in place instead. It certainly doesn't seem as easy as simply returning Mexican society to a pre-NAFTA status quo ante. Female workers who have moved from working in the home to factory employment in the city could reasonably resist returning to their previous roles, for example.

The difficulty with this version of the argument is that an open borders policy might also be highly disruptive and prevent the Mexican government from enacting successful long-term policies. We will look more carefully at so-called brain drain in the next chapter, but one potential problem is that some of the most economically productive and politically competent members of Mexican society might immediately leave for the United States, while the poorest Mexicans remain behind. What we need to ask, then, is whether sustainable development in Mexico, and justice for Mexicans on the whole, would be best served by a fully open border or a more tempered migration policy, such as a temporary worker program and efforts to admit as permanent residents only those people whose bonds with the United States are sufficiently strong already.

Second, Wilcox may be assuming that open borders are more readily "available" because there is no political will to change the background structures that she considers oppressive. But even if changing the structures seems like a political non-starter in the short term, open borders are also extremely controversial and might be even harder to make progress on. The political possibilities require further investigation also. Again, a temporary worker scheme, for example, might be more feasible than fully open borders (though such schemes also raise issues of exploitation that we will look at in Chapter 7).

ii. Colonialism

Before concluding this section, let us briefly consider a final harm-/exploitation-based argument for opening borders (a more extensive version of which can be found in Velásquez 2016). This argument is more historical: It treats increased migration as a remedial step in addressing the harms of colonialism and imperialism. Some harms of colonialism include the massive violence used to create and sustain colonial authorities. Consider General Thomas Robert Bugeaud's methods of quelling Abd al-Qadir's resistance to French rule in Algeria: He "pursued a scorched-earth policy in the Algerian interior, designed to undermine popular support.... . Men, women, and children were killed, and officers were told to take no prisoners. Any of Abd al-Qadir's men who tried to surrender were simply cut down" (Rogan 2009, 117–118). Land was expropriated, natural resources exploited for the gain of the colonial power, and crippling taxes levied on colonial subjects. Even if we set aside specific forms of mistreatment of colonial subjects, injustice of colonialism also includes the sheer fact of one set of people ruling over another. It violates the values of both freedom and equality for there to be such stark asymmetries of power, allowing some people to control others and treat them as inferiors (Ypi 2013, 158–191).

The effects of colonialism have persisted into the modern period. For example, following the Haitian Revolution, France forced Haiti to pay huge sums to offset the loss of its slave colony. The equivalent of $17 billion in modern currency was ultimately paid, and the associated interest was not paid off until 1947, with lasting economic impact (Marquand 2010).[11] What if there are cases where colonialism has ultimately produced some benefits, such as a set of stable and effective political institutions after the departure of the colonial power? Even in these instances, we might say that reparations are owed. One cannot generally justify the creation of massive harm and injustice to a group just by the fact that it may have had (or has had) benefits to that group. Suppose, for example, that in the present day one country, without provocation, proposed to invade another. Many civilians are expected to die in the process, and the soldiers on the ground are likely to engage in sexual violence and torture. For many years, members of the invaded country will be unable to make political decisions for themselves. But at the end of this process institutions will be in place that are more democratic than those present prior to the invasion. This hardly seems acceptable: The scale of the harms and injustices inflicted could not be justified by the later benefits.

Here too the issue remains of what the appropriate *remedy* is for historical injustices: Should we focus on monetary reparations or on migration? As with Wilcox's argument above, we might ask whether opening borders would actually benefit the totality of people in the former colonies or just the subset who succeed in migrating to the former colonial center. And even if all members of the country could be resettled, that seems directly contrary to one of the central points of decolonization: Allowing formerly colonized groups to exercise self-determination, rather than become subjects once more of the colonizing state.

G. Chapter summary

In this chapter, we have looked at potential justifications for opening territorial borders to immigration. There are several important arguments for opening borders *entirely* – allowing unrestricted movement – including that doing so would make the world more fair and that borders violate people's basics rights to freedom of movement and contract. These arguments, if successful, provide a radical goal to aim for in the long run. However, they face some significant objections, and even if they are successful it's not clear how much guidance they provide in the short run, where fully open borders are unlikely to be politically feasible. In this case, we might ask whether there is still a case for having borders that are *more* open (even if not fully open), and we have seen some strong arguments for this. Immigration can provide large economic benefits to both migrants and host countries. And it can also have substantial non-economic benefits, such as the social progress produced when people have to confront diverse ideas and practices. It can also provide one potential tool for addressing global poverty as well as wrongs of exploitation and colonialism (though in each case it must considered alongside other possible routes for dealing with these problems).

Study questions

1   What are the potential economic benefits of immigration? How about non-economic benefits? Are these significant?
2   What is the difference between cosmic unfairness and unfair treatment? Which, if either, should immigration policy aim to reduce?
3   What is the best argument for freedom of *intra*national movement? Does it extend to freedom of *inter*national movement?
4   Do border restrictions violate people's freedom to contract with others?
5   Why does Wilcox think that a closed border between the U.S. and Mexico enables exploitation? Is she correct in thinking this?
6   Consider a particular state that you are familiar with. What is the best argument you could give for increasing immigration to that country? Does it matter how those immigrants would be selected and on what terms they would be admitted? (Reading the later sections of the book may help you answer this final question.)

Notes

1 For a discussion of whether evaluation of immigration policy should begin with the question of open borders, see Wilcox (2014).
2 See also Mill (1859) for more on the value of diversity.
3 Versions of this approach can be found in Nagel (2005) and Blake (2001). See also the alternative "stakeholder" conception of government responsibilities in Bauböck (2007), which provides a somewhat wider scope of fair treatment duties.
4 I don't mean to endorse Carter's opinion here, just to note the use he makes of the idea of cosmic unfairness. Indeed, I think he is wrong to describe inequalities between rich and poor women in their access to abortion as merely part of the unfairness of "life," since in fact they issue from unfair treatment on the part of the state.
5 For a version of this objection, see Miller (2009).
6 I discovered this point in conversation with David Owen.
7 Murphy and Nagel (2002) make a similar general point.
8 For complexities in libertarian thought about patents, however, see, for instance, D'Amato (2014).
9 Though it should be noted that many studies show thin benefits to the United States, perhaps even smaller than those for Mexico: see Caliendo and Parro's (2015) estimates of the impact of tariff reduction. And NAFTA has also arguably substantially harmed some communities within the United States that were heavily reliant on industries like textiles and manufacturing: see Rodrik (2017).
10 See Nagel (2005) for an argument of this kind.
11 Marquand, Robert. 2010. "France Dismisses Petition for It to Pay $17 Billion in Haiti Reparations." *Christian Science Monitor*, August 17. https://www.csmonitor.com/World/Europe/2010/0817/Fra nce-dismisses-petition-for-it-to-pay-17-billion-in-Haiti-reparations.

References

Abizadeh, Arash. 2008. "Democratic Theory and Border Coercion: No Right to Unilaterally Control Your Own Borders." *Political Theory* 36, no. 1 (February): 37–65.

Aguayo-Téllez, Ernesto, Jim Airola, and Chinhui Juhn. 2010. "Did Trade Liberalisation Benefit Women?: The Case of Mexico in the 1990s." VoxEU.org (Centre for Economic Policy Research), August 24, 2010. https://voxeu.org/article/does-trade-liberalisation-emp ower-women-evidence-1990s-mexico.

Bauböck, Rainer. 2007. "Stakeholder Citizenship and Transnational Political Participation: A Normative Evaluation of External Voting." *Fordham Law Review* 75, no. 5 (April): 2393–2447.

Blake, Michael. 2001. "Distributive Justice, State Coercion, and Autonomy." *Philosophy and Public Affairs* 30, no. 3 (July): 257–296.

Caliendo, Lorenzo, and Fernando Parro. 2015. "Estimates of the Trade and Welfare Effects of NAFTA." *Review of Economic Studies* 82, no. 1 (January): 1–44.

Carens, Joseph H. 1987. "Aliens and Citizens: The Case for Open Borders." *Review of Politics* 49, no. 2 (Spring): 251–273.

Carens, Joseph H. 2013. *The Ethics of Immigration.* New York: Oxford University Press.

Carter, Jimmy. 1977. *Public Papers of the Presidents of the United States: Jimmy Carter, 1977,* 2 vols. Washington, DC: Government Printing Office.

Castles, Stephen, Hein de Haas, and Mark J. Miller. 2014. *The Age of Migration: International Population Movements in the Modern World.* 5th ed. New York: Guilford Press.

Clemens, Michael. 2011. "Economics and Emigration: Trillion-Dollar Bills on the Sidewalk?" *Journal of Economic Perspectives* 25, no. 3 (Summer): 83–106.

D'Amato, David S. 2014. "Libertarian Views of Intellectual Property: Rothbard, Tucker, Spooner, and Rand." Libertarianism.org (Cato Institute), May 28, 2014. https://www.liberta rianism.org/columns/libertarian-views-intellectual-property-rothbard-tucker-spooner-rand.

Economist. 2013. "Secure Enough." June 22, 2013. http://www.economist.com/news/ united-states/21579828-spending-billions-more-fences-and-drones-will-do-more-harm -good-secure-enough.

Freiman, C., and Javier Hidalgo. 2016. "Liberalism or Immigration Restrictions But Not Both." *Journal of Ethics and Social Philosophy* 10, no. 2 (May): 1–22.

Hosein, A. 2013. "Immigration and Freedom of Movement." *Ethics and Global Politics* 6, no. 1: 25–37.

Kukathas, Chandran. 2005. "The Case for Open Immigration." In *Contemporary Debates in Applied Ethics,* edited by Andrew I. Cohen and Christopher Heath, 207–220. Oxford: Blackwell.

Lister, Matthew. 2013. "Who Are Refugees?" *Law and Philosophy* 32, no. 5 (September): 645–671.

Marquand, Robert. 2010. "France Dismisses Petition for It to Pay $17 Billion in Haiti Reparations." *Christian Science Monitor,* August 17, 2010.

Mill, J. S. 1848. *Principles of Political Economy.*

Mill, J. S. 1859. *On Liberty.*

Mill, J. S. 1863. *Utilitarianism.*

Miller, David. 2009. "Why Immigration Controls Are Not Coercive: A Reply to Arash Abizadeh." *Political Theory* 38, no. 1 (February): 111–120.

Miller, David. 2016. *Strangers in Our Midst: The Political Philosophy of Immigration.* Cambridge, MA: Harvard University Press.

Murphy, Liam, and Thomas Nagel. 2002. *The Myth of Ownership: Taxes and Justice.* New York: Oxford University Press.

Nagel, Thomas. 2005. "The Problem of Global Justice." *Philosophy and Public Affairs* 33, no. 2 (March): 113–147.

Ngai, Mae M. 2014. "Undocumented Migration to the United States: A History." In *History, Theories, and Legislation*, edited by Lois Ann Lorentzen, 1–24. Vol. 1 of *Hidden Lives and Human Rights in the United States: Understanding the Controversies and Tragedies of Undocumented Immigration*. Santa Barbara, CA: Praeger.

Nozick, Robert. 1974. *Anarchy, State, and Utopia*. New York: Basic Books.

Obermann, Kieran. 2016. "Immigration as a Human Right." In *Migration in Political Theory: The Ethics of Movement and Membership*, edited by Sarah Fine and Lea Ypi, 32–56. Oxford: Oxford University Press.

Rodrik, Dani. 2014. "Mexico's Growth Problem." Project Syndicate, November 13, 2014. https://www.project-syndicate.org/commentary/mexico-growth-problem-by-dani-rodrik-2014-11.

Rodrik, Dani. 2017. "What Did NAFTA Really Do?" *Dani Rodrik's Weblog* (blog), January 26, 2017. http://rodrik.typepad.com/dani_rodriks_weblog/2017/01/what-did-nafta-really-do.html.

Rogan, Eugene. 2009. *The Arabs: A History*. New York: Basic Books.

Sangiovanni, Andrea. 2007. "Global Justice, Reciprocity, and the State." *Philosophy and Public Affairs* 35, no. 1 (Winter): 3–39.

Scanlon, T. M. 2003. *The Difficulty of Tolerance: Essays in Political Philosophy*. New York: Cambridge University Press.

Singer, Peter. 1972. "Famine, Affluence, and Morality." *Philosophy and Public Affairs* 1, no. 3 (Spring): 229–243.

Singer, Peter. 2009. *The Life You Can Save: Acting Now to End World Poverty*. New York: Random House.

Stiglitz, Joseph E. 2004. "The Broken Promise of NAFTA." *New York Times*, January 6, 2004. http://www.nytimes.com/2004/01/06/opinion/the-broken-promise-of-nafta.html.

Stiglitz, Joseph E., and Andrew Charlton. 2007. *Fair Trade for All: How Trade Can Promote Development*. New York: Oxford University Press.

Timmerman, Travis. 2015. "Sometimes There Is Nothing Wrong with Letting a Child Drown." *Analysis* 75, no. 2 (April): 204–212.

Wilcox, Shelley. 2014. "Do Duties to Outsiders Entail Open Borders?: A Reply to Wellman." *Philosophical Studies* 169, no. 1 (May): 123–132.

World Bank. 2018a. *Moving for Prosperity: Global Migration and Labor Markets*. Washington, DC: World Bank.

World Bank. 2018b. "Poverty: Overview." World Bank, April 11, 2018. Accessed August 2018. http://www.worldbank.org/en/topic/poverty/overview.

Velásquez, Ernesto Rosen. 2016. "States of Violence and the Right to Exclude." *Journal of Poverty* 21, no. 4: 310–330.

Ypi, Lea. 2013. "What's Wrong with Colonialism." *Philosophy and Public Affairs* 41, no. 2 (Spring): 158–191.

Further reading

Arash, Abizadeh. 2016. "The Special-Obligations Challenge to More Open Borders." In Sarah Fine and Lea Ypi (eds.) *Migration in Political Theory: The Ethics of Movement and Membership*. Oxford: Oxford University Press: 105–124.

Bertram, Christopher. 2018. *Do States Have the Right to Exclude Immigrants?* Medford, MA: Polity Press.

Carens, Joseph H. 2013. *The Ethics of Immigration*. New York: Oxford University Press, chapt.11.

Hidalgo, Javier. 2018. *Unjust Borders: Individuals and the Ethics of Immigration.* New York: Routledge, chapters. 1–4.

Hosein, A. 2013. "Immigration and Freedom of Movement." *Ethics and Global Politics* 6: 25–37.

Wilcox, Shelley. 2014. "Do Duties to Outsiders Entail Open Borders?: A Reply to Wellman." *Philosophical Studies* 169, no. 1 (May): 123–132.

2 Arguments for border controls

Relatively few people endorse open borders, and many people seem to think it's just *obvious* that states are permitted to put significant limits on migration across their borders. Why? What, if anything, makes this obviously permissible? One immediate answer is that regulating immigration is an aspect of *sovereignty*: the right of states (and their members) to be self-governing, making their own rules free of outside influence, including rules about who gets to enter their territory and under what conditions.

This answer, as it stands, seems too quick. As Carens points out, "It confuses the question of who ought to have the authority to determine a policy with the question of whether a given policy is morally acceptable" (2013, 6). His point is: we can think separately about who should be in charge of making a certain decision and which decision they should make. We can agree that states should be able to make their own decisions about how to regulate their borders – free from outside interference – without also agreeing that every decision they make is correct. Compare: it might be that (up to a certain point) states should be left free to make their own decisions about how to regulate speech within their borders, hence it would be wrong for the United States, which is relatively permissive with respect to speech, to try to force Germany to abandon its laws banning Holocaust denial. But that doesn't itself mean Germany's policy is the right one: we can still ask whether Holocaust denial ought to be permitted or not.

So an argument for limiting immigration must explain just why states have good reasons to limit immigration. In this chapter we'll look at several such arguments.

A. Public finances, jobs, and fairness

One familiar concern about immigration is its economic impact. We saw in the first chapter that according to some theorists, states (and their members) are obligated to take seriously the interests of their own members, prioritizing them (within limits) over the interests of others. This includes taking seriously the economic interests of members. People who favor limits on immigration point to several different kinds of economic impact. First, they suggest that immigration can burden public finances. States vary in the goods that they provide, but all at least attempt to provide security and basic infrastructure, and they generally also take steps to provide or subsidize their citizens' education, health care, and housing. Many also have welfare provisions designed to protect citizens from the full brunt of unemployment (especially involuntary unemployment), low wages, and so on.

Advocates for limitations on immigration raise the concern that immigrants will take advantage of these public goods, making them more expensive, and ultimately making it harder for states to provide the same quantity or quality of these goods to their own citizens (Miller 2016, 62). British politician Michael Gove, for instance, argued in 2016 that unlimited immigration from the European Union to the United Kingdom would ultimately make the National Health Service (NHS) completely unsustainable by 2030.

One question about this argument is the extent to which immigrants really do use public goods or can be limited in their access to those goods. For instance, states can decide to condition access to welfare benefits on a sufficiently long period of residence, and so, if workers are admitted on a temporary basis, they may not become eligible for such benefits. In Part III of this book we will look at the morality of providing and restricting benefits to immigrants, including in the context of temporary worker schemes. A second crucial question about this argument is whether immigrants really create a net burden on public finances, even when they take relatively significant advantage of the public goods provided by the state. For while their use of public goods may be an economic burden, immigrants also contribute to public finances by working and by paying income tax, property tax, sales tax, and so on. According to a study of the United States by the National Academies of Science, Engineering, and Medicine,

> In terms of fiscal impacts, first-generation immigrants are more costly to governments, mainly at the state and local levels, than are the native-born, in large part due to the costs of educating their children. However, as adults, the children of immigrants (the second generation) are among the strongest economic and fiscal contributors in the US population, contributing more in taxes than either their parents or the rest of the native-born population.
>
> (National Academies 2016)

In the United States, as in Germany (Hansen 2016), fiscal benefits seem to accrue at the federal level, while the several states/the *Länder* bear more of a cost, since they pay more for the education and (in Germany) health care of migrants. This perhaps speaks to the need to distribute the benefits and costs of immigration more evenly across federal systems rather than rejecting immigration for its burden on localities.

The fact that immigrants typically take up employment in their new homes raises a second kind of economic concern: that immigration will cause unemployment and drive down wages. The concern is generally focused especially on jobs and workers at the lower end of the wage and skills spectrum. Lower-skilled workers will sometimes be displaced by immigrants and become unemployed. And the influx of labor means that businesses will be able to offer all lower-skilled workers lower wages. All of this means that not only will immigration have potential costs for citizens, the costs will be concentrated on those who are already least well off. And since social justice requires not only that states pay attention to their own citizens' needs but also that they pay special attention to the needs of their least well-off citizens, limiting immigration is often a necessary step for states to fulfill their responsibilities.[1]

Is limiting immigration really a necessary step in securing social justice? There are several important questions here. The first empirical question regards the overall impact of immigration on the lives and jobs of low-skilled workers. While those workers may suffer lower wages, their cost of living would also likely go down following the impact of immigration on the price of goods. So that may offset whatever burden immigration places on those workers. There is also the question of whether immigration actually does drive down wages or create unemployment. The National Academies report cited earlier found that immigration to the United States has had an impact on lower-skilled workers, but a very limited one.

The second question is whether there is a way to design an immigration program in a manner that prevents any such impact on wages. As mentioned above, one possible route is a temporary worker program. Such programs can potentially be designed so that migrant workers enter only industries where they will be unlikely to heavily affect the wages or employment of domestic workers. Another route is to select immigrants who are likely to work in sectors where they won't compete with domestic workers.

Third, we need to consider how the impact of a more open border interacts with other policies that the state can put in place. Economists often suggest that the government can take various steps to prevent or offset any potential costs of immigration. One way in which this might happen is if immigration expands the pool of better-paying jobs. Even if low-skilled citizens are not immediately well placed to take advantage of these positions, the government might be able to help them acquire the skills and training needed to eventually perform these jobs.

Another option is to strengthen the bargaining rights of workers to ensure that they are in a better position to push for higher wages. On the assumption that immigration can grow the economy as a whole, this strategy is supposed to help workers (including the new migrant workers) reap more of the benefits of this growth relative to their employers. (Though some economists would argue that strengthening bargaining rights reduces the overall economic benefits of immigration, by making it harder to hire the new workers.)

A third option is to find a way to make transfers, using taxation, from those who gain from increased immigration to those who lose out from it

(Chang 2007). Let's assume that businesses will benefit from immigration by having cheaper labor available. The government might tax the increased profits of these businesses and use that money to benefit lower-skilled workers. For instance, the money could be put toward generous public-financed health care for all or tax breaks for poorer members of society. (Of course, if new public benefits – such as health care – are also made available to all new immigrants – itself a policy choice, as we discussed – then that would create one form of fiscal burden.)

In sum, we need to get clear on what exactly the impact of immigration is on low-skilled workers: to what extent does it in fact affect their wages? And to what extent are such costs offset by potential economic gains? We also need to think of immigration policy as one part of an overall package of policies that might be geared toward both growing the economy and protecting the least well off, seeing just how far these goals can be made compatible.

The economic effects of immigration that we have looked at so far are the relatively direct ones of changing market wages and so on. But some theorists suggest that there are also important indirect economic effects of immigration that occur as a result of the increased diversity and cultural changes that immigration can bring. We'll now consider arguments of this kind.

B. Culture

A very familiar argument for controlling immigration is its potential effect on culture. Nationalist movements often claim that unfettered (or, in their view, excessive) immigration will weaken bonds of national identity within a territory by introducing people who do not share in or identify with the national culture. Michael Walzer offers a version of this argument: "The distinctiveness of culture and groups depends upon closure and, without it, cannot be conceived as a stable feature of human life." In the same vein, David Miller writes,

> People mostly identify themselves politically with national communities that stretch backward and forward over the generations, and this membership is regarded as lifelong: it begins at the moment of birth and ends only with death.
> (Miller 2016, 6-7)

Part of what binds members of these national communities together over space and time is their common culture and identity, and national communities have an interest in maintaining this cohesion.

Of what exactly does this "shared culture" consist? Miller suggests that we should focus on "public culture" over "private culture" (2016, 67–68). An individual's "private culture" is their set of beliefs about what matters in their own life, whether it be their artistic projects, how they hope to dress, or their spiritual goals. A "public culture" is a set of shared assumptions about how the common spaces of a society should be organized: what the formal political and economic structures should be like, and which social norms of conduct people should obey. The degree of overlap between private and public cultures can vary: someone might think that all members of society should wear the same religious garments, and even be compelled to wear the same, or they might think that other people should be free to depart from their personal code. The more "thin" the public culture of a place – the less extensive the set of shared norms – the less of a concern there will be that new immigrants will have a distinct culture that alters the existing one. Miller claims that even liberal societies, which advocate toleration and sometimes celebrate diversity, have substantial public cultures.[2]

Take, say, Ireland. What defines the Irish nation? One definition is an ethnic one: we might think of the Irish people as, at its core, those descended from the Celtic peoples who settled the island in pre-Roman times. Another way to define Irishness is in linguistic terms: the group of people who speak the language descended from those spoken by early Celts. We could also try to separate out various cultural strands of Irishness. For instance, we might point to shared myth and stories about, for instance, the hero Cú Chulainn. Historically people have often associated Irishness with religion, specifically Roman Catholicism. More informal customs and ways of interacting might be thought distinctively Irish, such as the sense of humor described in the novels of Roddy Doyle or a general spirit of friendliness and joy in good company ("*craic*"). Or, lastly, being Irish might be defined in terms of shared political values, especially those found in the Constitution of Ireland. Now, liberal principles likely limit the ways in which nationality can be defined for political purposes: we'll return to arguments about these limits in Chapter 4. But let us set those aside for now to look at some more basic questions about what might motivate a concern with nationality in the first place.

Why care about the maintenance of a national culture? Miller claims that it matters both instrumentally – because of its effects – and in itself. The maintenance of a public culture is instrumentally important, according to Miller, because of its effects on social cohesion. These bonds are essential if people are to support social programs made for the common good, such as the welfare state. The instrumental reasons Miller proposes have received mixed empirical support. Robert Putnam (2007)'s famous study of communities in the United States found that levels of trust were higher in places, like North Dakota, with relatively homogenous populations than in places, like Los Angeles, with greater racial and ethnic diversity. But this diversity does not seem to translate into policy differences. Kymlicka and Banting (2006) find that increased diversity caused by immigration does not seem to correlate with reductions in levels of social assistance. (Although they do find that the *rate* of change can matter: social spending increases relatively slowly in places where diversity increases relatively quickly.) Finally, it may be that immigration *restrictions* can themselves sometimes undermine social trust and solidarity by stigmatizing people with ethnic connections to those who are excluded (Mendoza 2015).

In addition to arguing that maintaining an inherited culture matters instrumentally – because it helps to buffet the welfare state and so on – Miller claims,
second, that maintaining these cultures is important in itself. Some evidence that
national cultures matter in themselves is the sheer fact that many people in fact
cherish these cultures and are highly motivated to maintain them. They are concerned, as Charles Taylor puts it, with "remaining true to the culture of [their]
ancestors" (1994, 58). We can think of the Irish nation, for instance, as a collective with an important interest in expressing itself fully and independently. Or we
might just think that its individual members have an important interest in living
in a place that reflects their culture and in passing it on to the next generation.

Let's now look at some further questions about Miller's arguments for cultural preservation.

i. Homogeneity and malleability

One question about Miller's argument is whether it really fits with what actual
nation-states look like: are there really stronger commonalities between
people within particular nation-states than across national territories? In the
world as we know it, there are many liberal democracies with very substantial
diversity of cultural, linguistic, and historical ties.

There are also many examples of linguistic, cultural, and historical commonalities that cross borders. Colonial decisions in Africa about how to divide territory often drew political boundaries in ways that cut across cultural and linguistic
bonds. For instance, many people in present-day Burundi and Rwanda have at
least as much in common – linguistically and culturally – with certain groups in
Uganda and Tanzania as they do with some of their co-citizens (Shimeles 2010).
These observations suggest that national identities can often be relatively thin.

The histories that nationalists often appeal to when positing a deeply
rooted national community are frequently more imagined than real (Appiah
2005). Consider again Ireland: a formative moment that was often pointed to
by some Irish nationalists is the Battle of Clontarf in 1014, at which, as they
describe it, the Irish king Brian Boru – ethnically Celtic and religiously
Christian – drove the "heathen" Vikings out of Ireland. The legend of Boru
has often played a crucial role in the national consciousness: the official
national symbol of Ireland is the Brian Boru Harp, which appears on coins,
the presidential seal, Irish passports, and the branding of Guinness, Ireland's
famous stout. Boru has sometimes been relied on to justify a connection
between Irishness and a Celtic and Christian inheritance.

This version of history is rather distorted, however. Vikings fought on both
sides at Clontarf. Sitric Silkenbeard, often depicted as the leader of the Viking
forces in opposition to Boru, had both Celtic and Norse ancestry, unsurpris-
ing given that Vikings had been present in Ireland for about two hundred
years and were often substantially integrated into the rest of the population.
He was also a Christian – he had taken a pilgrimage to Rome – complicating

the religious nationalist's take on the battle. The historical ethnic mix in Ireland has included (in addition to Celts) Vikings, Romans, Anglo-Saxons, and so on. Linguistically, Gaelic has certainly played an important role in the history of Ireland, but it is also clear that many important and celebrated Irish writers produced their work in English, such as W. B. Yeats, J. M. Synge, James Joyce, Brendan Behan, Mary Lavin, and Maeve Brennan. Of course, more recent immigrant groups – from India, Nigeria, and so on – have also played an important role in contributing to the national culture.

Does falsehood and distortion really affect the importance of national identity? Defenders of the value of national identity argue that it clearly doesn't affect the instrumental role of national identity – its beneficial effects on social trust and so on – and also ultimately doesn't undermine the intrinsic value of national identity either. National identity can play an important instrumental role independently of any falsehoods or distortions in national myths because what allows it to bind people together – generating trust, solidarity, and so on – is just the sheer fact that it is shared. The content of the identity – the particular imagined history, myths, and so on – doesn't matter at all: as long as people strongly identify with their national identity and thus their fellow nationals, they act as a unit, whatever the "truth" about that national identity. More surprisingly, nationalists like Miller also claim that the shaky history and mythic inventions typically at the base of national identities shouldn't prevent us from caring deeply about those identities for their own sake. What matters is that there be a group of people that understands itself as a unit, extended in space and time, and which can reproduce itself over time by involving new members, such as children, in this same self-conception.

These claims by nationalists are in fact significant concessions. They suggest that the naïve nationalist view that there is such a thing as *the* national culture of their ancestors that must be adhered to is mistaken. Ethnic conceptions of the nation, for instance, can be replaced with more expansive definitions of what it is to be a national. If national identities can be made and remade over time and still have value, then why is it problematic if those identities are somewhat changed through immigration? What seems to matter is that there be some kind of commonality among people who share a state, not that it be the "real" culture of the ancestors. Immigration is not a problem, then, if it alters the direction of the national culture. It is only a problem if it destroys the national culture entirely, making it impossible to maintain bonds of trust and a cohesive political unit generally. So it seems that an important empirical question is at what level immigration generates not simply *change* in the national culture but a *breakdown* in that culture.

ii. Stultification

Another issue is whether efforts at maintaining a national culture will in fact be *effective* in maintaining that culture, at least in a form where it is still worth having. Cultures must evolve in order to survive (Scheffler 2007). This is partly because they must adapt to changes in the world: a practice of traditional quilt making may have to respond to market forces if it is to survive; literary endeavors must be matched to the available media, whether they be novels or Twitter poems. There is a danger, then, of stultifying a culture by trying to preserve it.

Cultures often thrive only through contestation and seemingly radical challenges to the status quo.[3] The literary inheritance of Ireland is a point of great national pride, with many of the writers mentioned earlier celebrated on stamps, in literary tours of Dublin, and on posters in pubs across the country and indeed the world. But few of the celebrated writers were easily accepted by the Irish majority while they were writing. The first performance of Synge's *The Playboy of the Western World* was met with rioting and could not be properly completed. When rioting some years later also met Seán O'Casey's *The Plough and the Stars*, Yeats castigated the Irish theatre-going public: "You have disgraced yourself again. Is this to be the recurring celebration of the arrival of Irish genius?" It's far from clear that states, backed by majorities, have the appropriate capacities or incentives to maintain a lively culture that endures rather than suffocates. This doesn't mean the government can do nothing to encourage and support cultural projects. Weak forms of cultural support can come in the shape of, for instance, subsidized housing for writers, regardless of writing tradition. Likewise, the government might give special support to visa applications from writers. What it does potentially rule out is the government taking a strong stand on what exactly the culture should look like going forward.

iii. Selection and integration

Finally, the impact of immigration on the national culture is not fixed simply by the sheer *number* of people admitted into a territory. One element that matters is the extent to which the particular migrants admitted really differ in their "public" culture from members of the host state, bearing in mind the points above about just how much cultural overlap is really needed to sustain a political community. The cultural impact of immigration is also affected by what the state's approach to "integration" is, and how private institutions and individuals interact with immigrants. With the right policies, it may well be possible to have diversity while also having cohesive national identities and proper respect for each individual and group in society. Here too it is important not to think of policies concerning admission in a vacuum: they must again be evaluated as parts of a potential *package* of policies.

We'll look at "cultural selection" procedures and integration policies as an alternative in Chapter 4, Section D. But let us look (extremely) briefly here at what "integration" might involve and how it might affect the national culture. This is a large topic that unfortunately cannot be fully discussed here, but the

key point to consider is whether whichever cultural commonalities and affi-
nities it is appropriate for states to promote can be produced as a side effect
of ensuring full participation in a society for immigrants, where this means
ensuring that they have extensive opportunities for advancement in that
society and for interaction with other members on a footing of equality.
Equality of economic opportunity seems to be an especially important force
in this regard (Hansen 2012, 2016).

As Anderson (2010) argues, when people meet personally and work together,
on a footing of equality, they gain a greater understanding of one another's
viewpoints and ways of life, ultimately leading also to reduced stereotyping and
prejudice. Equal opportunities can also cause greater identification between
immigrants and the host society, since feelings of alienation on the part of
immigrants, where they exist, are often due to a sense of being denied the
advantages offered to others in a society (Adida, Laitin, and Valfort 2016).

What affects the ability of immigrants to achieve social advancement? The
empirical debate continues. Some potential factors include linguistic abilities
of migrants, the role of discrimination, the degree of social assistance (which
might help people find work or might sap their motivation for doing so),
levels of education, access to information, and exclusion from social networks
(Koser 2007, 97; Hansen 2012, 2016). These different factors require quite
different policy levels. But the main point here is that whether immigrant
communities share commonalities with and identify with the rest of a society
is not fixed by sheer levels of immigration.

Now, it's often said that while immigrant co-participation in society might be
desirable, states ought to worry about whether this will in fact happen because
immigrants may cloister themselves in "separate societies," away from the
native population. Immigrants do sometimes cluster in particular neighborhoods and social networks, but we need to bear in mind two points. First,
where such clustering occurs it is often due in part to the difficulty immigrants
can have in being fully accepted by members of the receiving society. In the
most extreme cases, housing discrimination, harassment, and so on can drive
immigrants out of mixed neighborhoods. Second, insofar as immigrants make
their own decision to live in more homogenous neighborhoods it's not clear
that is necessarily a problem.[4] The state can still take steps, such as investing in
education in these neighborhoods, to make sure that immigrants can achieve
social mobility and interact with others within the spheres of economic and
civic life. The sheer fact that some people may wish to live near to others that
they identify with can be seen as a corollary of familiar liberal commitments to
freedom of association and the acceptance of pluralism.

C. Freedom of association

The next important argument that we will look at tries to sidestep some of the
problems we've seen for other accounts. Instead of focusing directly on

potential *costs* of cultural change induced by migrants or immigration's economic impact, it focuses on the right of a community to *choose* the way it develops. Even if immigration merely alters a culture rather than destroying it or changes its economic structure without seriously harming workers, existing members of a political community might still want to have control over the economic and cultural shape of their society. The need for such control means that political communities must have freedom of association. And to have this freedom they must have more or less complete discretion over whom to admit.

Why exactly does immigration limit the ability of political communities to choose the directions of their societies? The freedom of association argument – laid out by Christopher Heath Wellman – appeals to the fact that immigrants who settle in a new territory will become new members of the political community, with all of the entitlements granted to other members. We'll look later, in Part III, at the basis for this entitlement, but it is plausible on its face: if a country admits an immigrant on the understanding that they will settle permanently in that country, and they do indeed settle there, surely there is a point at which they must be granted a right to vote and so on, just like any citizen of that country. This means, Wellman argues, that accepting new immigrants is effectively similar to admitting new members into a club or another association. Once in the club, they won't just be in the same physical space: they will also participate in its social events and be able to vote for its leaders. This means that these new members will have an influence on the direction of the club, through both formal and informal channels.

Further, Wellman continues, we generally think that clubs and other associations have a right to freedom of association: they have a right to determine for themselves who gets to join. Liberal democracies generally protect (within limits) this freedom, putting constraints on the ability of the state to control people's associations. The state may not, say, dictate that a Methodist church must allow non-adherents to join or that a cricket club must merge with a rival team. And it certainly may not dictate to people whom they will marry.

Does this argument provide a justification for the state to limit immigration? One difficulty is that it appears to establish only that states have the right to make decisions for themselves about their membership: that others cannot force them to make one decision rather than another. And, as we saw at the beginning of this chapter, the fact that states have a right to settle their own immigration policy free of outside influence (if indeed they have that right) does not by itself tell us anything about which policy they should ultimately adopt.

Wellman's response is that we not only think people shouldn't be forced to associate with others, we also think that they don't have a duty to associate with others. Not only would it be wrong for the government to coerce people into marrying against their will, we also think that people do not have a moral obligation to marry against their inclinations. This is true, Wellman suggests, even if there would be important social good secured. Can we really demand, morally, of someone that they get married to someone from a lower socio-economic background just for the sake of promoting social mobility?

We might ask here whether Wellman's analogy with private associations is helpful. For one thing, the burden of having to accept someone into your club or your home – so that you now have to see them every week and accept their involvement in your personal projects – seems on its face quite different from the burden of living in the same country as someone you didn't want to enter, or having to share political institutions with that same person. When you share a home with someone, they are inextricably involved in your personal affairs – your religious practice, your love life, the objects you surround yourself with at night – while someone you share a state with only has an impact on the public sphere – the way your society is governed, what its public spaces look like, and so on. And generally speaking, we treat these spheres quite differently: for instance, liberal democracies generally put significant constraints on the ability of legislatures to regulate people's private lives, while leaving them comparatively free to make decisions about the public sphere. As we saw above, the public spheres of many societies already contain many heterogeneous influences, and it is not obviously a problem if those influences evolve over time.

Wellman suggests that these differences between marriages, clubs, and states are merely a matter of degree. Of course, it is worse to have no discretion over one's marital partner, but we still also think it would be bad, Wellman says, for clubs to have no discretion over their membership. Similarly, we should think that it is problematic (though less problematic) for a political community to have no say on who becomes a member. Is this correct? People enter into and value these various relationships with others for very different reasons, such as the deep bonds of intimacy and mutual concern, the pleasure of being part of a cricket club appropriate for one's level of ability, and the pursuit of a society matching one's conception of justice. Given the very different functions of these "organizations," one might think that the reasons people have for limiting membership are very different in kind and not just degree.

Another problem with Wellman's analogical reasoning is that exclusion from a small association within a society takes place against a very different background than exclusion from an entire state. When someone is excluded from one golf club, they generally have the option to join another broadly comparable one. And if another doesn't exist, individuals are able – assuming their state is appropriately supportive – to acquire the resources, space, and so on to create new associations. There is no comparable background in place when it comes to migrants trying to enter a state. Honduran migrants who are turned away from the United States cannot easily join another state, still less set up one for themselves. There is no global legal framework making sure that they can set up a new society for themselves if they want to. What about genuinely monopolistic private associations, where it really is impossible – for reasons of scale maybe – for non-members to find an alternative or set one up for themselves? These associations are more analogous to states, but it is rather less obvious that they are under no duty to admit new members. Maybe the only social club in a small, geographically isolated, town is under moral pressure to admit the townsfolk who would otherwise lead lonely existences on the outside.

Let's set aside Wellman's analogies between political communities and other kinds of associations. Even if these are very different, Wellman could still base his argument on the distinctive impact on the political community of admitting someone into a territory. Wellman points out, as we saw earlier, that people who settle in a territory ultimately acquire (at least after a sufficient period of time) various rights, including the right to vote. This means that they will have a say in the direction of the country: its economic structure, its cultural policies, and so on. Thus, we might say, admitting them has an impact on the ability of the society to be self-determining: its ability to make fundamental political decisions for itself. As Wellman writes, "Freedom of association is ... a central component of the more general right to self-determination" (2008, 13n5).

Self-determination, Wellman points out, is considered an important value in other contexts. Take, he says, regional associations among states, such as the North American Free Trade Agreement (NAFTA). Surely, Wellman says, countries must have a say in whether they join these organizations. It would be wrong for the United States to proceed as if Canada were part of NAFTA without any agreement from the Canadian government. Even more clearly, wouldn't it be seriously wrong for the United States to forcibly annex Canada if the majority of Canadians were against it? "I assume without argument," Wellman writes, "that, even if the United States could execute this unilateral merger without disrupting the peace or violating the individual rights of any Canadians, this hostile takeover would be impermissible" (2008, 112). The sheer destruction of Canadian self-determination would be wrongful, even if it weren't especially harmful.

Let's now consider some objections to this self-determination argument. The first points out that this version of the argument can justify at most limiting the admission of new permanent residents (Fine 2010). The version of Wellman's argument we are considering begins by assuming that those who are permitted to cross the border will ultimately become entitled to the full set of rights enjoyed by citizens. But many people who are admitted into a territory will never acquire these entitlements. Most obviously, spending a few weeks in a country as a tourist does not mean that you can now demand a right to vote. It's also plausible that, say, people on student visas or very short-term work visas are not entitled to full membership in the political community. Thus, admitting these people doesn't carry with it any significant cost in terms of self-determination.

What if Wellman were to confine his argument to the acceptance of new permanent residents, accepting that states may have to allow temporary immigration? Here are some concerns that apply even to this more restricted argument.

First, we need to consider the extent to which admitting certain immigrants really threatens the ability of a political community to determine its own future. This involves a mix of moral and empirical considerations. Once we note that states have distinctive functions from other kinds of association – functions very different from marriages, churches, cricket clubs, and so on – we need to think about the constraints on which goals it is proper for the state to pursue. For example, it is not acceptable – as we see from the rules laid out in many liberal constitutions – for a state to promote any particular religion. It also is not acceptable for a state to tell people that it is better to be straight than to be gay or (as Wellman acknowledges to an extent) to favor any racial or ethnic group. These constraints on the proper goals of states may in fact be quite tight: just as it is impermissible for a state to promote a sectarian religion, perhaps it is also unacceptable, in a pluralistic society, to promote a sectarian cultural project. Just how tight these constraints are is something that we will look at in more detail in Chapter 4. For present purposes, what we should note is that the narrower the range of goals states can permissibly pursue, the more diverse the range of immigrants that can be admitted without threatening the ability of the political community to be self-determining. For example, suppose that some potential admittees practice a religion that is in the minority in the receiving state. Their admission will increase the proportion of people in the territory practicing that religion. But since maintaining the majority religion – or trying to determine the religious makeup of the country more generally – is not a proper goal for the state, the sheer fact that immigrants might alter the religious balance in the state is not an acceptable reason to prevent them from entering. It is not a constraint on self-determination if immigration affects the ability of a political community to control its religious composition, since political communities have no right to control their religious composition in the first place.

Once we have determined which kinds of goals political communities can legitimately pursue, and which of these goals are especially important, there are also empirical questions about the extent to which admitting various immigrants would actually prevent the existing political community from pursuing its current goals. For example, suppose that those goals include trying to enact a certain view of justice. If the potential immigrants are broadly on board with that view of justice, then their admission will have no impact on the political community's ability to pursue its goals. There will also be many cases where admitting additional immigrants will have a negligible impact on the country's ability to maintain its majority language if the immigrants already speak that language and are happy to promote its use. The sheer number of migrants admitted, relative to the size of the country, is also relevant. One hundred thousand new immigrants would constitute almost one-fifth of the population of Luxembourg, but the same number of immigrants in the United States would be a very small fraction of the approximately 328 million people in the United States. Finally, as with the cultural preservation argument, we need to consider whether the immigrants once admitted and properly integrated will really differ substantially from the host population, especially by the time that they acquire the right to vote. If they come to share the same basic political values as people in the receiving society, then they will have no significant impact on the self-determination of the antecedent political community.

Finally, as Wellman points out, the self-determination argument provides only a prima facie case for limits on admission: it offers one consideration, but it's a consideration that must be weighed against potential arguments for accepting more immigrants. This means that even if self-determination matters, its importance might still be outweighed by the considerations in favor of open borders we looked at in Chapter 1. Wellman provides objections to some of those arguments (2013, 119–137), and you can weigh the various considerations for yourself.

D. Forced obligation

The freedom of association account that we just looked at focuses on the rights that individuals must be granted if they reside in a territory for a substantial period of time, and thus struggles to explain why states may be permitted to exclude people whose stay will be briefer. The argument that we will now look at attempts to cover all potential migrants, irrespective of the length of their stay.

There are rights that individuals gain simply by being present in a territory (we'll give these rights a closer look in Part III of this book). For instance, once someone is present in a territory, the state is obliged to ensure that they have access to at least emergency medical care, even if it is not obligated to provide them with the same full welfare benefits that it provides to its citizens. It must also protect their bodily security. Political institutions must secure the basic rights not just of their citizens but of all people within their territory. Thus, Blake (2013) writes,

> The mere fact of [a migrant's] presence within the jurisdiction is sufficient to place these institutions under an obligation to act in defense of these rights. The individuals within the United States, moreover, have a moral and legal obligation to act in defense of these rights, an obligation they did not have prior to her entry into the territory of the United States. They are obligated to act in particular ways, so that her rights are effectively protected and fulfilled: they are obligated to help pay for the police that will defend her physical security, they are obligated to serve on juries that will serve to convict those who attack her, and indeed, they are obligated to help create and sustain institutions sufficient to protect her basic human rights. This obligation, it should be noted, emerges from the simple fact of presence; no particular legal status within the jurisdiction is required.
>
> (Blake 2013, 113)

The forced obligation argument is that states (and their citizens) can exclude immigrants in order to avoid taking on these obligations. Are states permitted to exclude people just to avoid taking on obligations to protect their basic rights? Blake suggests that in other contexts we would agree that people can resist having obligations imposed on them. Suppose that a sick person requires considerable attention in order to survive.[5] They are currently receiving adequate attention. But, let's suppose further, that just by tapping you on the shoulder they can make you morally responsible for taking care of them. Do they "have a right to touch you, and place you under an obligation to provide [them] with those goods to which [they are] morally entitled?" (Blake 2013, 116). No, according to Blake: they are already getting all the care that they are entitled to, and they are not allowed to transfer to you the responsibility to provide that care. Moreover, you can resist being saddled with that responsibility: you could run away to prevent them from touching you and even use some degree of force to stay free of the responsibility.

Similar reasoning applies in the case of states, Blake argues. Suppose that a migrant lives in a place where their basic rights are protected: the state they live under provides proper police support when they are under threat, and so on. In that case, it would be wrong for them to insist on making some other state responsible for protecting their basic rights. To do so is to wrongly inflict new obligations on this other state and its members. And that state may enforce its borders in order to resist incurring these obligations.

Now, of course, many people do not live in places that protect their basic rights. So, Blake concludes, the right to exclude is conditional: states may only refuse entry to people whose basic rights are protected elsewhere. They have no right to exclude people whose basic rights are not protected in the countries they wish to leave. What exactly it is to lack proper protection for one's basic rights – in essence: who should count as a refugee – is itself a difficult question, and it's one we'll look at in more detail in Chapter 5. Blake's account entails that states may not exclude these people, and however we define refugees there are likely, as Blake notes, to be very many of them in the world today (2013, 126). What the account does allow is excluding people who in live in a state that adequately protects their rights: the majority of people in Norway, for instance, would not be wronged if Australia refused to admit them.

Why exactly is it so problematic to inflict new obligations on someone? And why is incurring those obligations so onerous that people (and states) are justified in using force to resist them? The key reason, Blake claims, is not the cost of fulfilling those obligations: the resources needed to provide proper attention to a sick person in one's home, for instance. It may be, for instance, that becoming responsible for someone's major illness is an overall benefit, given the intimate bond and exercise of distinctive caring capacities that it can bring with it. The problem, rather, is the limitation on one's freedom that comes with new obligations. If I have to care for a person with a major illness in my house, this affects the plans I can make for my life. I will have to exclude, for instance, projects that would prevent me from being at home sufficiently often. I may be able to write my novel, but I might have to give up on my dream of joining a touring circus. In sum, my options are limited. Blake proposes that there is likewise a burden placed on the freedom of states (and their members) when they incur new obligations to new immigrants.

Let's look at some potential advantages of Blake's account as an argument for (somewhat) closed borders. First, Blake offers an explanation for why restrictions might be acceptable, even where there is no apparent cost to host states. Immigrants are often an overall benefit, given everything that they can do for the economy, cultural diversity, and so on in the receiving state. But they can still limit freedom, according to Blake's argument, and thus be excluded.

Second, the argument seems capable of explaining why states may restrict all entry into the territory, not just limiting the permanent residence that ultimately brings with it full rights of citizenship. Because the duties Blake focuses on are owed even to people who are only in the territory briefly, the forced obligation argument suggests that states can limit the entry of even short-term immigrants, not just the long-term immigrants that the freedom of association argument focuses on.

Let's now consider some questions about Blake's account. Do immigrants really limit the freedom of states (and their members)? Are these limits sufficiently substantial to justify exclusion? States, unlike individual people, do not have personal projects like writing novels or achieving spiritual enrichment (Kates and Pevnick 2014, 182). As we saw earlier, the projects states can legitimately pursue are more limited than those of private people or organizations: they cannot pursue religious objectives, for instance. Does incurring obligations to new immigrants limit the legitimate projects of states in any substantial way? To some extent this will depend on exactly what basic rights people have, but let's focus on the rights that Blake emphasizes: rights to personal security. Securing this right will mean spending additional money on the police force and may also require, to some degree, rethinking current law-and-order policy. For instance, if the new immigrants are especially vulnerable to violence (in the form of hate crimes, for example), then perhaps prosecutorial priorities will have to change somewhat. We might question the degree to which this really limits the freedom of the state to pursue its objectives. After all, the state will already have some form of police force and criminal justice system generally (Kates and Pevnick 2014, 182), and the new migrants will be taxed to help pay for this system. The main burden will just be some time spent on thinking about how best to divert funds to and deploy this system, given the additional population. While this time could've been spent on other projects, it doesn't seem all that substantial a constraint of the state's freedom. It doesn't mean any major change to the available policy options in key areas, such as whether to have a minimum wage and how much post-tax redistribution there should be to less well-off citizens.

Still, Blake might insist, while the burdens on freedom of additional immigrants might not be that substantial, especially compared to taking responsibility for a person with a severe illness, there are still some constraints. And it is always wrong to inflict such constraints on an institution and its members.

Conceding that the burdens on freedom of admitting additional migrants are not substantial leads to a different kind of problem for Blake's account. Let's consider some different obligations and their differing impact on freedom. Acquiring a new dependent limits my choices substantially, whereas an obligation to bring my neighbor's newspaper in when I fetch my own from the garden (we live across the hall from one another) has much less impact on my freedom of choice. The rest of my day can still be planned out as I please.

This variation in how onerous various burdens are affects what I may do to avoid those burdens. Suppose that if my neighbor asks me to, I will have to collect his paper along with mine. It might be reasonable for me to resist this obligation by avoiding my neighbor, so that he doesn't get a chance to ask me. It seems much less reasonable – very likely impermissible – for me to put my hand over his mouth to stop him asking me. And it is still more clearly impermissible to stop him by saying, "Don't you dare ask me to take in your newspaper: if you do, I'll box your ears." My response must be proportionate, let's agree, to the burden placed on me of incurring the obligation.

States use force to prevent migrants from entering, and so we should ask whether that use of force is proportionate to the burden on freedom of admitting new migrants. If that burden is not substantial – more on the order of fetching the neighbor's paper than taking responsibility for a dependent – then it is much less likely that the state may use force to resist that burden. We'll look in more detail at the precise methods states use to enforce their borders in the next chapter, along with the nature of proportionality constraints.

E. Brain drain

A common concern with allowing substantial immigration, especially from poorer states, is that it will impose costs on the sending countries. We'll focus in particular on "brain drain" – the movement of skilled workers from less developed countries, where they have often received state-supported training, to take jobs in more developed ones – and the burdens this can place on sending countries. The movement of health care workers is a prime example of this.

> In 2000, for example, Ghana trained 250 new nurses – and lost 500 nurses to emigration.... In 2002 alone, Malawi lost 75 nurses to the United Kingdom – a cohort that represented 12 percent of all the nurses resident in Malawi.
>
> (Brock and Blake 2015, 2)

Why is the movement of health care workers troubling? First, it can be very costly for the countries losing a significant part of their skilled workforce

(Brock and Blake 2015, 38–39). As we just saw, brain drain can deprive developing countries of very significant proportions of their health care workers, making it very difficult for them to staff their hospitals and depriving them of specialists whose knowledge would otherwise diffuse through and bolster the economy generally. The loss of these workers also reduces the tax base available to the government.

Brain drain can also have a more indirect impact on developing countries: as Valdez (2010, 227) points out, the loss of skilled workers means the loss of educated citizens who might help to support and improve the country's institutions by helping to hold the government accountable, serving in government themselves, and so on. This has bad effects as well as being a problem in itself: well-functioning institutions are widely considered a crucial force in fostering development. Government corruption, for example, channels state funds into the pockets of elites rather than programs to support agriculture and health care for the poor.

Second, brain drain seems to create unfairness. Developing countries devote significant amounts of their scarce resources to training health care workers. They also support those workers in more subtle ways, providing not just the health care training, but also the personal security, infrastructure, and childhood education needed to take advantage of that training. Yet developing nations often lose much of the "return" from their investments in these workers. The workers benefit from the higher wages that they can now receive, and foreign, more developed nations benefit from their talents, while their home countries are left needing to fill their hospitals, find alternative sources of tax revenue, and so on. Isn't this unfair, especially to the people left behind in the less developed countries, whose taxes supported the ability of these workers to develop their skills?

These concerns suggest that developed countries should make sure to limit the entry of migrants where their admission would cause harm to their home countries and create unfairness. The United Kingdom should not draw its health care workers from Malawi.

But perhaps there are ways for developed countries to draw on this labor while mitigating any potential harm and unfairness. Gillian Brock supports a "Bhagwati tax," originally designed by economist Jagdish Bhagwati to offset the fiscal burden to sending countries of brain drain (Bhagwati 1976). This is a small surcharge on the taxable income of émigrés from developing nations that is collected and administered by an international body, such as, under Bhagwati's original proposal, the United Nations. The tax would be levied on a migrant for a limited period of, say, 10 years from the date they take up residence in their new country. This tax on the émigré workers themselves could be combined with a requirement that the developed countries that receive them, and benefit substantially from them, also pay developing countries in compensation for these benefits. Or, if it seems unfair to require the migrants to pay the tax (Brock thinks it isn't, given the benefits they have received from their home countries), then the more developed country can make all of the compensatory payments.

This still leaves the problem of the loss of skills and leadership that can affect the sending state's institutions. One proposal for offsetting this would be to admit the workers on a temporary basis. Since they will ultimately return to their home country, it may be that their skills and leadership would still be deployed there to good effect. Temporary worker schemes are controversial, however, and we will look at those controversies in Chapter 7.

F. Security

As a general matter, security is one of the few considerations that almost all theorists agree can be permissibly taken into account by the state. Where disagreement begins to set in is when we look at exactly which steps the state may take to protect security. Some security-protecting measures are relatively *individualized*, relying on careful investigations into, for instance, the criminal records of particular applicants and other assessments of the threat that they specifically pose. These are relatively uncontroversial, at least when applied fairly and consistently.

More controversial situations arise where the government seeks to exclude broad classes of people – such as members of a particular religion or people from certain parts of the world – on the basis of concerns about their security threat. These cases often arouse suspicions that the underlying motivation for the policy is racial and ethnic animus. US politicians often use the guise of security, Silva (2015) argues, when discussing the Mexican border, when in fact they are trying to appease members of their political base who wish to maintain racial hierarchies within the country. Border enforcement limits the sheer number of Latinx people who are able to enter, attempting to keep them in the minority, but can also communicate a message of racial inferiority. Racialized images of migrant security threats have also often created a wholly unrealistic perception of the risks posed by migration.

How should the competing demands of protecting national security and respecting racial equality be taken into account? As a case study, we'll look in more detail in Chapter 4 at the "travel ban" instituted by US President Donald Trump.

G. Chapter summary

In this chapter, we looked at arguments for the permissibility of states putting limits on immigration, including supporting the wages of local workers, limiting the obligations that states incur, and protecting the national culture. Each of these justifications faces significant challenges, as we have seen. First, one must consider the magnitude of any burden put on the state by admitting more immigrants: for instance, in many cases the impact of immigration on wages or the local culture will be small, and the obligations incurred by the host country relatively trivial. Second, one needs to consider not simply how many migrants will be admitted, but how exactly particular immigration programs will be designed, including how migrants are selected for entry and on what terms they will be present in the country. A state that is worried about the economic impact of immigration, for instance, can try to design a temporary worker program where the migrants work only in industries with severe labor shortages and thus do not negatively impact domestic wages. A state that is concerned about the effects of immigration on language use can try to select migrants who already speak the dominant language and/or provide support so that all new migrants can learn that language. Third, we need to consider immigration policies as part of an overall package of policies that the state institutes. For example, whether the state in general takes steps to lessen inequality will likely affect which citizens gain and lose from increased immigration.

For reasons of space, I had to cut an entire chapter on integration from this manuscript, but I would be happy to share it with anyone who requests it.

Study questions

- Must states limit immigration in order to promote equality within their territory?
- Why does Miller think it is important to maintain national cultures?
- To what extent are cultures malleable? Does this affect the case for cultural preservation?
- Is Wellman's analogy between states and smaller associations, such as clubs, helpful?
- Both Blake and Wellman think that states acquire obligations to people who enter their territory (at least for a sufficient period of time). Which obligations? Is avoiding these obligations a good reason for states to limit immigration?
- Which of the arguments in this chapter for limiting immigration do you think is the strongest? How should we weigh the considerations presented in that argument against the justifications for open borders given in the previous chapter?

Notes

1 The classic argument that social justice requires a focus on the least well off is in Rawls (1971).
2 At least sometimes: Miller's description of how liberal societies operate may be rosier than their reality, as we'll discuss in Chapter 4, and as implied by Hafez's (2014) title and argument.
3 See Orosco (2016) for an extensive argument for this claim.
4 I draw here on a parallel argument that Shelby (2014) makes in relation to African American neighborhoods.
5 This is a simplified version of the example that Blake (borrowing from Judith Jarvis Thomson) offers (2013, 116).

References

Adida, Claire L., David D. Laitin, and Marie-Anne Valfort. 2016. *Why Muslim Integration Fails in Christian-Heritage Societies.* Cambridge, MA: Harvard University Press.

Appiah, Kwame Anthony. 2005. *The Ethics of Identity.* Princeton, NJ: Princeton University Press.

Bhagwati, Jagdish N., ed. 1976. *The Brain Drain and Taxation: Theory and Empirical Analysis.* Amsterdam: North-Holland.

Blake, Michael. 2013. "Immigration, Jurisdiction, and Exclusion." *Philosophy and Public Affairs* 41, no. 2 (Spring): 103–130.

Brock, Gillian, and Michael Blake. 2015. *Debating Brain Drain: May Governments Restrict Emigration?*Oxford: Oxford University Press.

Carens, Joseph H. 2013. *The Ethics of Immigration.* New York: Oxford University Press.

Chang, Howard F. 2007. "The Economic Impact of International Labor Migration: Recent Estimates and Policy Implications." *Temple Political and Civil Rights Law Review* 16, no. 2 (Spring): 321–333.

Fine, Sarah. 2016. "Immigration and Discrimination." In *Migration in Political Theory: The Ethics of Movement and Membership*, edited by Sarah Fine and Lea Ypi, 125–150. Oxford: Oxford University Press.

Hafez, Kai. 2014. *Islam in "Liberal" Europe: Freedom, Equality, and Intolerance.* Translated by Alex Skinner. Lanham, MD: Rowman and Littlefield.

Hansen, Randall. 2012. "The Centrality of Employment in Immigrant Integration in Europe." Migration Policy Institute, Washington, DC.

Hansen, Randall. 2016. "Making Immigration Work: How Britain and Europe Can Cope with Their Immigration Crises." *Government and Opposition* 51, no. 2 (April): 183–208.

Kates, M. and Pevnick, R. 2014. "Immigration Jurisdiction and History." *Philosophy and Public Affairs* 42, no. 2: 179–194.

Koser, Khalid. 2007. *International Migration: A Very Short Introduction.* Oxford: Oxford University Press.

Kymlicka, W. and Banting, K. 2006. "Immigration, Multiculturalism, and the Welfare State." *Ethics and Global Politics*20. no. 3 (September): 281–304.

Mendoza, J.J. 2015. 'Latino/a Immigration: A Refutation of the Social Trust Argument', in H. Bauder and C. Matheis (eds.), *Migration Policy and Practice: Interventions and Solutions.* New York: Palgrave-Macmillan: 37–57.

Miller, David. 2016. *Strangers in Our Midst: The Political Philosophy of Immigration.* Cambridge, MA: Harvard University Press.

National Academies of Sciences, Engineering, and Medicine. 2016. "Immigration's Long-Term Impacts on Overall Wages and Employment of Native-Born US Workers Very Small, Although Low-Skilled Workers May Be Affected, New Report Finds; Impacts on Economic Growth Positive, While Effects on Government Budgets Mixed." National Academies of Sciences, Engineering, and Medicine, September 21, 2016. http://www8.nationalacademies.org/onpinews/newsitem.aspx?RecordID=23550.

Orosco, José-Antonio. 2016. *Toppling the Melting Pot: Immigration and Multiculturalism in American Pragmatism.* Bloomington and Indianapolis: University of Indiana Press.

Putnam, Robert D. 2007. "*E Pluribus Unum*: Diversity and Community in the Twenty-First Century; The 2006 Johan Skytte Prize Lecture." *Scandinavian Political Studies* 30, no. 2 (June): 137–174.

Rawls, John. 1999. *A Theory of Justice.* Cambridge, MA: Belknap Press of Harvard University Press.

Shelby, Tommie. 2014. "Integration, Inequality, and Imperatives of Justice: A Review Essay." *Philosophy and Public Affairs* 42, no. 3 (Summer): 253–285.

Silva, Grant. 2015. "On the Militarization of Borders and the Juridicial Right to Exclude." *Public Affairs Quarterly* 29, no. 2 (April): 217–234.

Taylor, Charles. 1994. *Multiculturalism: Examining the Politics of Recognition*. Princeton, NJ: Princeton University Press.

Valdez, Jorge M. 2010. "Is Immigration a Human Right?," in R. Pierik and W. Werner (eds.), *Cosmopolitanism in Context: Perspectives from International Law and Political Theory*. Cambridge: Cambridge University Press: 221–248.

Walzer, Michael. 1983. *Spheres of Justice: A Defense of Pluralism and Equality*. New York: Basic Books.

Wellman, Christopher Heath. 2008. "Immigration and Freedom of Association." *Ethics* 119, no. 1 (October): 109–141.

Further reading

Blake, Michael. 2013. "Immigration, Jurisdiction, and Exclusion." *Philosophy and Public Affairs* 41, no. 2 (Spring): 103–130.

Brezger, J. and Cassee, A. "Debate: Immigrants and Newcomers by Birth – Do Statist Arguments Imply a Right to Exclude Both?" *The Journal of Political Philosophy* 24, no. 3: 367–378.

Kollar, Eszter (ed.). 2016. "Symposium on Brain Drain: The Merits and Limits of Furthering Normative Solutions in Source Countries." *Moral Philosophy and Politics* 3, no. 1.

Miller, David. 2016. *Strangers in Our Midst: The Political Philosophy of Immigration*. Cambridge, MA: Harvard University Press. Chapter 4.

Oberman, Kieran. 2013. "Can Brain Drain Justify Immigration Restrictions?" *Ethics* 123, no. 3: 427–455.

Song, Sarah. 2018. *Immigration and Democracy*. New York: OUP. Chapter 4.

Wellman, Christopher H., and Philip Cole. 2011. *Debating the Ethics of Immigration: Is There a Right to Exclude?* New York: Oxford University Press.

3   Enforcement

Most of the arguments we looked at earlier in the open borders debate propose ways in which it would be desirable for there to be greater movement of people – for instance, because it would increase global equality – or ways in which greater movement of people would be problematic – for instance, because it would impose excessive fiscal burdens on receiving states.

Some theorists claim that these arguments miss a crucial aspect of immigration policy, namely mechanisms of *enforcement*: the *means* by which states actually prevent or deter people from crossing borders. In the modern world, there are multiple enforcement mechanisms, including screening people at airports, erecting fences along borders, detaining migrants in locked facilities, using drones and patrol officers for border surveillance, and searching for and deporting migrants who have crossed the border without authorization. A further complexity is that each of these mechanisms comes in different varieties. Detention can be for varying lengths of time, and the facilities can vary widely in their conditions. Searches for people who have entered without authorization could be conducted specifically by immigration officials, or they might be delegated to police officers who would combine traffic stops and so forth with requests for documentation. Which of these enforcement strategies, if any, is an acceptable means of restricting migration? Are some more problematic than others? Recent theorists have insisted that these questions require careful attention to the details of enforcement policy rather than just the general desirability or not of increased migration.

A. Enforcement and efficacy

A good way to see the difference between the closed borders arguments we looked at earlier and an argument for increasing enforcement is to see that increased enforcement can sometimes actually thwart the goals of closed borders theorists.

People who argue for closed borders generally present reasons why states have a strong interest in limiting, or a right to limit, the number of migrants that enter their territory, especially the number of migrants who enter and *settle* permanently. These arguments are generally taken to lead fairly straightforwardly to conclusions about enforcement at the border: if a state would be justified in seeking to reduce the immigration rate by 40 percent, then it is justified in directing its immigration administration to admit 40 percent fewer people at the border in the future and use some degree of force to prevent others from entering.

But there are some mechanisms by which enforcement can actually *increase* the total population of settled immigrants. Where borders are more porous, some migrants are attracted to "circular" migration, where they enter a country for limited periods, typically to work. For much of the twentieth century, for example, Mexican migrants often entered the United States purely to perform seasonal agricultural work (earlier as part of an official temporary migration program, and later as unauthorized migrants) (Ngai 2014). Between crop seasons, these workers returned to Mexico, and they generally left their families at home while working. Heightened US enforcement starting in the latter part of the twentieth century seems to have broken this pattern. The new enforcement strategy included much greater patrolling of areas that were easier to cross and less patrolling of areas where crossing is very dangerous due to the physical terrain. This meant that a migrant who made it to the United States was less likely to leave, since on the return journey they might get stopped at the border or even die in the desert. And it also meant that they were more likely to try to bring their families to the United States, since they would not be able to go home to see them.

So increased enforcement along the US-Mexico border may well have thwarted the very goals that people who support closed borders have in mind. Those theorists, as we saw, are especially concerned about the impact of settled migrants on culture, public finances, democratic deliberation, and so on. Some philosophers infer from this history that enforcement should *now* be decreased, even by the lights of the closed borders theorist, since it is counterproductive (Mendoza 2017, 98). What is hard to establish, though, is whether patterns of cyclical migration, once broken, can be re-established. The important empirical question is: if the United States were to reduce its border enforcement tomorrow, would this create a return to earlier trends or just result in a greater population of settled immigrants?

B. Moral constraints on enforcement

Setting aside whether and when enforcement is counterproductive, we can also ask whether present-day methods are *morally* acceptable. Even if states have good reasons to limit entry, that doesn't mean they can use just any means to do so. Perhaps I have good reasons to limit entry onto my farm, for instance, but it wouldn't be acceptable for me to prevent someone coming in by scaring them away with racial abuse or threatening to lock them in my basement indefinitely. Modern-day immigration enforcement uses a variety of methods that are controversial and that require more direct scrutiny than is present in the traditional open borders debate (Mendoza 2015). This is most obvious if we consider arguments for border controls, which tell us that migration can be limited without telling us *how* it can be limited. Even arguments for open borders don't necessarily settle current enforcement issues: those arguments tell us that *ideally* there would be no immigration controls at all, but they provide little guidance on present debates about whether some enforcement mechanisms are more morally problematic than others: telling unauthorized migrants that they are likely to be apprehended at the border and telling them that they will potentially be detained for a long period may both deter migration, but are they morally on a par? Let's now survey some of the specifics of contemporary border enforcement.

Enforcement mechanisms are varied and have changed over time, making it especially clear that different options are available to governments. There are several striking trends (we'll focus mainly on the United States). One, alluded to earlier, is the sheer increase in spending on border enforcement. Overall spending on immigration enforcement in the United States increased from $1 to $4.9 billion between 1985 and 2002. A significant majority of this money was put toward enforcement at the border itself, including increased patrols and inspections (Dixon and Gelatt 2005, 4). During the 2016 US presidential campaign, then-candidate Donald Trump proposed to build a "wall" along the border with Mexico. At the time of writing, the policy has not been implemented, and its details remain somewhat unclear, but in any configuration, it would likely require very significant expenditures: about $21.6 billion according to one estimate, made by the Department of Homeland Security. How large are these figures really, as an element of government spending on the whole? A 2013 report gives us a sense of the priority put on border enforcement: "the US government spends more on its immigration enforcement agencies than on all its other principal criminal federal law enforcement agencies combined" (Meissner et al. 2013, 9).

Increased spending has been accompanied by changes in the manner of enforcement. The 1994 "prevention through deterrence" strategy involved large amounts of spending focused on enforcement at the major points of entry, such as the Juarez–El Paso border. In addition to simply increasing the chances of apprehension at the border, the strategy involved "consequences enforcement," increasing the costs of apprehension for migrants and smugglers through, for instance, increased criminal penalties for smugglers (Meissner et al. 2013, 4).

The prevention through deterrence program relied on the assumption that migrants would be deterred from crossing the less patrolled areas of the border by the extremely inhospitable natural environment, including long stretches of perilous desert. The effect, however, was a shift in migration routes, with migrants increasingly attempting to cross through those dangerous desert areas. Deaths rose rapidly, as people died through dehydration in the summers and hypothermia in the winters (Helmore 2013). In the first six months of 2017 there were 217 migrant fatalities (Holpuch 2017).

In addition to simply deploying more border guards and other traditional mechanisms of limiting entry, there has been greater use of fencing, surveillance, and unmanned drones. More generally, there has been, theorists such as Grant Silva (2015, 218) claim, a "militarization" of the border, with border enforcement involving "military tactics, strategy, technology, equipment and forces."

Another striking feature of contemporary enforcement practices is the detention of migrants. Stephanie Silverman (2016) explains the following major developments. In 1996, the official US detention population was 70,000 people; by 2016, it was 380,000–420,000 people. Non-citizens may be detained while Immigration and Customs Enforcement (ICE) determines whether they are eligible to remain in the country, and as a means of holding them if it is determined that they may be deported. The length of time for which these non-citizens are detained can substantial: the Supreme Court case *Zadvydas v. Davis* (533 U.S. 678 (2001)) established a six-month mark as, in Silverman's words, "a presumptive limit." She notes further that detention, especially prolonged detention, can have a substantial psychological impact, creating "anxiety, depression, post-traumatic stress disorder, self-harm, and suicidality" (2016, 110).

The next feature of contemporary enforcement that we'll look at is the rise of criminal punishments for immigration-related offenses. In the United Kingdom, for example, three main immigration crimes are regularly prosecuted, according to Aliverti (2017, 377): "seeking leave to enter or remain or postponement of revocation by deception, assisting unlawful immigration, and being unable to produce an immigration document at a leave or asylum interview."

A last element of enforcement policy is the attempt to return more settled unauthorized immigrants to their countries of origin, either through deportation or by "attrition" (essentially, by making life in the receiving country sufficiently undesirable that unauthorized immigrants leave the country). These forms of "internal enforcement," especially the use of deportation, will be looked at in more detail in Chapter 8.

We can distinguish three ways in which enforcement methods might wrongfully treat migrants. The first is that some enforcement mechanisms involve ways of treating people that are inherently wrong, irrespective of circumstance: forms of treatment that universally violate human rights. The second concern is about *proportionality* in the burdens placed on migrants by certain enforcement tools, relative to the potential gains of those tools. The third concern is about the *necessity* of current enforcement methods where there are alternative means of reaching the same goals. Let's look at these in turn and how they might help us evaluate enforcement practices.

i. Absolute rights

There are certain forms of treatment that are arguably unacceptable under any conditions. International human rights law includes some prohibitions of this kind: various multilateral treaties declare that torture is always and everywhere a rights violation (Henkin et al. 2009, 9). According to Article 7 of the International Covenant on Civil and Political Rights, "No one shall be subjected to torture or to cruel, inhuman or degrading treatment or punishment." This is understood as an absolute prohibition. A country cannot justify torture by pointing to potential intelligence benefits or to special circumstances of national emergency. The Convention against Torture and Other Cruel, Inhuman or Degrading Treatment or Punishment (UNCAT) makes this clear: "No exceptional circumstances whatsoever, whether a state of war or a threat of war, internal political instability or any other public emergency, may be invoked as a justification of torture."

Critics argue that contemporary detention practices have often violated human rights. For example, Human Rights Watch (2017) claims that detained migrants are frequently denied basic medical treatment. There are widespread reports of violence within detention facilities in the USA, with an especially serious failure to protect LGBTQ migrants. Transgender women, for example, have often been detained in all male facilities where they are at serious risk of sexual assault. According to a 2018 study, LGBTQ migrants held in detention are 97 times more likely to be sexually assaulted than other detainees.[1] A recent lawsuit challenges the way certain detention centers have relied on migrants' labor. A detention facility in Colorado offered detainees the ability to work but for a wage of $1 an hour – in a state where the minimum wage is $9 – for performing tasks including cleaning bathrooms and showers and preparing meals. This minimal wage is especially troubling, critics argue, given that detainees can only access crucial goods, such as warmer clothes and the ability to make phone calls, via payments to the detention center. According to one report, detainees have sometimes had to work for two weeks in order to make a single phone call (Starr 2015).

A core principle in liberal democracies is that forced labor cannot be justified – it stands, with slavery, as one of the key historical practices that have been found utterly unacceptable. What counts as forced labor? In the clearest cases, the state or an employer simply threatens someone to work on pain of punishment. Slightly more subtle forms have also been recognized. "Debt peonage" involved employers compelling people to work in order to pay off debts to the employer. In classic examples of this, the employer would ensure that workers never succeeded in paying of the debt by making it the case that basic necessities of room and board near the factory could only be paid for using loans. In the United States, Congress prohibited debt peonage in 1867. We might likewise think that detention facilities that make detainees work long hours just for access to basic necessities are forcing them to work and are thus unjust.

Other practices associated with immigration enforcement surely don't violate any absolute rights. The sheer use of detention, for example, is a standard feature of any criminal justice system, so short of rejecting these systems altogether we must accept that detention is *sometimes* permitted. Thus

detention – and other practices that can be justified under certain circumstances – cannot be rejected outright in the context of enforcement. Is there
any way to criticize these practices?

ii. Proportionality

Even if relying on force is sometimes acceptable, there are moral constraints
on its use, including (as mentioned briefly in the discussion of Blake's argument for closed borders) requirements of proportionality. Put simply, proportionality constraints tell us that the harms averted by enforcing borders
must be sufficiently large relative to the costs put on migrants. But how large
is sufficient? To answer this, we need to look at some philosophical subtleties
relating to proportionality. The basic contrast which we will explore in some
detail, is between thinking of border enforcement as an evil done to unauthorized migrants for the sake of a greater good to the state and thinking of
border enforcement as a means of protecting states (and their members) from
wrongdoing on the part of migrants. Which approach we take affects how
much force it would be proportionate to use to prevent entry.

To understand proportionality constraints better, let's stand back for a
moment and consider some different kinds of justification for using force.
Generally speaking, people have *rights* that we not harm or coerce them (for
ease, we'll focus on harming for the time being). How then can harming
sometimes be permitted? Two types of justification for harming are especially
germane to thinking about immigration.[2] The first is a "lesser-evil justification." In these cases, harming someone is justified by the amount of harm one
will prevent overall (or, perhaps, by the overall benefits one would produce).
For example, suppose that I'm rushing a dying person to hospital, and on the
way I must soak some pedestrians in order to get there on time. I harm these
pedestrians by soaking them, but their right not to be harmed is outweighed
by the need to save my passenger's life. Generally speaking, if you are going
to harm an innocent person to prevent harms to others, the harm you are
preventing has to be substantially larger than the harm inflicted on the innocent. For example, if in order to get my passenger to the hospital I would
have to run over someone else's legs, I would not be permitted to do it.

A second form of justification – a "liability justification" – kicks in where
the person to be harmed has made themselves *liable* to being harmed because
they are going to inflict wrongful harm themselves. Suppose someone deliberately lunges toward me in an attempt to stamp on my toe. I can use force to
prevent this happening: some degree of self-defense is morally allowed (we'll
assume). And this is not simply because my preemptive kick will prevent
some harm, as is the case with lesser-evil justification. The additional element
is that because the attacker is intentionally seeking to harm me, I do not
violate any right of theirs when I use this force to defend myself. One way to
see this is to notice that I would not have to later compensate the attacker for

the harms of my kick, nor apologize for them, as I would have to do if I was relying on a lesser-evil justification. Since my self-defense doesn't violate any rights, I don't have to make up for any rights violations later.

Why exactly does the attacker lack a right not to be kicked by me? By lunging at me, the attacker *forfeits* their right not to be harmed. Wrongdoers give up the rights they ordinarily have not to be harmed. There are proportionality constraints on liability justifications also. Even though the attacker is going to violate my rights, I can't do just *anything* to them. It would be wrong for me to whip out a gun and kill them just to protect myself from a sore toe. That would be *disproportionate*: the harm I inflict on them is too great relative to the wrong they are going to do me. The wrong of intentionally inflicting a squished toe is too slight to make someone liable to death.

How exactly do we determine how much defensive harm someone is liable to? Two main factors have been proposed in the literature. The first factor, which seems relatively incontrovertible, is the degree of harm the attacker will potentially inflict. Surely more force can be used to defend oneself from a knife attack than from a water spray gun, and this is because the great potential harm in the first instance makes the attacker in turn liable to more defensive harm. A second, slightly more controversial, proposed factor in determining liability is the degree of responsibility on the part of the attacker (or, more generally, on the part of a person who is going to inflict wrongful harm).[3] Consider the contrast between the following examples, taken from McMahan (2009, chap. 4.1.1).

1   **Drugged**: A threatener is attempting to destroy your prized vase. The reason for their attack, however, is that they are under the influence of a drug that makes it hard (though not impossible) to control themself. They are under the influence of the drug because a villain secretly put it in their drink earlier in the evening.
2   **Clear Mind**: A threatener is attempting to destroy your prized vase (making just the same motions as in **Drugged**). However, they are under no chemical influence and have an entirely clear mind. They simply want to hurt you.

Even if we agree, as most people do, that you may defend your vase in both of these cases, the maximum amount of force you may use seems to differ. Maybe you could clout the threatener in **Clear Mind** over the head but doing so would be excessive in **Drugged**. You needn't agree with this precise judgment: just that the maximum amount of harm you can inflict in **Drugged** is *less* than in **Clear Mind**. This much suggests that responsibility plays some role in determining what you may do in cases of self-defense. So it appears that responsibility must affect liability to harm: it determines how much defensive harm the threatener is liable to.

In sum, there are two kinds of justification for using force against someone: lesser-evil justifications and liability justifications. And these justifications have different proportionality constraints. It's very important to see the difference between lesser-evil justifications and liability justifications because – all else being equal – the degree of harm it would be proportionate to inflict on someone is *greater* if one has a liability justification rather than just a lesser-evil justification. I cannot kill one innocent in order to save another innocent's life. But I can kill someone in order to prevent them from killing someone else.

Thus, if we want to know how much force can be used to protect a border, we need to know whether states have a liability justification for that force: we need to know whether the force is being used as a form of defense against wrongdoing. Do unauthorized migrants inflict wrongful harm on states (and their members)? And if they do just how much defense force are they liable to? To evaluate the first question, you should return to the defenses of closed borders that we looked at in Chapter 2. Those defenses rest on very different kinds of harm (I'm use the term "harm" broadly here) that migrants might cause. Some of these harms are costs, such as weakening cultural bonds within the state, while others are violations of freedoms, such as freedom of association. Which of these burdens (if any) is it wrongful to inflict, and which create significant liability on the part of the migrant?

As seen above, one relevant factor here is the *degree* of harm. We saw in Chapter 2 that almost all of the burdens that theorists think increased immigration can put on a receiving state come in degrees. Migrants are only liable to defensive harm to the extent that they create burdens on the state, and to the extent that those burdens are weak, the migrants' liability is also weak. For example, if immigrants are having little or no impact on the welfare state, then they also bear little or no liability to harm used in defense of the welfare state. The second relevant factor is their responsibility for the harm. And this factor seems to play a large role in many people's reasoning about how much force may be used against a migrant. The clearest example of this is with respect to children who are brought across the border. We standardly assume that children lack the capacity to make responsible choices, and this suggests that they are not liable to defensive force.

This means that policies that harm children are extremely hard to justify. Take, for example, the Trump administration's spring 2018 policy of deliberately separating families of unauthorized immigrants, detaining almost two thousand children in May and June away from their parents, with the goal of discouraging unauthorized migration. The policy had a severe impact on those children: in the words of American Academy of Pediatrics President Colleen Kraft, "The foundational piece of their health and development is the relationship with their parents. When you take that away, you take away the basic tenets of pediatric health."[4] The deliberate separation of the children for social ends is comparable to, say, putting the children of politicians who take bribes in detention camps in order to curb government corruption, a strategy that is plainly unacceptable.

What about adults? "Look," critics of enforcement say, "people attempting to cross the Mexican border are often willing to risk their lives in order to get across." This shows, the reasoning goes, that those unauthorized migrants (plainly this argument would not apply to, say, a middle-class Canadian who tries to enter the United States without authorization or a Belgian who over-stays their visa in Japan) are under extreme duress in their decisions about whether to enter without authorization. They should be thought of as akin to people who steal something in order to save themselves from hunger. We can understand this argument as relying on the idea of proportionality within a liability justification. The duress these migrants act under means that – like the person who is drugged into threatening another – they have minimal responsibility. And this means that they are liable to very limited defensive force on the part of the state. A special case is where the people crossing the border are entitled to asylum, perhaps because of persecution on the basis of their political views: these people are acting under the kind of duress that in fact *entitles* them to admission and thus are not to be held responsible for entering without permission. The bounds of this category are of course a matter of dispute, and we will explore these issues in Chapter 5.

Returning to border enforcement, let's look at some different enforcement practices and consider whether they involve proportionate use of force (taking into account the different forms of proportionality).

First, recall the funneling of migrants through more dangerous routes – especially the desert – as a result of the "prevention through deterrence" policy. Can the deaths created by this policy be considered proportionate, or are they, as Mendoza (2017) claims, unjust? Whether enforcement is given a lesser-evil justification or a liability justification, it seems very unlikely that death is a proportionate response. If we think of enforcement as a lesser evil, it seems very unlikely that any fiscal gains of enforcement are sufficiently large to outweigh the harm of *death*, something that, as Clint Eastwood's character in *Unforgiven* puts it, "takes away everything a man has and everything he's ever going to have." Even if states have a liability justification for enforce-ment, it still seems unlikely that causing migrant deaths is proportionate. For example, suppose that we think of immigrants entering a country and using its resources as a kind of theft. Surely it is unacceptable to *kill* someone that I spot trying to steal even a valuable possession, such as my car. In the words of Andy Adame, a spokesman for Border Patrol in Arizona, "It is a crime to enter the United States illegally, but it's not a crime for which you should pay with your life" (Helmore 2013).

Now, it might be said that the state doesn't have to take responsibility for these deaths, since the migrants voluntarily take the more dangerous routes. Can this choice absolve the state of any responsibility? First, some of those who die in the desert are children with their parents, and as we saw earlier policies that harm children are very difficult to justify. Second, even if migrants make a choice of some kind to enter the desert, that choice may not be fully informed about the extent of the risks involved, especially when the migrants are often taking their cue from smugglers who play those risks down. In response to this, the US government has taken some steps to provide greater information to people who are considering the crossing, for example by asking border patrol on the Mexican side to make public service announcements (Meissner et al. 2013, 34). Third, someone's responsibility for the consequences of their choices is more limited when that choice is made under duress, and, as we saw earlier, the difficult starting position of many migrants crossing the US-Mexico border arguably puts them under substantial duress. Fourth, even if the migrants are making choices to cross, the policies of the United States contribute to those deaths and do so despite (by now at least) clear evidence of these contributions. Compare, for example, someone who attempts to protect their property by putting deadly spikes on the interior side of the wall around their house, knowing that there will be multiple trespassers who will get impaled. Even if potential trespassers are informed of these measures by a sign outside the house, it still seems that the owner has an especially strong humanitarian duty to phone for emergency assistance when someone is dying at the end of their garden.

US Border Patrol has taken some steps to fulfill these humanitarian duties – such as introducing specially trained teams, capable of providing emergency assistance – but the number of deaths still remains high.[5] But even with such substantial efforts there are still likely to be deaths given the size and extremely harsh conditions in these stretches of the border.

How about detention practices? Can these meet constraints of proportionality? Detention inherently involves depriving someone of freedom: a burden that is generally taken very seriously in liberal democracies, many of which have constitutional rights against arbitrary detention. Silverman (2014, 604) emphasizes that detention can also inflict further psychological and physical damage – including anxiety, depression, and self-harming. It involves invasions of privacy, since detainees are subject to strip searches and monitoring, and is financially very burdensome for detainees and their families, given that detainees have no access to employment (other than the poorly paid work sometimes offered within the facilities themselves) (Marouf 2017).

Can detention – given all of its burdens on detainees – be given a lesser-evil justification? We again need to look at how much harm is likely to be averted by giving the state more time to determine who can be removed. We also need to consider whether the prevention of any such harm is sufficient to override the burdens put on detainees. Since we're considering a potential lesser-evil justification, we are operating on the assumption that the detainees are all innocents, who are not committing any wrong against the state. Given this assumption, it seems very difficult to justify sustained detention. Sustained detention of innocent citizens is almost never used simply as a means of preventing further harms. Very brief quarantines, for example, might be employed in order to prevent a major threat of deadly pandemic, but outside of such extreme circumstances substantial detention of innocents is considered an unjustifiable civil rights violation. The same standard should be applied in the context of immigration.

Thus, if substantial detention is to be justified, it seems to require a liability justification: it must rest on an assumption that unauthorized migrants cause harm to the host state for which they are morally responsible.

A first problem with giving a liability justification is that many of those detained are children, and – as noted earlier – children brought across the border are not responsible for any harms caused to the state and are thus not liable to any defensive action on the part of the state. Even in cases where the children themselves are not detained, the detention of parents can still separate children from their families and thus be highly detrimental to their well-being. In 2015, US District Court Judge Dolly M. Gee noted such problems and ruled (following an earlier decision in *Flores v. Meese*) that detention of children who entered without authorization, and whose parents are not present, ought generally to be released to relatives or foster care instead of being detained (Marouf 2017).

A second problem with relying on a liability justification is that we don't know in advance which people have in fact entered without authorization or without good reason for such entry, such as fleeing persecution. Indeed it is often part of the point of detention to give the state time to determine whether someone who entered without authorization is entitled to asylum, and so on. Moreover, detained people who have not been charged with a crime are not granted any public-funded access to legal representation. They can thus remain in prolonged detention without any real opportunity to challenge it, even when they are in fact legally entitled to go free because, for instance, they have a valid asylum claim. So even on the assumption that some migrants have made themselves liable to defensive action on the part of the state, detention still frequently sweeps in people who, even by the state's own lights, ought to be left free to live their lives in the host state.

Still, what if there are migrants who genuinely are liable to defensive action and can be identified as such? How do we determine whether detention of these people is a disproportionate response? In other contexts, we generally assume that prolonged detention is only acceptable where someone presents a serious threat or has committed a significant crime. Petty theft, such as shoplifting some food, carries merely a fine, while grand theft, such as stealing a vehicle worth thousands of dollars, carries with it significant time in prison. Certainly some defenders of detention would count unauthorized entry, especially repeated unauthorized entry, as on a par with various more serious criminal offenses. This view is reflected in the increasing number of immigration-related criminal offenses – noted earlier – that states have instituted and punished with increasing severity. Can unauthorized entry be considered a wrong on a par with various significant (non-immigration-related) criminal offenses: offenses that rise to the level of, say, vehicle theft rather than shoplifting?

Here again we need to consider the questions raised above about the degree of harm done by unauthorized entry. And we also need to consider issues of responsibility. As Aliverti (2017) notes, there are typically some important and distinctive elements to the form of responsibility required for a criminal conviction. She emphasizes the need for a *mens rea*: to be convicted of a criminal offense, someone must not just inflict harm, but do so with a "guilty mind." Exactly what counts as having a guilty mind for particular crimes varies somewhat between jurisdictions. In the clearest cases, someone inflicts harm intentionally, as when they deliberately kill another person. With the exception of the extremely small minority of people who enter in order to commit terrorism, migrants do not cross borders with the aim of damaging the host society; instead, they are generally looking to work or perhaps unite with family and friends. Other familiar *mens rea* standards are "recklessness" – where someone foresees that certain actions will cause a significant risk of harm, but performs them anyway – and "negligence," where someone does not foresee the degree of harm that their actions will cause but performs them anyway.

Do unauthorized migrants assume that their actions will create any significant risk of harm to the host society? Do they create risks that they ought to have taken into account in deciding to cross the border? Here too we need to consider the various possible burdens – those discussed in Chapter 2 – that migrants might create. Take, for example, fiscal burdens that migrants might create for the host society. Typically migrants enter with (and carry out) plans to work, pay taxes, and avoid accessing welfare provisions. These behaviors could plausibly count as taking sufficient precautions to avoid becoming a fiscal burden to the host society. Other burdens that unauthorized migrants can create might be more predictable as well as difficult to mitigate. For example, it should presumably be relatively clear to migrants that once they enter the territory the host society will have to offer them police protection, as emphasized by Blake. Finally, considerations of duress, of the kind mentioned above, will again be relevant here. The question to consider then is whether there are cases where migrants create a burden (a) of sufficient magnitude and (b) with sufficient responsibility that their entry could make them liable to the kind of detention associated with criminal punishment.

iii. Necessity

In additional to constraints of proportionality on the use of force, there are constraints of necessity. Take again a person who is attempting to stand on my toe. Suppose that I am considering a defensive maneuver that is proportionate: giving them a light kick in the shin to stop them getting to me. But I don't *need* to kick them. I could just as easily step aside to avoid the stomping. I ought not to kick them: it's an unnecessary use of force.

We can apply the idea of necessity to immigration policy by asking whether particular enforcement methods are *needed* to secure the goals that people care about when they argue for more limited immigration: whether there are equally effective alternatives that use less force. We'll first focus on detention and then look at some necessity arguments that apply to border enforcement of any kind.

Critics of detention, such as Silverman (2014), argue that there are alternative methods that are equally effective but less burdensome to migrants. What makes a method effective or ineffective? The standard goal of detention is to ensure that unauthorized migrants don't *abscond*: sever ties with immigration officials and attempt to live free of their oversight. Absconding prevents the state from judging who is eligible to remain or be removed and from exercising its ability to act on these determinations. Are there alternative methods that are at least as effective in preventing absconding?

One alternative method that has been deployed is the use of electronic monitoring, such as ankle bracelets. These are often combined with requirements that migrants make themselves available for visits from immigration officials, roughly on the model of parole requirements for people released from prison. As the analogy with parole requirements suggests, these methods are less burdensome than detention (parole is something that inmates seek as a desirable alternative to life in prison). But they are still restrictive of a migrant's freedom, since they still must lead a life that makes them available for official oversight. We should thus also look, Silverman (2014) and Marouf (2017) argue, for alternatives to these enforcement methods.

The alternative that both of these authors favor is community-based case management. Instead of having immigration enforcement officials as their primary point of contact, they have "case managers," whose primary role is to help migrants have access to important services, such as medical care, housing, and language classes. For example, a 2015 ICE program created a community for migrant families, specifically those headed by women, and tried to help those families access key services (Marouf 2017) via case managers. Now, in some programs of this kind, case managers are also assigned a duty to relay information about the migrants back to central immigration enforcement officials. Marouf (2017) argues that in these cases, it is harder for case managers to gain the trust of migrant families that is needed to help them access the relevant services. Whereas in a "purer" community-based program, absconding is prevented without any form of supervision and instead through the "carrot" of encouraging migrants to remain where they are so that they can maintain access to, for example, important health care benefits for their children. Such programs have been implemented with some success in jurisdictions including Australia, Hong Kong, and the Netherlands. The Australian program produced a compliance rate of 94 percent, while the program in Hong Kong secured 97 percent compliance (Marouf 2017, 2170).

Now, community-based programs, of course, cost money in terms of case manager time and the funding for the resources that migrants are provided with, but detention is extremely expensive, given the facilities, officers, and so on required, so it's quite possible that community-based programs will still be cost effective. US Representative Bill Foster argued for a bill reducing detention levels on the grounds that "[it] costs roughly $150 per person, per day, to put them in a detention facility. For roughly a tenth of that – somewhere between $17 and 15 cents or 20 cents a day, you can put them into either electronic monitoring programs or community-based programs where people are frequently monitored" (WNYC 2017).

So alternatives to detention may be more efficient. But even if they aren't, Silverman and Marouf would argue, justice still requires taking the option that is less burdensome to migrants.

Moving on from detention, some philosophers have argued that taking necessity into account has much broader implications for enforcement practices as a whole. When we looked earlier at various arguments for closing borders, we saw that in various cases it might be possible to ease potential burdens of immigration by means other than simply decreasing the *level* of immigration. For example, burdens on freedom of association might be lessened by increasing temporary migration rather than permanent migration. Wages that are decreased by immigration might be supplemented with some of the fiscal benefits of increased immigration. Local languages might be protected by encouraging immigrants to learn those languages. And so on. We might think that if border control isn't needed to prevent burdens on the state, then there is no good reason for those controls, especially if there are important interests – of host state members and of potential migrants – in having increased immigration.

Wellman and other theorists will reply that states may restrict immigration, even for fairly weak (or arbitrary or irrational reasons): freedom of association means that people make their own choices about whom to marry, even when those choices seem foolish. But Martín Chamorro (2013) makes a distinct point that isn't susceptible to this reply. If border controls are not really needed to avoid any burdens on the state, then those controls are *unjust*. It is wrong, Chamorro emphasizes, to use unnecessary force, and since border controls deploy force, they may not be used where other means are available. Of course, this argument is only successful to the extent that alternative means really are available, but it does seem to shift the burden of proof onto people who would like to enforce border controls to show that they really are needed to promote important goals.

Let's briefly review the proportionality and necessity points that we have surveyed. The key point to notice is that even if states have good reasons to prevent unauthorized immigration, this doesn't license just any potential use of force to prevent unauthorized entry. Politicians often simply defend enforcement practices by saying that unauthorized entry is "illegal." Where a law is being broken, they say, the state simply must take steps to stop this. Not to do so is to fail to respect the democratic enactment of the law, as well as the purposes behind it, and to potentially encourage lawbreaking more generally.

This form of argument moves too fast: we cannot assess immigration practices without considering broader principles that guide the infliction of harm on people by the state. We must consider general constraints on inflicting harm on innocents, as with the migration of unauthorized children. And if we think there are migrants who make themselves liable to defensive force by the state, we need to consider just how much defensive force they are liable to, based on principles of proportionality and necessity. It might still be possible to justify certain enforcement techniques – for example, the use of ankle bracelets and relatively brief detention – but that case needs to be made and not assumed.

C. Enforcement and burdens on minority groups in the host society

We have so far looked at objections to enforcement practices that focus on the burdens for *migrants* of those practices. Often these practices can also affect members of the host society who get caught up in, for instance, the workplace searches that are used to identify unauthorized migrants and other forms of "internal enforcement." We'll look at two kinds of potential wrongs that enforcement can inflict on current members of society, as well as, often, migrants: first, that they can infringe the rights to privacy and freedom, and, second, that they can violate norms of equality and anti-discrimination.

i. Privacy and freedom

Consider some steps that authorities take to identify unauthorized migrants:

- Searching a vehicle that roaming patrol officers have stopped.
- Erecting checkpoints near the border for all cars passing through a certain area.
- Stopping people on the street for questioning.
- Searching the wallets of people stopped on the street.
- Sending officers to a workplace suspected of employing unauthorized migrants and interviewing workers there.
- Raiding a house where unauthorized migrants are suspected of living.

Philosophers have pointed out that these steps are, in varying degrees, invasive – they involve the government making people disclose private facts about themselves, what takes place in their homes, and so on. And philosophers have also pointed out that these steps are, again in varying degrees, constraining – requiring people to give up some of their freedom to drive where they please, and so on. This means, Mendoza (2015) argues, that there is a presumption against these enforcement practices.

That may be true, but how strong is that presumption, and when is it overturned? In the United States, these questions are primarily asked with reference to Fourth Amendment to the Constitution, which states that there is a right against "unreasonable searches and seizures." Courts have interpreted this right, plausibly enough, in a way that makes various distinctions among different kinds of investigative practice. If we return to the list above, it seems clear that some of the steps involve much more substantial infringements of people's privacy and/or liberty than others. A brief set of questions from an officer – especially if the questioning is voluntarily assented to – seems very different from having one's house turned over by immigration officials while being subject to lengthy and non-voluntary questioning.

This means, the courts have indicated, that different standards are needed to justify different practices. In particular, the *evidence* needed to justify different forms of investigation varies. Suppose that roving patrols are searching for people who have committed immigration-related infractions. Officers may only stop and hold a car and those riding in it if they have grounds for "reasonable suspicion" of wrongdoing: "articulable" grounds for thinking that this particular vehicle contains unauthorized migrants, beyond a mere "hunch" (Aleinikoff et al. 2016, 1147). When a roving patrol doesn't merely stop a vehicle but searches it more thoroughly and makes arrests, this must be based on a still higher standard of "probable cause": evidence good enough to establish a "fair probability" of criminal activity.

Are these standards too weak or too strong? A balance must be struck between respecting the rights to liberty and privacy and the government's ability to control immigration. We cannot here engage in a lengthy exploration of the former rights, but we have spent considerable time on assessing how important the latter ability it is. What do you think is a reasonable balance?

ii. Equality and discrimination

The second set of issues we'll look at here rests on the prominent use of race and/or ethnicity (in what follows I'll write "ethnicity" for short) in searches for unauthorized migrants. In their attempts to identify unauthorized migrants, authorities have often – whether officially or unofficially – relied on the fact that someone "seems Mexican" or "looks Nigerian." Can this ever be acceptable?

There is a long history of ethnicity being used in searches, whether sanctioned by the government or just used in practice by officers. Take the border patrol officers in *United States v. Brignoni-Ponce* (422 U.S. 873 (1975)), who were stationed at a fixed checkpoint but – once the checkpoint was closed because of poor weather conditions – decided to patrol a highway, eventually chasing after a car and questioning its riders, who were revealed to be unauthorized migrants. The officers said that their only basis for suspicion was their apparently Mexican descent.

Bill Ong Hing (2009) claims that in the recent past ethnically based searches became especially common with increasing investment in enforcement, beginning with the presidency of George W. Bush. He describes an ICE raid on a packing plant. The immigration officers insisted that all workers remain within the plant during the officers' questioning. Citizens and non-citizens were directed to different parts of the plant, and different lines were established for authorized and unauthorized migrants. Multiple people were told, "You have Mexican teeth. You need to go into that line [for unauthorized migrants] and get checked" (Hing 2009, 307).

The justification for relying on racial and ethnic traits is that they correlate to some degree with the likelihood of someone being an immigrant, especially an unauthorized immigrant. A person of East Asian ancestry driving through Texas, the argument goes, is relatively unlikely to have entered El Paso without authorization, compared with someone who, given their appearance, may have been living in Juarez. Thus, profiling will target government resources on people who are more likely to be unauthorized migrants.

One sort of objection to this argument questions whether using race or ethnicity actually helps authorities to identify a greater number of unauthorized migrants. For example, in *U.S. v. Montero-Camargo* (1999) – which concerned a checkpoint in El Centro, California – the U.S. 9th Circuit Court noted that a majority of citizens and authorized migrants passing through the checkpoint could be described as having a Latinx appearance. In this area, someone's having a Latinx appearance was not a strong basis for suspecting them of being an unauthorized migrant, and it may have been better to use other traits as a basis for identifying unauthorized migrants.

Would profiling be acceptable, though, if it actually does make it more likely that officers will identify unauthorized migrants? And even if profiling isn't helpful, is it especially important to make sure that officers don't profile, or is it merely an inefficiency that doesn't warrant special attention and investment to correct it?

A second set of objections to profiling set aside the issue of whether profiling is *effective* at identifying unauthorized migrants and ask whether it violates norms of equality and anti-discrimination. There are several such objections. One such objection focuses on the fact that profiling places disproportionate burdens on some people over others. If the government targets Latinx people, then a greater number of Latinx citizens and authorized migrants will be subject to stops and searches relative to other members of the population. Mendoza (2014, 77) objects that this violates an "equality of burdens" standard that he thinks is required by justice.

Are unequal burdens always unjust? Discussing racial profiling of black people, Ta-Nehisi Coates (2013) suggests that it should be viewed as something like a special tax on black people. Is it unjust for the government to place more substantial burdens on some groups than others? The tax analogy suggests that in fact the *sheer* inequality may not be sufficient to trigger a serious complaint of injustice. Governments regularly take steps that have the effect of burdening some people more than others. Whether these steps comport with justice seems to depend in significant part on just how large those burdens are. For example, it seems much more acceptable for the government to impose a special tax on cigarettes – even though this creates a special burden for smokers and manufacturers – than for the government to shut down certain industries entirely – perhaps because of the pollution they create – without taking any steps to make sure that the people employed in those industries are able to regain employment. Likewise, subjecting some people more than others to very brief and infrequent stops in migration searches is surely much easier to justify than putting some people on notice that they are especially likely to have their homes searched, their places of employment raided, and so on.

So, if there is a problem with even brief stops targeted especially at Latinx people, it must be something beyond the sheer inequality. What troubles us about a special tax on black people is not simply that some people are paying more in taxes than others but that they are doing so *on the basis of their race.* What is so bad, then, about imposing inequality on this basis? A common concern is that doing so creates social *stigma.* In the case of black people, the concern is that by profiling, the government creates an association between blackness and, say, gun crime. In the immigration case, the concern is that profiling will create associations between being Latinx and being a non-citizen (or a non-member of the political community). One way this association can be problematic is because of what it expresses to Latinx citizens and authorized migrants: that they are not considered full members of society (Sánchez 2011). A second problem is that these associations can affect how Latinx people are treated by other members of society (Mendoza 2014). By associating their ethnicity with unauthorized migration, the government can cause other members of the populace to, consciously or unconsciously, adopt this association and come to treat Latinx people as second-class members of society. This means being taken less seriously in political discussions, shut out of the networks needed to gain better jobs, underserved by the government, and so on. Racial profiling of groups who already have a history of mistreatment by the government can also seriously damage their relationship with the government. By implying that the government takes some people in a society to be more objects of control than full members – who are entitled to be taken seriously and supported by the government – racial profiling can make members of these groups feel afraid to bring their claims to the police, sue in court, and so on (Hosein 2018).[6]

In addition to being substantial, many theorists argue, these burdens are sufficient to make Latinx people into a *subordinated class* within the United

States: a socially visible group that is consistently less well off across a range of dimensions. Subordination is often taken to be especially inimical to fundamental ideals of social equality.[7] Caste systems, for example, in which people's life chances are heavily determined by which caste they are born into, seem especially antithetical to the idea that in a liberal democracy people should live as equals, without there being superior and inferior members of society. The same criticisms can be made of feudal societies, in which an aristocracy clearly occupies a position of superiority over the serf class. And the systematic disadvantages faced by African Americans, most obviously during the periods of slavery and segregation, seem problematic for similar reasons. Critics of contemporary enforcement practices analogize the situation of present-day Latinx people with these other forms of subordination and reject them on those grounds.

Are there ways to search without relying on ethnicity? One option is to target searches on people using alternative traits. For example, officers might be directed to rely on whether certain drivers appear to be furtive near immigration officers, driving in the opposite direction when they see a patrol car. A potential difficulty with this approach is that racial profiling may still occur in immigration enforcement even when it is officially discouraged and other traits emphasized instead. Moreover, it may be important to provide minorities with clear reassurance that they *won't* be profiled, given the historical prevalence of profiling in immigration enforcement, and perhaps this means clearly removing any potential discretion from officers. A second option, which may avoid this problem, is to avoid all officer discretion by having purely fixed checkpoints where all cars or people are stopped, irrespective of their ethnicity or any other traits.

Let's put together the concerns about privacy and freedom and the concerns about equality and discrimination that we have examined. Which enforcement practices are able to satisfy all of these moral desiderata? Consider random searches, such as roadblocks, which, as we just saw, seem to avoid the risk of allowing racial profiling. Some philosophers might suggest that indiscriminate searches will inevitably be unjustifiable given the widespread infringement of freedom they would entail. But this seems to depend on just what form the searches take: relatively brief stops at roadblocks, for example – perhaps accompanied by more extensive secondary screening where the initial stop provides clear evidence of potential immigration violations – might not be a major infringement of freedom or of privacy and might be justified where the number of unauthorized migrants is known to be high. Compare immigration screening at an international airport. Almost all flyers go through some such screening, and there are also sometimes randomized checks elsewhere in the facility. These steps are generally taken to be relatively unproblematic, given that airports are places that migrants flow through.[8] Is it so different to have checkpoints *near* the border in areas where there are especially strong migrant flows? To answer this question, we need to consider exactly what counts as "near" the border. The US government has taken a broad interpretation, treating all places within 100 miles of a US land or coastal border as within the "Border Zone." About 200 million people – which is around two-thirds of the US population – live within that zone. Is this overbroad? Is there a reasonable interpretation of "near the border" that would justify heightened screening within that zone?

D. Chapter summary

While the first two chapters focused on in-principle reasons why states should or shouldn't restrict immigration, this chapter considered the *means* by which states restrict immigration. A theorist who thinks borders should be (at least somewhat) closed must explain exactly which steps states may take to exclude migrants, and even an open borders theorist must ask, in a world where restrictions are prevalent, whether some methods of enforcement are more problematic than others. We looked at several different enforcement mechanisms, including guarding the border itself, using detention, and using searches to find unauthorized migrants who might then be deported. Some criteria for analyzing these mechanisms include their *effectiveness*, whether they are a *proportionate* means of enforcement, and whether they are a *necessary* means. Proportionality and necessity constraints seem to be heavily affected by whether the person being excluded can be considered responsible for an injustice done to the home state, as well as how significant that injustice is. If the migrant is a child, or an adult with little or no responsibility of their actions (because they are acting under serious duress, for instance) then it is much harder to justify using substantial force against them. Other moral considerations that are relevant to enforcement policy concern not the harm done to migrants through enforcement but to members of the host society, especially those who are ethnically similar to the migrants and thus may be racially profiled.

Study questions

1 What is the relationship between the open-borders debate and issues of enforcement?
2 Consider an enforcement mechanism discussed in the text or some other that is currently in use. Is this method proportionate? Which factors are relevant?
3 Why do states detain unauthorized migrants? Is it permissible for them to do this?
4 Is racial profiling by immigration enforcement officers ever justified? Why or why not?

Notes

1 https://www.nbcnews.com/feature/nbc-out/lgbtq-migrants-97-times-more-likely-be-sexually-assaulted-detention-n880101
2 See McMahan (2009) for a more general discussion of these two kinds of justification in the context of war.
3 This remains subject to debate, and my own considered view is that in fact responsibility is not relevant to liability. But even on this alternative view responsibility still typically features in some way in determining how much defensive force may be used against someone. See Hosein (2017).
4 https://psmag.com/social-justice/trumps-child-separation-policy-will-scar-migrant-children-forever
5 There are also even now reports of border agents chasing migrants into especially dangerous parts of the desert and sabotaging water supplies (Carroll 2018).
6 See Hosein (2018) for development of this argument and a defense of it against objections.
7 Hing (2009) draws a parallel between the effects of contemporary enforcement and earlier systems of racial subordination. For a broader discussion of the "anticaste principle" in general, see Sunstein (1994).
8 See Mendoza (2014) and Hosein (2018) for further discussion of randomized screening.

References

Aleinikoff, T.Alexander, David A.Martin, Hiroshi Motomura, Maryellen Fullerton, and Juliet P. Stumpf. 2016. *Immigration and Citizenship: Process and Policy.* 8th ed. St. Paul, MN: West Academic Publishing.

Aliverti, Ana. 2017. "The Wrongs of Unlawful Immigration." *Criminal Law and Philosophy* 11, no. 2 (June): 375–391.

Carroll, Rory. 2018. "US Border Patrol Routinely Sabotages Water Left for Migrants, Report Says." *Guardian*, January 17, 2018. https://www.theguardian.com/us-news/2018/jan/17/us-border-patrol-sabotage-aid-migrants-mexico-arizona.

Chamorro, Martín. 2013. "A Theory of Just Immigration Policy." PhD diss., University of Colorado.

Coates, Ta-Nehisi. 2013. "The Banality of Richard Cohen and Racist Profiling." *Atlantic*, July 17, 2013. https://www.theatlantic.com/national/archive/2013/07/the-banality-of-richard-cohen-and-racist-profiling/277871.

Dixon, David, and Julia Gelatt. 2005. "Immigration Enforcement Spending Since IRCA." Migration Policy Institute, November 2005. https://www.migrationpolicy.org/research/immigration-enforcement-spending-irca.

Helmore, Edward. 2013. "'Death Map' of Deserts Aims to Save Lives of Desperate Mexican Migrants." *Guardian*, June 1, 2013. https://www.theguardian.com/world/2013/jun/01/map-us-mexico-migrant-deaths-border.

Henkin, Louis, Sarah Cleveland, Laurence Helfer, Gerald Neuman, Diane Orentlicher. 2009. *Human Rights.* 2nd ed. New York: Thomson Reuters/Foundation Press.

Hing, Bill Ong. 2009. "Institutional Racism, ICE Raids, and Immigration Reform." *University of San Francisco Law Review* 44, no. 2 (Fall): 307–352.

Holpuch, Amanda. 2017. "Migrant Deaths at US-Mexico Border Increase 17% This Year, UN Figures Show." *Guardian*, August 5, 2017. https://www.theguardian.com/us-news/2017/aug/05/migrants-us-mexico-border-deaths-figures.

Hosein, Adam Omar. 2017. "Responsibility and Self-Defense: Can We Have It All?" *Res Publica* 23, no. 3 (August): 367–385.

Hosein, Adam Omar. 2018. "Racial Profiling and a Reasonable Sense of Inferior Political Status." *Journal of Political Philosophy* 26, no. 3 (September): e1–e20.

Human Rights Watch. 2018. "Code Red: The Fatal Consequences of Dangerously Sub-standard Medical Care in Immigration Detention." https://www.aclu.org/report/code-r ed-fatal-consequences-dangerously-substandard-medical-care-immigration-detention.

Marouf, Fatma E. 2017. "Alternatives to Immigration Detention." *Cardoza Law Review* 38, no. 6 (August): 2141–2192.

McMahan, Jeff. 2009. *Killing in War.* New York: Oxford University Press.

Meissner, Doris, Donald M. Kerwin, Muzaffar Chishti, and Claire Bergeron. 2013. *Immigration Enforcement in the United States: The Rise of a Formidable Machinery.* Washington, DC: Migration Policy Institute. http://www.migrationpolicy.org/pubs/enforcementpillars.pdf.

Mendoza, José Jorge. 2014. "Discrimination and the Presumptive Rights of Immigrants." *Critical Philosophy of Race* 2, no. 1: 68–83.

Mendoza, José Jorge. 2015. "Enforcement Matters: Reframing the Philosophical Debate over Immigration." *Journal of Speculative Philosophy* 29, no. 1: 73–90.

Mendoza, José Jorge. 2017. *The Moral and Political Philosophy of Immigration: Liberty, Security, and Equality.* Lanham, MD: Lexington Books.

Ngai, Mae M. 2014. "Undocumented Migration to the United States: A History." In *History, Theories, and Legislation*, edited by Lois Ann Lorentzen, 1–24. Vol. 1 of *Hidden Lives and Human Rights in the United States: Understanding the Controversies and Tragedies of Undocumented Immigration.* Santa Barbara, CA: Praeger.

Sánchez, Carlos A. 2011. "On Documents and Subjectivity: The Formation and De-Formation of the Immigrant Identity." *Radical Philosophy Review* 14, no. 2: 197–205.

Silva, Grant. 2015. "On the Militarization of Borders and the Juridicial Right to Exclude." *Public Affairs Quarterly* 29, no. 2 (April): 217–234.

Silverman, Stephanie J. 2014. "Detaining Immigrants and Asylum Seekers: A Normative Introduction." *Critical Review of International Social and Political Philosophy* 17, no. 5: 600–617.

Silverman, Stephanie J. 2016. "The Difference That Detention Makes: Reconceptualizing the Boundaries of the Normative Debate on Immigration Control." In *The Ethics and Politics of Immigration: Core Issues and Emerging Trends*, edited by Alex Sager, 105–124. London: Rowman and Littlefield.

Starr, Alexandra. 2015. "At Low Pay, Government Hires Immigrants Held at Detention Centers." NPR, July 23, 2015. https://www.npr.org/2015/07/23/425511981/at-low-pa y-government-hires-immigrants-held-at-detention-centers.

Sunstein, Cass R. 1994. "The Anticaste Principle." *Michigan Law Review* 92, no. 8 (August): 2410–2455.

WNYC. 2017. "Immigration Detention Quotas Costs Taxpayers Billions." WNYC, August 1, 2017. https://www.wnycstudios.org/story/billion-dollar-price-tag-immigration-detention-centers.

Further reading

Aliverti, Ana. 2017. "The Wrongs of Unlawful Immigration." *Criminal Law and Philosophy* 11, no. 2 (June): 375–391.

Mendoza, José Jorge. 2015. "Enforcement Matters: Reframing the Philosophical Debate Over Immigration." *Journal of Speculative Philosophy* 29, no. 1: 73–90.

Sager, Alex. 2017 "Immigration Enforcement and Domination: An Indirect Argument for Much More Open Borders." *Political Research Quarterly* 70, no. 1: 42–54.

Silverman, Stephanie J. 2014. "Detaining Immigrants and Asylum Seekers: A Normative Introduction." *Critical Review of International Social and Political Philosophy* 17, no. 5: 600–617.

Part II

Selection procedures

In the first part of the book, we considered whether states should open their borders entirely to migrants. But most states do not behave in this way; they regulate their borders at least somewhat, limiting who can and cannot enter. And they make distinctions among different categories of people, giving priority to some over others. For instance, those who have some family ties to existing citizens are often given some degree of preference. In this chapter, we will focus on the criteria that states use in choosing whom to admit and not. Sometimes states have attempted to exclude particular groups, such as ethnic groups they deemed undesirable, while in other cases, they have privileged certain groups, such as people with family ties to existing members. We will look at a variety of these criteria in the next chapter, and then focus in on an especially important class of (sometimes) privileged migrants: refugees. Discussion of particular selection criteria will also be used to introduce some broader theoretical issues that are relevant more generally. For example, in looking at ethnicity, we will consider "expressive harms," with gender we'll consider "disparate impact" standards, and our discussion of refugees will bring in questions about how to conceptualize human rights.

4 Selection for admission

The range of criteria used for selecting immigrants historically and in the contemporary world is wide. States have relied on factors including a (potential) immigrant's race, ethnicity, religion, skills, family ties, linguistic knowledge, and persecution in their home country. In this chapter, we will explain the limits of the state's discretion over immigrant selection by examining which criteria are *impermissible* (may not be used by the state). In the next chapter we will turn to criteria that the state is *required* to use, especially refugee status.

A. Race and ethnicity

The history of immigration policy, even in liberal democracies that now profess a strong commitment to racial equality, is tightly bound up with the use of race, and it is worth reckoning properly with that past to properly understand the nature and scale of that moral failing. One example is the "White Australia" policy adopted in the early twentieth century, the central goal of which was to exclude Asian immigrants from Australia. Furthermore, the use of race and, especially, ethnicity in selection policies has persisted in liberal democracies into the recent past. Christian Joppke (2005) has detailed how, for instance, Germany, Italy, and Spain all had programs in the late twentieth century that gave privileges to people who could show simply some hereditary connection to those nations. And, finally, resistance to immigration in recent years, even when racial criteria have not been *explicitly* used in policy, often seems closely bound up with the politics of race, and we should consider what morality says about this situation.

So let us now consider some potential reasons for rejecting the use of race in immigration policy. Surely, many people will think, race is unacceptable simply because it is *irrelevant*. Race does not correlate with intelligence or good character or anything else that might make someone a useful new member. So, someone's race provides no more of a basis for accepting or rejecting their immigration application than their eye color provides a basis for giving them a job as a mathematician. More strongly, one might question the very idea that people can be grouped into distinct races: Some philosophers – such as Kwame Anthony Appiah (1985) – think that since biologists have not found any fundamental genetic basis for categorizing people by their race, there simply *aren't* any races as traditionally understood. There are only arbitrary distinctions that we happen to make based on superficial differences of skin tone and so on. An immigration policy that incorporates these arbitrary distinctions lacks any justification.

These concerns suggest that using race in immigration is arbitrary or irrational. And it surely is. But that doesn't seem to fully explain the nature of the problem with using race (Fine 2016, Hosein 2016). It would be irrational to admit more engineers than doctors in a country that has a much greater shortage of the latter. Yet, this wouldn't be *wrong*, it seems, in the way that using race is wrong.

A second reason for rejecting the use of race is that it would be unfair. Michael Walzer argues that since Australia is such a "vast territory," and given that white people occupied only a small portion of that territory, it was unfair of them to cordon that space off from Asian migrants with the White Australia policy. They ought to have shared it more equitably.

This might indeed have been *a* problem with the "whites only" policy. It is less clear, though, that it is the main problem. Take the Johnson-Reed Act in the United States, which also seems extremely troubling because of its use of race. The point of the act was to limit people of color and Southern and Eastern Europeans from becoming new members of the United States on the grounds that, it was thought, their race made them unfit to contribute positively to the United States (Ngai 2004). The abandonment of this policy in the 1960s is now seen as a major instance of moral progress in US immigration policies. Yet that change in policy did not increase the overall number of immigrants. So Walzer's injunction to use space fairly cannot explain what was so significant about the change: the new policy was no more or less fair (in this regard) than the previous one.

Now, Walzer does say that racial selection in the United States was unjust. It involved, he claims, a mistake about the nature of the US polity. Policymakers thought "they were defending a homogeneous white and Protestant country," but in fact the United States was already highly diverse with respect to race, ethnicity, and religious practice, and the national culture already included some self-understanding of the United States as a pluralist nation.

Did the authors of the Johnson-Reed Act rely on factual mistakes about the composition of the United States? Not obviously. They were certainly aware that people of color were already present, as well as Southern and Eastern Europeans. Their argument for limiting immigration from these groups was not that total racial and religious purity would thereby be maintained, but that members of these groups are harder to "assimilate" – are resistant to values of hard work and good citizenship – and thus must be limited in number for the nation to survive (Ngai 2004). And as for national self-understandings, these racial supremacists could easily have conceded that there was a pluralist strand in the national culture; their goal was to *resist* that strand and stress the need for reaffirmation of white, Anglo-Saxon, Protestant values. Walzer needs an argument not for the *existence* of a pluralist strand in American political thought, but for the *favorability* of that strand over the racist alternatives.

Although insufficient as they stand, perhaps what Walzer's comments about the United States point toward is a third variety of problem with racial selection, one that also takes seriously existing diversity in societies. According to some theorists, such as Blake and Wellman, racial selection procedures are problematic not because they wrong *prospective migrants*, or other foreign residents, but because they wrong *existing members* who share the same racial characteristics.

The problem with racial selection arises because of the rights to equal treatment that existing members have against their state and each other.

> We have a special duty to respect our fellow citizens as equal partners in the political cooperative. With this in mind, I suggest that a country may not institute an immigration policy which excludes entry to members of a given race because such a policy would wrongly disrespect those citizens in the dispreferred category.
>
> (Wellman 2008, 31)

Why exactly do racial selection policies convey disrespect? We need to consider what could plausibly be *behind* these choices: what *reasons* those promoting racial selection have for doing so. The policies of White Australia and the Johnson-Reed Act were officially based on the assumption that people who are not white are less fit to be citizens: lacking in the intellectual and moral abilities needed to fully participate. The policies thus indicated that the government considered people who are not white to be unfit for citizenship.

Blake and Wellman's point is that minorities who are *existing* members of the political community have a right not to be told that they are unfit for citizenship; they ought to be treated as fully capable of equal participation in the political community. We might analogize racial selection, then, with policies such as racial segregation, which were wrong (in part) because of the message they conveyed to minorities: Apartheid, for instance, conveyed that black people who were forced to use different facilities and so on were too base and degraded to use the same public spaces as white people. And this was clearly incompatible with the equal status that black people ought to have had in South African society. It meant both that black people were mistreated by white people within civil society, because the state had endorsed that mistreatment, and it also meant that black people had to live under a state that was openly hostile toward them, making it very difficult for them to insist on having their rights and interests taken seriously.[1]

One concern about this argument is its scope: It only tells against racial selection policies in countries that are already at least somewhat diverse, for only then will the message of disrespect also fall on people who are existing members. Wouldn't it still be very troubling, though, if a hypothetically homogenous country were to exclude particular racial groups (Fine 2016)?

One option here is to say that the message of disrespect conveyed by this policy is wrong because of what it expresses to the potential (black) immigrants themselves. Even if they do not have the strong rights of equal treatment that citizens have, perhaps they still have a right not to be shown contempt? Blake and Wellman resist this option, claiming that people simply don't have a right against being shown contempt. They might say that for an existing citizen being shown such contempt undermines their ability to continue to interact with the state and other citizens on a footing of equality. When it comes to non-citizens, there is no comparable harm and hence no rights violation. A potential reply to this claim might be to note that there is *some* cooperation that takes place *across* borders, even if it is not cooperation of the same dense variety that occurs *within* territorial borders. And there are *some* moral constraints on that cooperation, even they aren't the same constraints that should guide cooperation within a territory: International cooperation is needed on issues such as trade, climate change, and indeed migration, and it seems morally problematic if some nations are persistently in a subordinate position in this cooperation. It is often said, for instance, that less developed nations have been consistently dominated in trade negotiations by more developed nations and that this is unjust (Stiglitz and Charlton 2007). Perhaps if Japan (even a hypothetical Japan with no black population) were to specifically exclude all black migrants that would put African nations into a subordinate position when they had to cooperate with Japan on trade policy. We will look in more detail at the issue of harms to foreign nationals in the discussion of religious selection and Donald Trump's "Travel Ban" below.

So far we have discussed only race, but what about ethnicity? Like race, ethnicity is conceived as an inherited characteristic, but it refers not to some supposed racial essence passed on through generations, but simply to the fact that someone's ancestors were from a particular place.[2] And, as briefly alluded to earlier, ethnic selection has been (perhaps surprisingly) resilient in liberal democracies. Germany's *Aussiedlung* ("resettlement") policy gave special immigration benefits to people who were able to show some German ancestry, even if their families had lived abroad for many generations, they spoke no German, and generally held few cultural ties to Germany (Joppke 2005). And Spain has given preference to people from "Hispanic" countries – such as Chile, Colombia, and Mexico – on the grounds that they are ultimately descended from Spanish settlers (Joppke 2005).

Although these policies have been frequently criticized – *Aussiedlung* was ultimately abolished following many moral critiques from inside and outside of Germany – they may avoid some of the obvious problems with racial selection. Ethnic ties have a genuine historical basis in continuities of descent, whereas racial distinctions have no genuine biological grounding. And perhaps this means that ethnic distinctions are also somewhat less arbitrary: perhaps there is more reason to care about where one is ultimately "from" than there is to care about imaginary racial essences. (Though we can certainly question whether there really is any great significance to the sheer fact of common descent, independent of any further cultural ties: People can have the same ethnic origin while having no values, language, etc., in common. Why should the *sheer* fact of similar descent make any real difference?)

What about the message conveyed by ethnic selection policies? Racial selection policies seem to convey that some people are biologically inferior to others. But the ethnic policies just mentioned were not primarily about excluding particular groups, presumed too debased to live in, say, Germany. Rather, their point was to celebrate a particular common ancestry and ensure that people bearing that ancestry could exercise their right to return "home." It was consistent with this idea to assume that non-Germans are equally important as persons and have similar rights: their rights just entitle them to live in their own homelands, not Germany. All the same, many people found the message of *Aussiedlung* problematic. And we can explain this using much of Blake and Wellman's framework. Here, too, we can point out that Germany had many residents from different ethnic backgrounds, mostly obviously people of Turkish origin. *Aussiedlung* allowed ethnic Germans to not only enter Germany but also naturalize more quickly than many ethnic Turks who had been present in Germany for multiple generations. Thus, even if it did not express that these ethnic Turks were biologically inferior, it did express that they were less entitled to support from the German state: that they were second-class members of society. And this seems, again, incompatible with the requirement that all permanent residents of a state be treated as equal members.

What happens on this view when an ethnic distinction is "benign": When it doesn't reflect open prejudice and so on? An example from domestic policy-making might be affirmative action policies intended to help under-represented groups gain access to institutions – such as higher education – from which they have traditionally been excluded. Blake (2002) suggests that there can similarly be racial and ethnic distinctions made in immigration policy, not out of malice but out of special concern for helping certain groups. For example, Israel, he suggests, may be construed as giving preference to Jewish people not out of hatred for others but out of a desire to protect a group that has frequently been persecuted elsewhere (mostly obviously during the Holocaust, but also through discrimination in employment, education, governance, and so on: Harvard University, for example, still had a 15 percent maximum quota for Jewish students in the early twentieth century).

This suggestion puts some pressure on how exactly a "benign" motivation is to be defined. If a state is not acting out of open prejudice, may it take as its mission promoting the interests of members of particular groups? Some policies of this kind seem more clearly acceptable than others. For instance, many states have given preference to people from former colonies. Britain, for example, historically was more open to immigration by people from former colonies such as India and Barbados. Though this preference was eroded by time, it seems relatively unobjectionable. By contrast, as we saw earlier, there was much more resistance to Germany's *Aussiedlung* policies, giving special preference to ethnic Germans to protect them from oppression.

How can we distinguish among these various preferential policies and determine which are genuinely acceptable? Since the underlying concern is with protecting equality, we might look at whether the group being given special preference has an antecedent elevated position in society. People of Indian and Caribbean origin in the United Kingdom were not an especially powerful or privileged group, so to give preference to Indian and Caribbean migrants ran relevantly low risk of expressing any superiority of these ethnic groups within the British polity or of harming other groups within that polity. By contrast, ethnic Germans were a more politically powerful and socially elevated group within Germany (compared with, say, people of Turkish origin), and so giving preference to ethnic Germans in admissions was more plausibly an expression of political superiority.

Now, we have been looking at policies that explicitly distinguish among candidates for admission based on their race. But this sets aside a large part of the politics of immigration, policies in which race seems to play a significant role even where the policies themselves do not explicitly single out any particular race. This brings up an issue often discussed in the philosophy of race: even where there are policies that aren't explicitly racial, they can still have important negative *effects* on particular racial groups (Mendoza 2017). Let's look at this kind of dynamic in more detail shortly when we analyze US President Donald Trump's "travel ban."

B. Religion

Religious selection, unlike racial selection, cannot be said to always rest on irrationality. The desire to associate with members of one's own religion need not be based on any discredited biological theory. The religion of one's compatriots can affect the public life of a country, including its physical structures and its social mores. And accommodating new religions can impose costs (for instance if members of a minority religion demand the right to take a different day off from work than that taken by the majority). Yet religion has often been considered an extremely problematic basis for selecting immigrants. What could be the problem?

One way to approach this question is to consider the relationship between the state and religion more generally. A basic assumption of liberal democracies is that there should be significant constraints on the state's ability to establish and enforce an official religion, though the precise nature of those constraints is of course contested. We take it for granted that the state may not punish people who do not share the majority religion. Nor may the state give special political powers – extra votes, an increased opportunity to hold office – to those who have a particular religious viewpoint (or an anti-religious viewpoint). While some liberal democracies, such as the Dominican Republic, have no official religion at all, others, such as Britain, limit their official religion and its officers to relatively ceremonial political functions. (Israel is of course an outlier – given the strong political role it gives to Judaism – one whose special historical role we cannot do full justice to here.)

Why these limits on the involvement of the state in the temple, or the church in the state? We can again consider expressive harms, as US Justice Sandra Day O'Connor proposed:

> [Religious] Endorsement sends a message to nonadherents that they are outsiders, not full members of the political community, and an accompanying message to adherents that they are insiders, favored members of the political community.
>
> (*Lynch v. Donnelly*, 465 U.S. 668, 688 (1984))

And so one could object to religious selection of immigrants on the grounds that it suggests state endorsement of the favored religion and thus state favoritism toward all members of that religion (Nussbaum 2010).

The standard concern about O'Connor's "endorsement test" is that it requires difficult judgments about what exactly a particular symbol or policy expresses. Does a holiday display in a US town that includes a crèche (along with some reindeer, candy canes, and Santas) express a commitment to the divinity of Christ – and thereby express that Jewish people are less favored members of the community – or does it simply express a general attitude of festive cheer? Similarly, someone might ask whether a policy of religious immigrant selection expresses official favoritism toward the majority religion or is instead just an attempt to ensure social cohesion and save costs of accommodating a wider plurality of religions. Broader context matters here. For example, suppose that members of the town have never had a crèche before in their Christmas display but have suddenly adopted one upon learning that some Jewish people are considering moving into town. Moreover, local media have been strongly suggesting that there is a need to discourage Jewish people from settling in the town because they are untrustworthy and their culture is corrupting. These circumstances would support the view that the crèche expresses an elevated status for Christianity within the community and that any other justification was pre-textual. What matters, we might say, is whether this interpretation of the motivation for the law is *reasonable*: if it is unreasonable then the government cannot be blamed for anyone's sense of an inferior status in society, and it is their responsibility to take better care in interpreting the policy. But if the interpretation is reasonable, then responsibility falls on the government for generating a sense of inferior status (Hosein 2018).

It is obvious that laws that explicitly attempt to exclude a certain religious group can be reasonably construed as expressing government disfavor for that religion. But, as mentioned earlier, we can also ask whether immigration laws that do not directly refer to particular religions (or races or ethnicities) or involve the use of religious symbols can all the same be discriminatory or unjust. For an example of this, let's look in detail at US President Donald Trump's travel ban, implemented in 2017, which almost entirely prohibited travel to the United States by people from seven (later revised to six) Muslim-majority countries, including Iran, Somalia, and Yemen. The order thus did not explicitly mention any religion, and the given rationale for this policy was to promote national security by denying admission to people disposed toward acts of terrorism. After pushback against the initial version of the ban, President Trump commissioned a US Department of Homeland Security report that endorsed the security rationale for the ban (though the report remained out of view from the public).

But despite this official appeal to security considerations, there were strong suggestions that the policy was ultimately based in broad antipathy toward Islam. In January 2016, then-candidate Trump stated that "Islam hates us... . [W]e can't allow people coming into this country who have this hatred of the United States ... [a]nd of people that are not Muslim" (*Trump v. Hawaii*, No. 17–965, 585 U.S. ___, 6 (2018)). The impression of a law grounded in dislike and distrust of Islam was not dispelled after Trump assumed office. A close aide said, "[W]hen [Donald Trump] first announced it, he said, 'Muslim ban.' He called me up. He said, 'Put a commission together. Show me the right way to do it legally'" (*Trump v. Hawaii*, No. 17–965, 585 U.S. ___, 7 (2018)).

Many people thus interpreted the ban to be an expression of animus against Islam, and this interpretation seems reasonable given the background. It thus seems parallel to the religious display example mentioned earlier. The official justification for this policy is neutral, but in context, it can reasonably be construed to express disfavor (in fact animus) toward a particular religion. So why not think that the travel ban was, like our religious display example, unacceptable?

Constitutionally speaking, US Supreme Court Chief Justice John Roberts claims in *Trump v. Hawaii*, the travel ban is in fact very different from examples involving religious displays. The context of immigrant selection is special, he claims. Settling some intricacies of US law, Roberts's argument has two main strands. First, he claims that any potential harms created by immigrant selection are very different from those that can be created by religious displays. Second, there are crucial and distinctive national security concerns that arise in the context of immigrant selection. Let's look at each of these arguments in turn.

Entry into the country Roberts begins, is a "privilege" and not a right (he's setting aside people with grants of asylum, green card holders, and so on). Denials of entry remove an option that no one is entitled to in the first place – an assumption grounded in the closed borders view we looked at in the first part of this book – and hence can be taken away on almost any basis. So potential immigrants are not harmed in any morally significant way by being excluded from the country as a result of a new selection policy. Now sometimes, Roberts accepts, denials of admission affect not only the people seeking entry but also US citizens who might, for example, wish to hear the immigrants speak. But these harms also demand only minimal justification: No one is entitled to interact with a person from another country (perhaps excepting certain special cases, such as family connections).

Suppose we agree that the *mere* fact of someone being excluded from a territory doesn't demand an extensive justification. What happens, though, if we focus on exclusion that can reasonably be construed as Islamophobic? Are the harms involved still of no great moment? First, notice that exclusion of this kind creates exactly the same harms that are and should be taken seriously in the religious display example discussed earlier. As Justice Sonia Sotomayor pointed out in her dissent, the travel ban likewise put Muslim Americans into a second-class status in society, making them "outsiders, less favored members of the political community." This is supported by Blake and Wellman's point discussed earlier: refusing to admit members of an ethnic group in that country has implications for the members of that ethnic group who live within that country (Blake 2003). The same goes for religious groups. Defenders of the ban will say that it merely points out some issues with Muslims *out there*, beyond the border, not Muslims *within the country*. But this ignores the fact that Trump in the main spoke simply of "Muslims," not making any real distinctions between the two groups.

Beyond harms to Muslim Americans, we can also look at harms to Muslims elsewhere in the world. We saw earlier that Blake and Wellman do not believe such harms are serious in the context of state expressions of religious (or racial, or ethnic) animus. We can question this by looking at the global significance of the ban and of immigration policy in general. States jockey for power within the sphere of global politics, but there are plausibly limits on what they can or should do in seeking it. In particular, they should not try to achieve greater leverage by engaging in racial and religious humiliation of foreign people and states. In support of this, consider colonialism. At least one major reason why colonialism was deeply wrong is the way it created racial and religious hierarchies, including through symbolic means. For example, colonizing powers often enforced new hierarchies of status according to which local forms of dress, customs, and so on came to be treated as signs of backwardness and indicators of the need for "civilizing" rule by ethnic and religious superiors. Members of the indigenous populations who became part of the colonial administration were often required to adopt "respectable" European dress in order to mark them off from the rest of the population. Remnants of these codes still have a strong influence today in postcolonial societies (Hundle 2017).

Now, in the absence of colonialism, we do not have formal rule by some countries over others. But the United States still interacts substantially with, and exerts power over, various Muslims and Muslim-majority countries. Consider the many Muslim citizens of Iraq, Pakistan, Syria, and so on, who were – before the ban and at the time of its enactment – cooperating closely with the US government. They have fought alongside US soldiers, acted as translators on behalf of the United States, approved US use of their airspace, etc. One criticism of the travel ban was that it would anger these people by expressing that they were unfit to enter the United States and thereby sap their willingness to cooperate in the future. If that's right, then perhaps the policy was counterproductive, reducing rather than bolstering the United States's capacity to fight terrorism. (The key enemy Trump was concerned with was *Daesh* – the so-called Islamic State – and the vast majority of people fighting *Daesh* globally were Muslims, including Muslims in countries like Syria that were targeted by the ban.) But beyond these pragmatic concerns, we might ask whether the message of the policy created an injustice. There is something wrong, one might think, with the United States continuing to make demands of Muslim people around the world while at the same time expressing a fundamental lack of trust in them. The US government also exerts power in these areas of the world, even when it is not formally ruling over them. It influences elections, builds military bases designed to change the balance of power in the region, and so on; and, again, it seems problematic to exercise power in part through the humiliation of foreign powers and peoples. Just as O'Connor rejected a *society* of inferiors and superiors, so too one might reject a *global* order in which some people and nations stand above others.

So far we've been looking at the harms of the travel ban, and we've seen that they have close moral commonalities with the harms of religious displays that create a strong impression of religious animus. But that still leaves Roberts's assertion that the two situations are significantly disanalogous because of the security concerns involved in selecting immigrants. Roberts argues that the Constitution must not be read in a way that constrains the executive – which alone has the necessary information and capacity – from responding in real time to threats to the nation, including from immigrants who might commit acts of terrorism. In the case at hand, the president may have made some intolerant statements, but this cannot become a strong barrier to his protecting the country. Roberts is especially concerned about having *courts* constrain the executive in this way, but we can also consider more broadly whether the executive ought to be trusted by Congress and by the public to promote national security goals given its special access to intelligence and ability to respond quickly to threats.

Does the executive need such flexibility? Let's consider some potential rebuttals of Roberts's arguments. First, insofar as there is an apparent conflict between security and equality here, it is one that presidents can avoid by not making disparaging statements of the kind that Trump made, and this seems like a relatively light constraint on the executive. One might wonder whether it is too constraining to say that just because a presidential candidate made some disparaging comments in the past, they are now indefinitely constrained from taking various security-protecting measures. But the constraint need not be indefinite: The standard we have looked at says that a policy must not create a situation where someone could reasonably interpret it as an expression of animus. And a president could alter the reasonable interpretations of a policy by changing the background context in which it is enacted. For example, President Trump could have worked to walk back his earlier statements about Islam and made an effort to engage with Muslim leaders and seek their advice. Doing so would have made it more credible to assert that the travel ban was not really motivated by anti-Muslim bias.

Second, if a conflict between equality and security seems to remain, then we might look for ways to jointly satisfy each consideration. For example, Sotomayor suggested a policy of rigorous individualized screening, which would look at the threat posed by particular people rather than placing a blanket prohibition on immigration from the countries singled out by the ban (and she claimed that there was already a rigorous congressionally approved scheme for such vetting).

C. Gender

In recent history, liberal democracies have not explicitly singled out gender groups for selection. There have not been specific quotas for women or men, nor have governments typically directly sought to achieve a particular gender balance. But all the same, gender has played an important role in immigrant selection. Until 1934, only male US citizens were able to pass their citizenship on to their children. Similar restrictions have been in place in the more recent past in many other parts of the world and survive to this day. At the time of writing, 26 countries – including Barbados, Burundi, and Kuwait – deny women an equal ability to pass on their citizenship (UNHCR 2017). Often these restrictions are inherited from colonial laws on nationality (Global Campaign for Equal Nationality Rights 2017).

In addition to directly disadvantaging women (as well as their children, who often become stateless), the generation and persistence of these laws reflect harmful stereotypes, such as the idea that only men are true citizens in the state – that only men have the capacity and standing to make political decisions – and thus the proper representatives of the state in determining whether a child should be naturalized. In what follows we'll look in more detail at gender stereotyping, its relation to immigration policy, and why it might be problematic. The theoretical ideas about stereotyping that we'll look at may also be useful for thinking about race, religion, and so on.

Consider, first, the situation in *Nguyen v. INS* (533 U.S. 53 (2001)). Nguyen was born in Vietnam to an American-citizen father and a Vietnamese-citizen mother who were not married. He was attempting to establish that he had inherited US citizenship from his father. But the law under review imposed – in situations where a child was born abroad and out of wedlock – different requirements for inheriting citizenship from a father than from a mother. Had Nguyen's mother been a US citizen, he would have acquired citizenship from her automatically, but a father was required to establish paternity before the child reached 18, for instance through a declaration of paternity under oath.

Why the special bar for inheriting citizenship via a father? The justification given was the "special relationship" between mothers and children. And there were two parts to this: first, the idea that it is simply easier to establish maternity at birth. The mere presence of a mother at birth is enough to prove that she is the biological parent, but the mere presence of a father is not. But this doesn't itself explain why paternity would have to be established by *the age of 18*. Why not allow a DNA test to be used at any age? The second justification spoke to this requirement: (biological) mothers, the argument went, are more likely to have a real bond with the child by virtue of their proximity at birth, while a biological father might not be present at birth or even aware of the child's existence. This means that the child is more likely to have social and cultural ties to the United States via a biological mother than via a biological father: ties via the father should be assumed only if an early life connection between father and child is established.

To critics, these justifications are unacceptably tied to gender stereotyping.[3] The second justification, especially, seems to reflect social presumptions that (a) women are especially inclined toward child-rearing or (b) it is especially appropriate for women to engage in child-rearing. But these presumptions are not rooted in any biological facts about womanhood, and historically they have been associated with clear errors about what is possible and acceptable behavior for women: for example, about whether women should have rights to vote or run for office.

Now, in defense of the law, someone might say that it doesn't really reflect stereotyping because stereotyping involves reliance on mistaken or ill-founded generalizations, whereas the two justifications given assert genuine statistical differences about the ease of establishing biological parenthood and the likelihood of developing social ties (though this, of course, would need to be established). In support of the latter, it might be pointed out that in the United States women do currently play a disproportionate role in the rearing of children. Critics can give the following response: Even if these statistical differences in fact hold, it is still important for the state not to *reinforce* prevailing social stereotypes about differences between women and men. By privileging the ability of mothers to pass on citizenship, the state makes it easier for them to be the people involved in socializing children and also gives the impression that this is a natural and appropriate state of affairs. This potentially steers mothers more than fathers into different roles, reinforcing older patterns of gender differentiation in society. This reinforcement can be problematic for multiple reasons. First, the fact that women and men are expected to perform particular functions in society can restrict the *freedom* of women and men who wish to buck the norm: women who want to be CEOs and politicians, men who want to be primary caregivers for children, and so on. It also makes it harder for people who identify as *neither* male *nor* female to find a place in a society that takes there to be just those two possible tracks for building a life. Second, the reinforcement of gender roles can perpetuate the *subordination* of women in a society. For example, gender norms can make it harder for women to gain political power, and this in turn makes it more likely that the state will systematically discount their interests in its decision-making.

Gender stereotypes often *interact* in complicated ways with racial and ethnic stereotyping. It may be useful here to have the concept of "intersectionality" to hand. First defined by Kimberlé Crenshaw (1989) in order to explain discrimination against black women, "intersectionality" refers to cases where someone is a member of two different groups, each of which is mistreated, and thus faces special forms of social disadvantage that result from being within the overlap, the "intersection," of those two groups. For present purposes, it is important to see that immigrant women are often subject not only to prevailing stereotypes about *women* and prevailing stereotypes about their *ethnic group*, but also more specific stereotypes about *women members of that ethnic group*.

Take female East Asian immigrants to the United States in the nineteenth century. As *women*, they were constrained – just as white women were – by the stereotypes we just looked at about what counts as "women's work." They were also subject to objectifying stereotypes – according to which women function mainly as objects for male desire – which made them vulnerable to sexual harassment. As ethnically East Asian, they were subject to prevailing stereotypes about East Asian people as an "impure" race, unfit to live among white people, making them targets for mistreatment. This double burden, however, is still not sufficient to capture the full nature of these women's experience. They were stereotyped more specifically as "prostitutes," Sucheng Chan (1994) reveals, who would degrade the national character by promoting licentious behavior, creating a public health risk, and fostering multiple children who would degrade the national character. Such stereotypes licensed special forms of discrimination against East Asian women. For example, in San Francisco, a general crackdown on brothels was announced, but it was enforced in a manner that was "desultory and racially selective" (97). This perception of East Asian women as disposed toward sexual misconduct also played a large role in limiting the admission of women from China. Often they were denied entry out of suspicion that they would engage in prostitution on arrival: At its highest, the percentage of women in the late nineteenth-century Chinese immigrant population was a mere 7.2 percent. And while the initial wave of immigrants from particular countries has often been gender unbalanced, this percentage remained low for more than a century (94). In the modern United States, East Asian women are still sexualized in problematic ways, often being stereotyped as submissive partners, appropriate for white husbands who will act as more dominant heads of the household (Sue et al. 2007).

As Natalie Cisneros (2013) points out, a similar phenomenon has occurred with unauthorized Latin American women in the recent past. They have been subject to both general stereotypes about women and about Latin Americans, but also to more specific intersectional stereotypes. The discourse around so-called 'anchor babies' is an example of this. One major fear around unauthorized Latin American migration to the United States has been that Latin American women will attempt to cross the border specifically to give birth in the United States so that their children will be entitled to US citizenship. Cisneros points to the rhetoric used to express fears about these women. In 2010, Curry Todd, a Tennessee state lawmaker, described them as "rats [that] multiply" (291), which is indicative, Cisneros says, of general social understanding of "pregnant immigrant women ... as sexually deviant and ... a threat to the well-being of the nation." The parallels with earlier conceptions of East Asian women – conceptions that are now deemed dehumanizing and unacceptable – are substantial. In addition to being directly damaging to the self-respect of immigrant women, these social understandings affect the material lives of these women. For example, they support attempts to prevent unauthorized immigrant women from accessing state-funded health care programs for their children, as well as calls to prevent the children of unauthorized immigrant women from naturalizing (291) (though this proposal has not been put into action yet, in part because of constitutional hurdles).

There are also more indirect ways in which stereotypes can affect women's interests. We saw earlier that women are often associated with particular roles in society, such as caring for children and performing other forms of work within the home. Feminists have pointed out that these roles associated with women have also been traditionally *devalued*: considered less important to society than male roles – such as employment outside of the home and participation in politics – and given a lower social status. Yet, care work performs an essential social function; without it, future citizens would be unable to perform their civic duties adequately, the economy would be deprived of skilled workers, older populations would lack adequate support, and so on. One important strand of feminist thought, sometimes called "difference feminism," tries to respond to this devaluation of roles and practices associated with femininity. Iris Marion Young writes that this approach ("gynocentric feminism")

> defines women's oppression as the devaluation and repression of women's experience by a masculinist culture that exalts violence and individualism. It argues for the superiority of the values embodied in traditionally female

experience, and rejects the values it finds in traditionally male dominated institutions.

(Young 1985, 173)

Practices and values associated with masculinity, Young is asserting, generally involve competitiveness and individuals trying to pursue their individual self-interest. Take the characters in the movie *Glengarry Glen Ross* (1992), one of whom tells a "failing" colleague: "You can't play in the man's game, you can't close [deals] – go home and tell your wife your troubles. Because only one thing counts in this life: Get them to sign on the line which is dotted." Such cutthroat environments, Young claims, are destructive and ought to be replaced with more cooperative ways of organizing society.

Even if we don't agree with Young that practices and values culturally associated with femininity are *always superior* – surely *some* degree of aggressiveness is valuable when, say, fighting a just war[4] – we can still accept that reflexive exaltation of masculinity must be challenged.

Returning to immigration, we can see important policies that devalue traditionally female roles. Shelley Wilcox (2005, 218) points to the Immigration Act of 1990 (IMMACT), which shifted the share of employment visas awarded in the direction of "skilled" workers, who were considered more valuable than care workers. Young might say here that we should celebrate the work that is predominantly done by immigrant women (rather than men), such as nursing the sick in hospitals and caring for the elderly, and that this means both welcoming their admission and ensuring their favorable treatment when they enter the country. Furthermore, given that women from developing countries as a matter of fact disproportionately perform care work, a policy that favors other forms of work has the effect of systematically disadvantaging developing world women relative to men (Wilcox 2005, 219). This violates a plausible feminist principle of rejecting any policy (or policies) that disproportionately disadvantages women, especially the poorest women.[5]

Can the various feminist ideals we have looked at be jointly satisfied? These are: avoiding role stereotyping, celebrating virtues that are coded "feminine," and ensuring that women are not disproportionately burdened by a policy. In calling for a celebration of "feminine" ways of doing things, Young can be accused of reinforcing the association of women with particular practices: precisely the role stereotyping that many other feminists hope to abolish. A potential solution to this problem is to revalue the particular roles that women have in fact performed – stressing the importance of care work to society, for instance – while at the same time trying to emphasize that there is nothing about these roles that makes women rather than men especially suited to them: that both men and women can make great parents, and that this is a really important form of work. For instance, rather than valuing care work by offering paid maternity leave, one could instead offer *both* paid maternity and paternity leave.

Can a similar combination be found in the context of immigration? If women are admitted mainly as caregivers, then this can have the effect of reinforcing stereotypes about women and work within the home. That potential problem might be corrected somewhat by the fact that migrant care workers often allow more advantaged women in the destination country – where their access to the labor market is often limited by the expectation that they will do disproportionate amounts of labor within the home – to go work as lawyers or doctors or in other fields that are structured in a manner that requires long hours (Wilcox 2008). But that correction can lead to another, intersectional stereotype, where migrant women – as well as other women who share their ethnicity (Filipino Canadian women, for example) – are stereotyped as having a caregiving role.[6]

To combat this, the state might take steps to ensure that a broader mix of women in different forms of employment is brought from the developing world: not just care workers, but also women who work in high-tech fields, for example. But if we assume that, given common policy constraints, only a fixed number of people are going to be admitted, this approach means admitting fewer caregivers, which in turn means admitting fewer of the poorest women from developing countries.[7] This violates the principle that immigration policies should work for and not against the very poorest women. So we have potential tension among various feminist ideals. Which should trump the others?[8]

Intersectional stereotypes can also affect men. For example, Latino men in the United States, as well as black men, are often associated with violence and danger, as Curry (2017) points out. One psychological study "consistently found that fictional Black or Hispanic men are envisioned to be physically larger, higher in aggression, and lower in status" (Holbrook, Fessler, and Navarrete 2016, 75, cited in Curry 2017). Muslim men are often associated with violent extremism. Insofar as breaking down gender stereotypes in general is a goal of feminism, including intersectional stereotypes, these associations with immigrant men are also an important subject of feminist concern. Breaking them down would not only be to the benefit of immigrant men but would also, at least in the long run, likely benefit immigrant women: The flipside of immigrant men being associated with violence and misogyny is the association of immigrant women with docility and also a sense that any problems faced by immigration women are primarily due to their involvement with immigrant men rather than due to their reception in the receiving society.

Finally, though we will not be able to give the topic due space here, stereotypes, including intersectional stereotypes, also matter for LGBTQ people. Queer migrants can face, for instance, special forms of distrust where the combination of their race and their gender presentation or sexuality is taken to be an especially strong marker of deviance and thus a basis for social exclusion.[9] Historically there have been, at times, outright prohibitions on the entry of gay and lesbian people. For example, the legislature of the United States passed a law in 1965 making it explicit that "afflict[ion] with sexual deviation" was a ground for exclusion from entry (Johnson 2003, 143). There have also been less direct forms of exclusion, as seen in the 1985 restrictions on entry into the US of people infected with HIV, which was partly based on fears of entry by gay people stereotyped as licentious and immoral (*ibid.* 146). (Those restrictions were lifted in 2010.) Another barrier for gay migrants has been a lack of access to "family ties" migration routes, which allow current citizens (and sometimes already admitted immigrants) to sponsor family members for immigration. Restrictions on gay marriage have often prevented same-sex couples from making use of those routes. And even now that same-sex marriage is more widely permitted in liberal democracies, there are still potential difficulties faced by couples migrating from countries that do not permit it.[10] Later in this chapter we'll discuss in more detail family migration and which kinds of relationships should be given priority by the state. In the next chapter we'll talk about another issue of importance to LGBTQ migrants: the way refugee status is defined.

D. National culture

Cultural selection seeks to maintain and bolster a "national culture." And if we think of cultures as mainly involving traits – language use, beliefs, traditional practices – that can be acquired through voluntary steps, then cultural selection seems much less exclusionary than ethnic selection policies. It thus is common to claim that while "descent-based approaches to national membership have obvious racist overtones, and are manifestly unjust," cultural approaches can be acceptable when "membership is open in principle to anyone, regardless of race or color, who is willing to learn the language and history of the society and participate in its social and political institutions" (Kymlicka 1995, 23).

Also, cultural practices seem to be different from religious practices in that people can be asked to adopt them without having to seriously violate their own conscience; on the face of it, it is much more reasonable for a society to ask someone to learn its dominant language than it is to ask someone to abandon their religion.

As we saw in Part I of this book, theorists have offered important arguments for the value of a shared national culture. A national culture, they say, can be an important resource for stabilizing democracy. It can help to establish trust between members, which, in turn, promotes the cooperation between members that is needed for democracy to flourish. They also argue that national cultures establish a degree of fellow-feeling between members of a society, and that this fellow-feeling is necessary to ensure the survival of social programs that promote the common good. For instance, it is sometimes claimed that Swedes have been willing to support a relatively generous welfare state, rather than voting out of narrow self-interest, only because they conceive of themselves as a unified people and share a commitment to the idea of a *folkhemmet*, or "people's home."[11]

Yet even cultural selection threatens to violate some of the moral requirements we have looked at already. By elevating one culture over others, it can
result in stigma and ostracism for minority groups, and certainly appeals to
national culture have often been associated historically with highly exclusionary practices. For instance, in the United States, even as explicit racial
prejudice and the biological theories underpinning it became discredited and
socially unacceptable, there were still many people who advocated the superiority of an "American" culture, ultimately associated with (supposedly)
Anglo-Saxon and Christian values (Klinkner 1999). African Americans have
suffered under the assumption that they are biologically incapable of progress,
but they have also suffered under the assumption that their communities have
a degenerate culture, one that prevents them from assimilating into the genuine national culture of a strong Protestant work ethic. Their poverty – even
when deeply rooted in discrimination, lack of adequate infrastructure, and so
on – has often been attributed wholly to their cultural difference and thus
considered outside of the state's responsibility. Women too, as we saw earlier,
were often subordinated because the "hard work" valued by this culture was
implicitly assumed to be "masculine work," performed by men outside of the
home.

In sum, there is both promise and peril to promotion of a national culture:
it can be both a resource for democratic goals and a source of exclusion and
subordination. Can this dilemma be solved? Can we have the benefits of a
national culture without the costs? Many philosophers have thought that the
answer must lie in the *details* of how we *define* the national culture. If only,
for instance, masculinist elements were excised from any American national
culture, then there would be no threat of gender subordination, the thought
goes. We will now consider various attempts theorists have made to define
nationality in ways that are compatible with liberal principles and democratic
equality in practice (the survey will draw substantially on Song [2009]).

i. Constitutional patriotism

"Constitutional patriotism," as defended by Jürgen Habermas (1992), proposes a definition of the nation in terms of shared political values. Constitutional patriots do not wish to anchor national identity in any narrow political
affiliation, such as being a member of a particular party; that seems incompatible with the democratic idea that political decision-making rests with the
people as a whole, not just one party. So they appeal to more abstract values
that all members of a democratic society can be reasonably expected to share.
For instance, one might define the United States, in the words of Abraham
Lincoln, as a nation "conceived in liberty, and dedicated to the proposition
that all men are created equal." To be an American, for the constitutional
patriot, is to be committed to these shared values of freedom and equality,
irrespective of one's ethnic origin, religion, personal projects, and so on. A

little more specifically, it is to be committed to the embodiment of those values in the US Constitution. Likewise, German-ness can be defined as a commitment to that country's constitution, the "Basic Law."

The advantage of constitutional patriotism is its apparent inclusiveness: All it takes to be German is to accept the principles set out by the Basic Law, and this is possible for people with extremely different ethnic, cultural, linguistic, and religious backgrounds. This makes it, supporters say, the most appropriate national identity for a modern pluralistic nation. Some potential problems with the approach are the following.

First, the basic values that constitutional patriots ask nationals to identity with are typically highly abstract: freedom, equality, and democracy. And these values are (in some form) broadly shared among liberal democracies. Why, then, should Haitian nationals, who strongly endorse the importance of *liberté*, associate themselves closely with *Haiti* and *Haitians*, rather than, say, Grenada and Grenadans, who also value liberty? Furthermore, abstract values may not have the kind of emotional resonance capable of generating bonds of identification and trust between members of any particular community (Smith 2003, 144–147).

The constitutional patriot can say that while national identity is to be defined in terms of values, nationals are asked to identify with their *particular* country's constitution: the 2012 Haitian constitution, for instance. But why? Why should people treat a certain constitution as *theirs*, beyond the fact that they happen to live in a certain place (Smith 2003, 144–147)? And it is here that ethnic and other problematic elements can easily creep into constitutional patriotism.

Take, for instance, the Tea Party movement in the United States, which made one of its central tenets a strict fidelity to the US Constitution. "We are dedicated," members set out in a mission statement, "to educating, motivating, and activating our fellow citizens, using the power of the values, ideals, and tenets of our Founding Fathers." Thus, while principles and values, especially liberty, may be at the forefront of their cause, it is clear that those values are put forward in significant part because of their association with a particular founding moment, a moment strongly associated with white Protestant men. If the answer to the question, "Why should I care about the US Constitution?" is "Because it was enacted by *our* – white, Protestant, male-forefathers," then we may once again have the problem of a nation defined in exclusionary terms. One way to counter this might be to assert the important role played by minority and historically disadvantaged groups in achievements of the nation. In Britain, one might point to the huge contribution to cultural and economic life played by people of Indian descent, for instance.

A second potential problem with constitutional patriotism is that even if the official national culture is defined in terms of abstract political values, there is still the question of how exactly people are to be identified as belonging to the culture or not. And there are important potential problems here. In the United States, for instance, the history of McCarthyist purges of

Communists and ideological tests for naturalization shows that a concern with national values can also lead to deeply undemocratic outcomes (Song 2009, 34), in this case because of the severe ideological conformity demanded to count as American. In our time, hostility to immigrant groups is often couched in the language of commitment to political values, and constitutional patriots face hard questions about when such hostility can be justified. For instance, the far-right *Rassemblement National*, in France, often criticizes France's Muslim community not directly for its religious perspective, but because of the supposed incompatibility of that faith with French Republican values. Similarly, Dutch politician Pim Fortuyn argued that Muslim immigration to the Netherlands ought to be limited because Muslim immigrants would not share the national commitment to freedom of sexual orientation.

The easy response for the constitutional patriot to these concerns is simply to dismiss such right-wing views as racial or ethnic hostility couched in more universalist language. But perhaps this is too quick; even if we accept constitutional patriotism as a view about how national identity should be understood, we still need to know how this national identity is to be incorporated into institutional decision-making. It seems that we are owed an account, not simply of how national identity is to be defined at the most abstract level, but also of how that abstract conception should be used in practice to select immigrants for admission and naturalization. This will be partly an empirical exercise in seeing the extent to which particular traits really are associated with certain values. But there is also an important moral dimension here: Some practices, such as using religious practice as a proxy for lacking the appropriate values, seem to be at least as stigmatizing as simply defining national identity in terms of a particular religion.

Finally, some philosophers raise concerns that even though constitutional patriotism is focused purely on shared values, it in practice inevitably leads to some cultures being promoted over others (Kymlicka 1995, 107–115). Most obviously, they say, politics must be conducted in some language or other; courts must make their pronouncements in a language, legislation must be written. Even constitutional patriots often favor some sort of language requirements for entry and, especially, naturalization. Sharing a language, obviously, facilitates communication between people. And immigrants who are better able to communicate with the existing population will likely be better placed to work, participate in democratic institutions, and integrate into a society more generally. Kymlicka emphasizes that once the state chooses a particular language for these purposes, it thereby favors people who speak and identify with that language and promote the culture associated with the language.

ii. Liberal nationalism

With these reflections on the inevitability of promoting some cultures and identities over others in mind, some theorists propose that the project of constitutional patriotism – of founding national identity purely on shared political values – ought to be abandoned. Instead, we should take an approach to national identity that unapologetically aims to secure a shared national culture that includes elements – such as a common language, traditions, and social norms – that go beyond merely shared political values. But these theorists are still mindful of the potential for a national identity to be exclusionary, so they endorse "*liberal nationalism*" (Miller 1995) or other forms of cultural nationalism that are intended to be inclusive enough to be suitable for a modern pluralistic society.

How is it possible for a state to associate itself with a set of cultural traditions and practices without being exclusionary? One suggestion, touched on earlier, is that the key distinction is between identities than can be voluntarily acquired and identities that cannot be. Language, many philosophers have thought, is an acceptable basis for selection because linguistic competence can also be acquired. It is acceptable to associate national identity with a particular language, they say, because all members are able to adopt that national language and can be reasonably expected to do so. Thus Kymlicka distinguishes the Quebecois commitment to maintaining French language and Francophone culture from German *Aussiedlung*, because anyone can learn French and thus become a full member (Kymlicka 1995, 23).

Perhaps, though, it is less straightforward to separate purely "cultural" and straightforwardly ethnic identities than Kymlicka's discussion suggests. We might ask not just who can learn French, but why many Quebecers are so wedded to the language and associated Francophone culture in the first place. What many of them really care about, Charles Taylor proposes, is "remaining true to the culture of [their] ancestors" (Taylor 1994, 58). So, while French can be spoken by people from many different ethnic backgrounds – and indeed *is* spoken by people from North Africa to Haiti – French is associated with Quebec ultimately because many people there wish to respect their descent from the (white Catholic) settlers who brought the language there. Thus, there is a concern that even if people can voluntarily learn French, they cannot so easily become part of the ethnic group whose identity is treated as fundamental to the province's government. In response, Kymlicka might argue that the celebration of Francophone culture need not be grounded in its connection to any white founders or their descendants. Is this how linguistic identity has in fact developed in Quebec? How about in other places with strong linguistic nationalism, such as Catalonia? Or Wales?

Another suggestion for ensuring that cultural identities are not exclusionary is to ensure that all current members, including members of minority groups, have an equally good opportunity to contribute to that culture and to promote their own cultural goals. This proposal seems attractive when we think about multicultural nations that celebrate multiple or complex cultural identities. It is a step toward inclusion, one might think, when New Zealand recognizes and celebrates Maori festivals and traditions as much as its British inheritance.

The approach offers an attractive interpretation of what it is for the government to equally accommodate different cultural and linguistic identities. There are major complexities, though, when we consider what exactly it entails, especially when it comes to linguistic identities (for some of these complexities, see Patten [2014]). For instance, if the state provides school in one language, must it provide schooling in every language spoken within the territory? What if there are many small minority groups who speak different languages? Applied to immigrant selection, does it mean that the state must admit equal numbers of speakers of all the different languages spoken in the territory? Or immigrant speakers of a given language in proportion to the number of current speakers of that language within the territory? And as an approach to linguistic variation, this "equal opportunity" approach is unlikely to satisfy linguistic nationalists in Quebec, Catalonia, and so on. The problem is that such languages are highly vulnerable to erosion, because of sociological dynamics that govern communication. Philippe Van Parijs (2011) points out that generally when a linguistically heterogeneous group of people comes together to communicate, the language in which they typically choose to communicate is the one that is *spoken best by the person who speaks it the least well*. An example might help illustrate: Suppose that five people have a conversation. Four of them speak fluent Spanish and fairly strong English. One of them speaks fluent English and poor Spanish. Within this group, the person who speaks Spanish least well speaks it poorly, while the person (people) who speaks English least well is still a strong English speaker. So, even though this might be mainly made up of people whose mother tongue is Spanish, the conversation will still be conducted in English. So in practice a "foreign" language – such as English in Quebec or Castilian Spanish in Catalonia – can quickly become the most used in conversation, even if it is not the mother tongue of the majority of speakers. This means that there are strong reasons for linguistic nationalists to limit the admission of people who only speak (say) English or want to have their children primarily educated in English.

If we think about aspects of culture beyond language, it may be easier to conceptualize what counts as an equal opportunity to participate and less of a problem of potentially fast erosion of cultural markers that are heavily endorsed by the majority. The major remaining difficulty, as Song points out, is that "national cultures are not typically the product of collective deliberation in which all have the opportunity to participate" (Song 2009, 35). Members of minority and historically stigmatized groups are frequently excluded from full social participation and thus denied an equal chance to influence the national culture. They might live in neighborhoods that are cut off from the rest of society or be taken less seriously in discussions. And even if steps are taken to provide them with equal opportunities now, there is still the problem that the inherited national culture – which theorists such as Miller would use as the initial basis for immigration policy – has typically been heavily shaped by more dominant groups.

E. Economic status

Economic criteria are another familiar basis for selecting people for admission. States frequently evaluate, for instance, which sectors of the economy would benefit from a greater supply of workers and give preference to people who could fill these jobs. Canada, for instance, has often looked to immigrants to fill medical jobs. Employers are often given channels by which they can sponsor the granting of a visa or permanent residency to an immigrant on the basis that they could fulfill special needs in the economy.

Another potential advantage of economic selection criteria is that by managing the flow of immigrants into particular sectors, the state may be able to ensure that existing domestic workers are not displaced, or at least are only displaced at a rate at which the state can feasibly protect them through retraining for different work or through compensation. So economic criteria seem to have a fairly clear basis that serves legitimate state interests in growing the domestic economy and promoting the jobs of existing members.

What about the expressive concerns we looked at earlier: If excluding certain ethnic groups can convey a negative message toward existing minority ethnic groups within a country, why not think that a ranking of migrants by their economic abilities similarly expresses that, say, less skilled workers are less valuable members of the community?

It's certainly possible for people to be stigmatized because of their socioeconomic class. In his novel *Super Sad True Love Story*, Gary Shteyngart imagines a dystopian near future in which each person can be immediately identified as an "L.N.W.I." (Low Net Worth Individual) or "H.N.W.I." (High Net Worth Individual) and shunned or revered accordingly. Neighborhoods are referred to using these categories, and press releases use them to describe the people involved in events. While actual societies are not (yet ...) quite so stark, there are still clearly class distinctions that are often highly visible – in people's dress, accents, and so on – and that correspond to variations in social stigma (consider the use of the phrase "white trash" in the United States or "chav" in Britain). Can't immigration policy create or exacerbate such distinctions and stigmas?

Perhaps the precise nature of the policy and the broader context in which it is presented makes a difference here. For instance, if medical professionals are favored in immigration, this might seem to imply that the state considers them simply of more desirable character than, say, plumbers: a stigmatizing message. But the state could make clear that the medical professions are being brought in specifically because it is taking seriously the needs of all members of the population equally. For instance, a policy that offers visas specifically to doctors who are willing to work in rural areas seems fairly clearly designed to ensure that potentially underserved populations also receive medical care rather than to admit people of especially high personal quality.

Another potential problem with economic selection is that it often equates someone's ability to make a contribution to a society with their ability to participate in its job market. But as we saw earlier in this chapter, this over-looks other crucial forms of contribution people can make to a society, such as the unpaid care work women often perform in the home. It also ignores the contributions immigrants can make by, for instance, sharing alternative cultural practices.

F. Family ties

Family unification criteria allow people to immigrate based on family ties to those who already have some form of legal status in the destination country. These policies are a familiar part of the policies of liberal democracies. While there is a degree of consensus that family ties should have *some* role in immigration policy, there is frequent controversy about the details of that role. For instance, in 2006, Nicolas Sarkozy launched a major attack on French family reunification policies. Since a policy reorientation in 1974, family connections had become the dominant basis for immigration to France, accounting for more than three-quarters of migrants admitted through regular legal channels. Sarkozy claimed that this trend needed to be reversed, with skilled workers given greater priority: "We no longer want an immigration that is inflicted (on us), but an immigration that is chosen. This is the founding principle of the new immigration policy I advocate," said Sarkozy.

By contrast, the Universal Declaration of Human Rights includes a right to "protection [of the family] by society and the State" (Article 16). And this basic right to protection of the family unit has been used to argue that immigration policy must include a right to family reunification. For instance, the European Court of Human Rights has claimed that "respect for ... family life" – enshrined in Article 8 of the European Convention on Human Rights – requires states to enable their citizens to sponsor family members for immigration (Yong 2016, 63). Which of these perspectives is correct? Philosophical reflection is needed on what exactly might justify privileging the use of family ties in immigration policy.

Another crucial question is how to define family ties, if they are to be used. For instance, should people only be able to sponsor their spouses and dependent children, as has been the case in Germany? Or should they also be able to sponsor siblings and parents, as in Australia (Yong 2016, 61)? Or should the category of "family ties" be abandoned altogether in favor of some other kind of important bond between people, one that might allow individuals to sponsor their caretakers or closer friends?

This question of how to define family ties (or some form of important relationship) is especially difficult if we try to respect, as theorists like Luara Ferracioli (2016) think we must, a constraint of *state neutrality*. According to this constraint, the state may not give preference to any particular view about what is of fundamental importance in life. Thus, for instance, the state may not favor any particular religion (or religion over non-religion). This constraint bears on the state's approach to the family, because family life is closely connected to people's fundamental decisions about what is important; take the US Supreme Court's finding that forming a same-sex relation is connected to an individual's "right to define one's own concept of existence, of meaning, of the universe, and of the mystery of human life" (*Planned Parenthood v. Casey*, 505 U. S. 833 (1992) at 851). So if the court is correct, then the state may not give greater weight to opposite-sex partnerships than same-sex partnerships in immigration. May it privilege *any* form of relationship over others?

To address all of these questions, let us now look at some potential justifications for privileging family ties, along with some discussion of whether policies privileging those ties can or should adhere to constraints of neutrality.

i. Benefit to the receiving country

One way to justify privileging family ties is by reference to its potential benefits to the receiving country. As we saw earlier, in the statements of Sarkozy, it is common to argue *against* family-based immigration by suggesting that it crowds out forms of immigration – especially skills-based admission – that might be more beneficial to the receiving country. Of course, people admitted through family ties schemes *might* well possess the needed skills. The complaint of Sarkozy and others is that family ties immigration essentially delegates immigration decisions to individuals – who are left able to decide which, if any, of their family members to sponsor – taking away the state's ability to select more carefully which migrants would be most beneficial to the society as a whole.

The benefits-based case in favor of family migration is that people admitted through this process are especially likely to bring benefits other than just their job skills. They might help their family members who are already residents to integrate more fully into society, since they will now have the comfort and support of close ones (Honohan 2009, 772). And the migrants themselves may be able to integrate into the receiving society more easily given their pre-existing ties.

Critics like Collier (2013) argue that these effects are likely to be outweighed given that family migration allows current members not just to sponsor particular individuals but also to create potential migration "chains," as the new migrants also become able to sponsor additional family members. Furthermore, the critics say, family migration tends to increase in rate over time because the costs to a migrant of getting to and settling in a country are lowered to the extent that there is already a significant diaspora in the country (Castles and Miller 2009, 29). So people are more likely to move from, say, Ghana to Italy if there is already a sizable Ghanaian immigrant population in Italy. Given this self-perpetuating aspect of family migration, Collier and others argue that it is especially likely to prevent the state from achieving economic goals through immigrant selection.

In sum, while there is a case for family migration based on its benefits to the receiving country, it is somewhat limited and might be overridden by other considerations.

ii. Subjective importance

One way to justify family ties is to claim that families are simply an especially valuable form of association. American political group "Focus on the Family," for instance, has at the core of its mission fostering romantic relationships within a context of marriage and ensuring that each child is raised within a family.

It is clear that Focus on the Family derives its mission from a religious outlook, specifically a conservative, evangelical Christian one that is opposed to same-sex partnerships and the rearing of children within those partnerships. It thus seems impossible for the state to endorse Focus on the Family's perspective while remaining neutral between different views of what matters fundamentally in life. Is there any way for the state to endorse the special value of family relationships over others, without relying on a sectarian viewpoint?

Ferracioli suggests not. Any attempt to privilege the family will inevitably deny and denigrate the views of people who think that families are not especially important compared with, say, close friendships. Her alternative test is to look purely at (what we might call) "subjective importance": the importance that an individual member of society gives to a relationship. Those who especially value family ties will be able to sponsor family members. Those who especially value close friendships will be able to sponsor close friends. This approach does seem clearly neutral between different views about what is of fundamental importance; each individual's perspective regarding relationships is given weight in policymaking, and no individual's perspective is privileged over others.

The trouble with this approach (as Ferracioli flags) is that it leads to a massive proliferation in the number of people that members of a society are able to sponsor for immigration. No one is limited to just family members; they can assert that a relationship is important to them and generate a sponsorship claim. This leaves a dilemma for states: Allow no relationship-based sponsorship, which seems too harsh, or allow a massive increase in relationship-based sponsorship, which seems unworkable and could crowd out almost all other forms of immigration.

Is there any way to satisfy neutrality without going all the way to endorsing the explosion of claims that the subjective importance approach leads to? We might look at little more closely here at what counts as a neutral policy. Does this really mean, as a Ferracioli implies, that *no* relationships can be privileged over others? That would be a somewhat surprising finding. If we look outside of the immigration context, we can see that states regularly give special status to some individual concerns over others. Compare someone who doesn't want to fight in a war because they are a committed pacifist – for religious or philosophical reasons – with someone who simply doesn't want to risk their life. Each of these people is trying to avoid the war because of something they are deeply invested in: respectively, their religious/philosophical beliefs and preserving their own life. Yet liberal states regularly give special exemptions from military service to conscientious objectors that they don't grant to others. Perhaps, then, we need a more fine-grained notion of neutrality – one that is able to distinguish acceptable from unacceptable distinctions that the state might draw between people and their ways of life. In the case of military service, the state might argue that while no one wants to lose their life in war, there is a special burden placed on people who are forced to serve in violation of their most fundamental beliefs. More generally, we might say that to be neutral the state just needs to have a strong non-sectarian *justification* for the distinctions it draws: what John Rawls (1996) called "public reasons." In addition to being non-sectarian, these public reasons are *political* considerations that apply specifically to the organization of government (rather than individual lives or other associations) and are drawn from the values that liberal democracies have coalesced around in resolving policy issues, such as protections for individual liberty and equality before the law (Rawls 1996). As an example of public reason in action, consider how the European Court of Human Rights or the Canadian Supreme Court justify their decisions. In reflecting on the limits of free expression, members of those institutions never consider banning hate speech simply on the grounds that it is blasphemous – a religious justification. Instead, they appeal to political considerations, such as the potential for hate speech to undermine some people's ability to participate fully in common life.

There remains a hard question, though, about what exactly these public reasons are. Let's now consider some possibilities.

iii. Intimacy

Iseult Honohan (2009) argues that family migration must be allowed as a matter of entitlement. That entitlement has two bases, which we will consider in turn. First, the state must respect people's ability to form intimate relationships, and, second, the state must allow people to fulfill their duties of care.

Families are generally intimate. They often involve, for example, living together in close contact (Honohan 2009, 771). The role of intimacy is likely a significant part of why many people are inclined to privilege, for instance, spouses over close friends in immigration. One concern about emphasizing intimacy is the difficultly of defining what exactly counts as an intimate relationship for these purposes and doing so without relying on a sectarian perspective. For instance, if we think about spouses, some immediate answers don't seem adequate. We might emphasize that spouses are sexually involved. But this ignores many marriages that don't give any important role to sex

(Ferracioli 2016). Likewise, if we broaden our focus to include all people who are romantically involved in some way, we still leave out those who live together and love each other, but not romantically.

All the same, perhaps a rough and workable notion of intimacy is available. At its core, we might say, is the idea of mutual sharing of our innermost selves, including our secrets and other things we feel most vulnerable about and protective of. Physical intimacy, which involves revealing our bodies and desires to others, is one form of intimacy, but not the only one.

How might levels of intimacy be gauged? The fact that people have lived together for a reasonable period of time – a gauge that Honohan mentions – is often an indicator of intimacy. It clearly isn't sufficient, though: people can of course arrange to share an apartment while leading largely separate lives. And they can also be highly intimate without living in the same place, as with long-term romantic partners who are separated because of work. A state that wants to privilege intimacy will need to be innovative in finding workable measures of intimacy.

Would this approach be compatible with neutrality? Clearly there are some people who like to live fairly solitary lives, or at least prefer to keep an emotional distance from others, never fully disclosing their inner lives. (Just as there are perhaps some "over-sharers" in the world!) Yet the need for intimacy is a fairly central feature of human experience, and its importance can be endorsed from a wide variety of perspectives. Some religious doctrines will view human intimacy as an important element in finding God together. St. Augustine describes a moment in which his close relationship with his mother allowed the two of them to experience an ecstatic communion with the divine: "Augustine and Monica experienced something remarkable: They felt themselves climbing higher and higher, through all the degrees of matter and through the heavenly spheres and, higher still, to the region of their own souls and up toward the eternity that lies beyond time itself. And 'while we were speaking and panting for it, with a thrust that required all the heart's strength, we brushed against it slightly'" (Greenblatt 2017). Many (though not all) non-theistic people consider the intimacy involved in romantic attachments to be a wonderful part of their lives. So, arguably, protecting intimate relationships has a non-sectarian justification. Alternatively, some philosophers will say that the constraint of neutrality should just be abandoned. If intimacy really enriches so many lives, why shouldn't the state promote it, even if this means the state taking a stand that some people (likely a small minority of people) will disagree with?

iv. Care

Some theorists, including Honohan and also Yong, propose that the family is especially important because of its connection with *care*. Caring involves, roughly, providing support for others, especially those who are dependent on us for fulfillment of their basic needs. Children, most obviously, are highly dependent on their parents, and parents have an obligation to provide support to them.

Why should the state emphasize the importance of care? Honohan claims that the state must respect people's ability to fulfill their individual obligations, and familial relationships, she argues, generally generate duties of care; most obviously, parents are morally required to ensure that their children's needs are met (as illustrated, perhaps, by the fact that they can be criminally liable if they maliciously or negligently let their children become malnourished). The state must respect these duties by ensuring that people are able to fulfill them.

Another way to defend the importance of care is by reference to the people who would receive it. Children, Yong argues, are in a special position where they require care to satisfy crucial "developmental interests" (2016, 74). These "include the interest in healthy physical development, but equally important is cognitive, emotional, and moral development." This means having a caregiver (s) who doesn't just supply them with nutrition and generic schooling in writing and arithmetic but is also knowledgeable about and attentive to the *specific* temperament of that child and what it would take for them to flourish in their individual projects and as a member of society. So where a child already has a developed relationship with a particular caregiver, it will be important to sustain that relationship, and migration policy must enable this.

What about important relationships where neither party is dependent in the way that children are on their parents? For example, what about long-term romantic partnerships? Honohan can say here that there are still important duties between these parties that the state must respect. Spouses, for instance, are plausibly required to pay special attention to each other's interests. It's not obvious that these duties always involve care, however, in the sense that children need to be cared for. Presumably I ought to support my husband in his pursuit of various career goals, even if his basic needs are already met.

Yong argues that there is in fact a special kind of care involved in these relationships. By showing special concern for each other, we support each other's basic sense of self-respect and worth, and we also enable each other to think about moral issues. These are important goods, since they enable people to pursue their personal projects and be fully participating members of society. Moreover, they are, Yong argues (following Brake [2012]), goods that the state can pursue without being objectionably sectarian: They are essential whatever the particular projects an individual might pursue or the particular form their participation in society might take. This approach means also prioritizing some non-familial relationships –such as where one individual has been a long-term caregiver for an elderly person – and de-prioritizing others – such as sibling connections, where there is no crucial caring function.

What if people involve themselves in quite different kinds of caring relationships and have different notions of caring obligations? For instance, as Honohan notes, while some imagine a small family with one or two parents to be the standard structure for caring for children, others raise children within a much larger unit that includes many aunts and uncles (who may or may not bear any biological connection to the child or parents). Here the problem of neutrality comes back into focus. The state again must either make a determination about which of these is a genuinely essential caring relationship – which threatens to undermine neutrality – or must allow people to determine for themselves which relationships count –which threatens to create a proliferation of claims to sponsor people for immigration.

v. Justice and particularity

Honohan claims that family reunification policies are required by *justice*. Why does this mean that a family must be reunified in any *particular* country? For instance, if a person in Sweden wishes to sponsor their spouse from Canada, why can't the government of Sweden say that this person should instead move to Canada? Honohan's response begins by claiming that the Swedish person has certain special rights against the Swedish government: there is "a universal obligation on states to allow those within the ambit of their authority to pursue family life" (774). (We will consider in the next part of the book how and why citizenship – and other forms of connection to a society – might affect someone's moral entitlements.) Another approach is to claim that there are human rights – rights not tied to membership in any particular society – to be connected with certain family members. Yong, for instance, argues that the special needs of children mean that they have a human right to be united with their primary caregiver(s).

Neither of these approaches fully solves the problem, though, as Honohan and Yong note: We still need to explain why the Swedish government has to enable the person to pursue their family life *in Sweden*, as opposed to Canada. Something needs to be added, and one plausible approach, suggested by Yong, says that the Swedish government must enable its existing subjects to continue to pursue their lives in Sweden: it is important that they not be forced to leave the country in order to pursue their central projects. Ultimately, then, it looks like the right to reside a particular country will have to be defended at least in part by reference to rights that people have in virtue of their membership in a particular society. What about families where no individual has a clear right to reside in any particular place – though they may have a right to be admitted *somewhere* outside of their home country – as is sometimes the case with stateless people and refugees? These raise difficult questions, which we will look at in the next chapter, about when a particular state has a responsibility to admit people in these categories.

Chapter summary

In this chapter we looked at selection procedures: the criteria states can use to determine who is permitted to enter their territories. We began by looking at race, ethnicity, and gender and also used each of these examples as case studies to illustrate moral concerns, including expressive harms and stereotyping, that can be applied to all of forms of selection. We then turned to cultural selection, which, we saw, raises some difficult questions about how to define nations and national belonging: for example, what is to be an Icelander. Narrower definitions risk failing to unite a society and preserve important cultural traditions, while broader definitions risk being exclusionary. Lastly, we focused on family ties, considering how the state might take some such ties into account while still being neutral between different views about which relationships are most valuable.

Study questions

- Selection on the basis of race seems clearly morally wrong. But why? What's the best explanation (or explanations) of what's wrong with it? Is there any moral difference between selecting on the basis of race and selecting based on ethnicity?
- Was President Trump's executive order creating the "travel ban" unjust? Why or why not?
- What's problematic, from a feminist perspective, about the law that was under review in *Nguyen v. INS*?
- Why might there be a dilemma for feminists who would like to find an immigration policy that both combats gender stereotyping and helps the least well-off women in the world? If there is a dilemma, how should it be resolved?
- Is it possible for a state to associate itself with a set of cultural traditions and practices without being exclusionary? How might it try?
- Why might it be problematic to justify giving preferential admission to family members on the grounds that families are an especially valuable form of association? What alternative policy does Ferraciolli propose? What policy would you endorse?

Notes

1 See Hosein (2018) for a lengthier discussion of the harms of racial profiling.
2 Sometimes "ethnicity" is used more broadly to include cultural connections passed over time, including perhaps religious affiliations. We will look at religious and cultural selection below, so this section focuses just on descent-based selection.
3 See Justice Sandra Day O'Connor's dissent in the same case.
4 Though, to be clear, feminists can plausibly argue that we should challenge existing assumptions about when war is necessary and also suggest that more cooperative behavior might make militaries stronger when they are necessary.
5 See Higgins (2013) for a version of this principle and a defense of it.
6 It also, arguably, often involves the exploitation of migrant women, who are paid low wages and live on the margins of society, and has costs for the sending countries since the caregivers are separated from their families. See Wilcox's (2008) argument.

7 This is a prospect that may be especially disturbing given that a lack of visas often means migrant caregivers must enter outside of legal channels, which in turns makes them vulnerable to exploitation and mistreatment (Wilcox 2008, 69).
8 For further discussion of this kind of dynamic (mainly in the context of race) and a defense of paying special attention to role stereotyping, see Cox and Hosein (2016).
9 This is discussed in some of the papers surveyed by Luibhéid (2008).
10 See for instance https://foreignpolicy.com/2018/10/01/trump-administration-to-deny-visas-to-same-sex-partners-of-diplomats-un-officials-gay-lgbt/.
11 Of course, there is disagreement in politics and philosophy about whether a strong welfare state is desirable: the general point is that pursuing any conception of the common good requires that individuals ask what will benefit not just them personally but their society as a whole. And national cultures may help support this kind of selflessness, the argument goes.

References

Appiah, Kwame Anthony. 1985. "The Uncompleted Argument: Du Bois and the Illusion of Race." *Critical Inquiry* 12, no. 1 (Autumn): 21–37.

Blake, Michael. 2002. "Discretionary Immigration." *Philosophical Topics* 30, no. 2 (Fall): 273–289.

Blake, Michael. 2003. "Immigration." In *A Companion to Applied Ethics*, edited by R. G. Frey and Christopher Heath Wellman, 224–237. Malden, MA: Blackwell.

Brake, Elizabeth. 2012. *Minimizing Marriage: Marriage, Morality, and the Law*. New York: Oxford University Press.

Castles, Stephen, and Mark J. Miller. 2009. *The Age of Migration: International Population Movements in the Modern World*. 4th ed. New York: Guilford Press.

Chan, Sucheng. 1994. "The Exclusion of Chinese Women, 1870–1943." In *Entry Denied: Exclusion and the Chinese Community in America, 1882–1943*, edited by Sucheng Chan, 94–146. Philadelphia: Temple University Press.

Cisneros, Natalie. 2013. "'Alien' Sexuality: Race, Maternity, and Citizenship." *Hypatia* 28, no. 2 (Spring): 290–306.

Collier, Paul. 2013. *Exodus: How Migration Is Changing Our World*. New York: Oxford University Press.

Cox, Adam B., and Adam Omar Hosein. 2016. "Immigration and Equality." Unpublished manuscript.

Crenshaw, Kimberlé. 1989. "Demarginalizing the Intersection of Race and Sex: A Black Feminist Critique of Antidiscrimination Doctrine, Feminist Theory and Antiracist Politics." *University of Chicago Legal Forum*: 139–168.

Curry, Tommy J. 2017. *The Man-Not: Race, Class, Genre, and the Dilemmas of Black Manhood*. Philadelphia: Temple University Press.

Ferracioli, Luara. 2016. "Family Migration Schemes and Liberal Neutrality: A Dilemma." *Journal of Moral Philosophy* 13, no. 5: 553–575.

Fine, Sarah. 2016. "Immigration and Discrimination." In *Migration in Political Theory: The Ethics of Movement and Membership*, edited by Sarah Fine and Lea Ypi, 125–150. Oxford: Oxford University Press.

Global Campaign for Equal Nationality Rights. n.d. "The Problem." Accessed 2017. https://equalnationalityrights.org/the-issue/the-problem.

Greenblatt, Stephen. 2017. "How St. Augustine Invented Sex." *New Yorker*, June 19, 2017. https://www.newyorker.com/magazine/2017/06/19/how-st-augustine-invented-sex.

Habermas, Jürgen. 1992. "Citizenship and National Identity: Some Reflections on the Future of Europe." *Praxis International* 12, no. 1 (April): 1–19. Reprinted in: Habermas,

Jürgen. 1997. *Between Facts and Norms: Contributions to a Discourse Theory of Law and Democracy*. Translated by William Rehg. Cambridge, MA: MIT Press.

Higgins, Peter W. 2013. *Immigration Justice*. Edinburgh: Edinburgh University Press.

Holbrook, Colin, Daniel M. T. Fessler, and Carlos David Navarrete. 2016. "Looming Large in Others' Eyes: Racial Stereotypes Illuminate Dual Adaptations for Representing Threat versus Prestige as Physical Size." *Evolution and Human Behavior* 37, no. 1 (January): 67–78.

Honohan, Iseult. 2009. "Reconsidering the Claim to Family Reunification in Migration." *Political Studies* 57, no. 4 (December): 768–787.

Hosein, Adam Omar. 2016. "'Where Are You Really From?': Ethnic Linguistic Immigrant Selection Policies in Liberal States." In *Citizenship and Immigration: Borders, Migration and Political Membership in a Global Age*, edited by Ann E. Cudd and Win-chiat Lee, 191–202. Switzerland: Springer.

Hosein, Adam Omar. 2018. "Racial Profiling and a Reasonable Sense of Inferior Political Status." *Journal of Political Philosophy* 26, no. 3 (September): e1–e20.

Hundle, Anneeth Kaur. 2017. "Uganda's Colonial-Style Dress Code." *Al Jazeera*, August 14, 2017. https://www.aljazeera.com/indepth/opinion/2017/08/uganda-colonial-style-dress-code-170808072148083.html.

Joppke, Christian. 2005. *Selecting by Origin: Ethnic Migration in the Liberal State*. Cambridge, MA: Harvard University Press.

Klinkner, Philip A. 1999. *The Unsteady March: The Rise and Decline of Racial Equality in America*. With Rogers M. Smith. Chicago: University of Chicago Press.

Kymlicka, Will. 1995. *Multicultural Citizenship: A Liberal Theory of Minority Rights*. Oxford: Clarendon Press of Oxford University Press.

Luibhéid, Eithne. 2008. "Queer/Migration: An Unruly Body of Scholarship." *GLQ: A Journal of Lesbian and Gay Studies* 14, no. 2–3 (June): 169–190.

Mendoza, José Jorge. 2017. "Discrimination and Immigration." In *The Routledge Handbook of the Ethics of Discrimination*, edited by Kasper Lippert-Rasmussen, 254–263. New York: Routledge.

Miller, David. 1995. *On Nationality*. New York: Oxford University Press.

Ngai, Mae M. 2004. *Impossible Subjects: Illegal Aliens and the Making of Modern America*. Princeton, NJ: Princeton University Press.

Nussbaum, Martha C. 2008. *Liberty of Conscience: In Defense of America's Tradition of Religious Equality*. New York: Basic Books.

Patten, Alan. 2014. *Equal Recognition: The Moral Foundations of Minority Rights*. Princeton, NJ: Princeton University Press.

Rawls, John. 1996. *Political Liberalism*. New York: Columbia University Press.

Smith, Rogers M. 2003. *Stories of Peoplehood: The Politics and Morals of Political Membership*. Cambridge: Cambridge University Press.

Song, Sarah. 2009. "What Does It Mean to Be an American?" *Dædalus* 138, no. 2 (Spring): 31–40.

Stiglitz, Joseph E., and Andrew Charlton. 2007. *Fair Trade for All: How Trade Can Promote Development*. New York: Oxford University Press.

Sue, Derald Wing, Jennifer Bucceri, Annie I. Lin, Kevin L. Nadal, and Gina C. Torino. 2007. "Racial Microaggressions and the Asian American Experience." *Cultural Diversity and Ethnic Minority Psychology* 13, no. 1 (January): 72–81.

Taylor, Charles. 1994. *Multiculturalism: Examining the Politics of Recognition*. Princeton, NJ: Princeton University Press.

UNHCR. 2017. "Convention on the Elimination of All Forms of Discrimination against Women: Quick Reference Guide; Statelessness and Human Rights Treaties." UNHCR

and the Global Campaign for Equal Nationality Rights (GCENR), April. http://equalna
tionalityrights.org/images/zdocs/CEDAW-Quick-Reference-Guide.pdf.

van Paris, Philippe. 2011. *Linguistic Justice for Europe and for the World*. New York: Oxford University Press.

Wellman, Christopher Heath. 2008. "Immigration and Freedom of Association." *Ethics* 119, no. 1 (October): 109–141.

Wilcox, Shelley. 2005. "American Neo-Nativism and Gendered Immigrant Exclusions." In *Feminist Interventions in Ethics and Politics: Feminist Ethics and Social Theory*, edited by Barbara S. Andrew, Jean Keller, and Lisa H. Schwartzman, 213–232. Lanham, MD: Rowman and Littlefield.

Wilcox, Shelley. 2008. "Who Pays for Gender De-Institutionalization?" In *Gender Identities in a Globalized World*, edited by Ana Marta González and Victor J. Seidler, 53–74. Amherst, NY: Humanity Books.

Yong, Caleb. 2016. "Caring Relationships and Family Migration Schemes." In *The Ethics and Politics of Immigration: Core Issues and Emerging Trends*, edited by Alex Sager, 61–84. London: Rowman and Littlefield.

Young, Iris Marion. 1985. "Humanism, Gynocentrism and Feminist Politics." *Women's Studies International Forum* 8, no. 3: 173–183.

Further reading

Blake, Michael. 2002. "Discretionary Immigration." *Philosophical Topics* 30, no. 2 (Fall): 273–289.

Cisneros, Natalie. 2013. "'Alien' Sexuality: Race, Maternity, and Citizenship." *Hypatia* 28, no. 2 (Spring): 290–306.

Fine, Sarah. 2016. "Immigration and Discrimination." In *Migration in Political Theory: The Ethics of Movement and Membership*, edited by Sarah Fine and Lea Ypi, 125–150. Oxford: Oxford University Press.

Joppke, Christian. 2005. *Selecting by Origin: Ethnic Migration in the Liberal State*. Cambridge, MA: Harvard University Press.

Smith, Rogers M. 2003. *Stories of Peoplehood: The Politics and Morals of Political Membership*. Cambridge: Cambridge University Press.

Song, Sarah. 2009. "What Does It Mean to Be an American?" *Dædalus* 138, no 2 (Spring): 31–40.

Wilcox, Shelley. 2008. "Who Pays for Gender De-Institutionalization?" In *Gender Identities in a Globalized World*, edited by Ana Marta González and Victor J. Seidler, 53–74. Amherst, NY: Humanity Books.

Yong, Caleb. 2016. "Caring Relationships and Family Migration Schemes." In *The Ethics and Politics of Immigration: Core Issues and Emerging Trends*, edited by Alex Sager, 61–84. London: Rowman and Littlefield.

5   Refugees

There is wide agreement that states have some kind of obligation to admit refugees. The modern refugee regime began with the realization that certain states and the international order as a whole had failed – in a deep and morally egregious manner – Jewish people fleeing the Holocaust. This agreement fades when we start to discuss what exactly the obligation to protect refugees means for present-day policy. In response to the Syrian refugee crises, precipitated by the civil war that began in 2011, German Chancellor Angela Merkel proposed that Germany ought to do more to help the millions of people fleeing Syria, proposing a policy that was generous by European standards: By 2016, more than 70 percent of approved Syrian asylum applications within Europe were in Germany. Many Germans were sympathetic to Merkel's project, but political backlash against the number of Syrians admitted damaged her poll numbers, lost her political capital within the Bundestag, and helped far-right parties, such as the Alternative for Germany (AfD), to gain momentum (Lane 2016). By November 2017, Merkel was struggling to find coalition partners with which to form a government, creating a crisis of stability within the Federal Republic. Disagreement about refugees was one of the major points of disagreement. Had Merkel in fact done the right thing by trying to welcome more refugees and asylum seekers, or had she mistakenly jeopardized the interests of her country?

Meanwhile – despite the focus of media outlets in the global North – the majority of Syrian refugees were not in fact admitted to countries in Western Europe or North America at all. The top five destination countries were Turkey, Lebanon, Jordan, Iraq, and Egypt. Was this distribution fair? In many cases, the refugees in these countries were in camps: the largest by 2017 – the Zaatari refugee camp in Jordan – was home to 80,000 people.[1] Are camps of this kind an acceptable solution, especially when people find themselves living in them for long periods?

Let's now see if philosophical theorizing can help resolve these and other controversies.

A. Who counts as a refugee?

Refugees are thought to have a very special status in both international law and the morality of immigrant admission. For asylum seekers, who seek admittance and refugee status in a foreign country, being granted refugee status can make an enormous difference. First and foremost, a requirement of *non-refoulement* applies: A refugee cannot be returned to a country where they would be in danger. For refugees whose stay in the host country is more permanent, there is also typically a requirement to provide them with a "durable solution" that involves gaining membership in the host country, including the right to remain indefinitely.

But who exactly counts, or should count, as a refugee? Some insist that we must maintain a definition of refugee that is narrow, limited to people who have fled certain kinds of egregious persecution by their own states. Others say that there is nothing special about this category. What really matters is just how dire someone's situation is: refugees are just people in extreme need who can be helped by being admitted to another state. Settling this question would have a huge impact on the lives of people seeking refugee status and on the states that are asked to admit them.

To see the full complexities involved, a useful starting point is to examine the most influential conception of a refugee thus far: the definition found in the 1967 Protocol to the United Nations Refugee Convention. According to the UN Convention, a refugee is someone who,

> Owing to a well-founded fear of being persecuted for reasons of race, religion, nationality, membership in a particular social group, or political opinion, is outside the country of his nationality and is unable or, owing to such fear, is unwilling to avail himself of the protection of that country; or who, not having a nationality and being outside the country of his former habitual residence, is unable or, owing to such fear, is unwilling to return to it.

Three features of this definition stand out (Gibney 2004). First, it requires that a refugee be *outside* of their country of origin. They must have fled from, say, Somalia to Ethiopia. Someone who was forced to leave their home in Mogadishu and fled to Berbera (still within Somalia) would not qualify.

Second, to count as a refugee, a person must be fleeing *persecution*. Escaping the threat of starvation due to a drought and subsequent crop failure, for instance, does not seem sufficient.

Third, this persecution must have a specific *basis*. A refugee is not just persecuted but persecuted because of their race or religion or other singled-out category.

Challenging any of these features (or some combination) would broaden the definition of a refugee. And some organizations have tried to do just this. For instance, the Organization for African Unity (OAU), beginning in 1968, proposed that a refugee can be fleeing their country of origin not just because of persecution but any form of "external aggression, occupation, foreign domination or events seriously disturbing public order" (Shacknove 1985).

Which direction is the right one? We'll now look at some different philosophical theories that attempt to settle the problem, starting with different ways of *defining* who counts as a refugee and then different ways that we might justify *responsibilities* to admit refugees, according to the different definitions. We'll then consider the issue of "climate refugees" and how the various theories might be applied to that case. Next, we'll consider how responsibilities to admit refugees might be fairly distributed among states. And finally, we'll look at challenges to the common focus on the *admission* of refugees that point out the centrality of refugee *encampment* in the world as we know it.

i. The humanitarian theory

One straightforward approach to refugees suggests that the obligation to help refugees is simply the obligation to help people who live in serious need. As Michael Dummett (2001, 37) puts it, "all conditions that deny someone the ability to live where he is in minimal conditions for a decent human life ought to be grounds for claiming refuge elsewhere." This proposal generates a definition of a refugee that is *much* broader than the UNCHR's. Assuming, as Dummett does, that the conditions for living a minimally decent life include being free of serious poverty, the humanitarian approach invites us to give up the common distinction between refugees and migrants who are fleeing poor economic conditions. As long as the latter are in sufficient need, they are entitled to refuge in another country just as much as someone who is fleeing, say, political persecution on the grounds of their race. Thus, the 767 million living on less than $1.90 a day (World Bank 2018) are all presumably entitled to refugee status on Dummett's account.

This account is attractive for its simplicity. It also draws attention to features of the UNHCR definition that may seem arbitrary on close inspection. If someone is doing extremely poorly, why should it matter whether the *source* of their need is direct persecution or lack of subsistence goods? Surely these other details of their circumstances are not relevant to whether they are worthy of help?

This is a serious challenge to the UNHCR definition, and it means that anyone who wishes to retain that definition must give a compelling explanation of why the distinctions it makes are morally important. We will consider some potential explanations below. In the meantime, though, notice that the humanitarian theory requires a very significant shift away from the dominant concept of a refugee. While history contains many examples of forced migration and people seeking refuge in foreign places, the modern international refugee regime began with the efforts of the League of Nations, which appointed a High Commissioner for Refugees in 1921. His initial specific charge was to create protection for people fleeing Russia in light of the revolution, and his task was later expanded to include, for instance, resettling Armenians attempting to escape genocide.

Since this initial phase, the concept of a refugee has continued to be deployed mainly in the context of dealing with political turmoil and persecution rather than when considering development or other humanitarian issues. The UN-established International Refugee Organization (IRO) of 1947, for example, was put in place mainly to deal with people displaced during the Holocaust and Second World War. The concept of a refugee is generally taken to single out a morally distinctive category of needy people who bear some important resemblance to the people singled out by the League of Nations, the IRO, and ultimately the UNHCR. To adopt the humanitarian approach would be to cease trying to single out any such special category. And to that extent the approach may seem to require not simply *expanding* our inherited notion of a refugee but *abandoning* it altogether in favor of a different set of concepts.

ii. The legitimacy theory

The legitimacy approach, associated most prominently with Andrew Shacknove, tries to give a little more weight to the way we ordinarily conceive of refugees while still, like the humanitarian approach, pushing us to broaden our definition of a refugee beyond the UNCHR definition.

Shacknove conceives of refugees as people who live in societies where the political institutions are not "minimally legitimate" (279). A legitimate state is one that has the right to make rules, demand obedience to them, and punish disobedience. An illegitimate state is one that rules overs its people without the entitlement to do so. Shacknove's account thus respects the intuitive idea that refugees are a special class of persons who are in some fundamental way being failed by their home state. Certainly, for instance, those who fled Nazism were living in a country that had no right to rule over them.

What does it take to meet the requirements of legitimacy? Shacknove suggests that a state certainly has no right to rule over people that it persecutes by, say, torturing them. But, he emphasizes, this isn't the only way for a state to lack legitimacy. A state that is not providing for an individual's basic needs—the things they need to lead a minimally decent life—is also failing in its basic functions and has no right to rule. A state that does not secure for its citizens basic sanitation and access to nutrition, for instance, is failing to perform a central duty toward its citizens. Mightn't a state of this kind be doing everything it can to serve its citizens yet still be simply *unable* to fully satisfy their needs? And wouldn't a state of this kind be fulfilling its duties to its citizens and thus legitimate? Shacknove points out that while there are some cases of genuine incapacity, often what look like problems caused solely by "natural disasters" actually occur in significant part because of human and institutional failings. Take famine: we often think of extreme hunger as a product of drought or hurricanes, but often these external factors only have a genuinely devastating impact when combined with political institutions that, for instance, fail to establish a good mechanism for identifying which rural areas are in need of food or that hoard grain for the rich.

Shacknove thus proposes that refugees are "persons whose basic needs are unprotected by their country of origin, who have no remaining recourse other than to seek international restitution of their needs, and who are so situated that international assistance is possible" (1985, 277). To lack protection for one's basic needs is to lack necessities of a decent life, such as food, shelter, and protection from physical harm. This means that on Shacknove's account, as with the humanitarian theory, we appear to end up with a definition of a refugee that is broader than the UNHCR's (and closer to the OAU's), since it does not require refugees to show that their governments are actively persecuting them. They just need to show that their governments are failing to ensure that their basic needs are met and that they cannot reverse this situation by appealing to the authorities to do better.

Shacknove's definition is also broader than the UNHCR's in a second way (Lister 2013): It does not require that a refugee be actually displaced from one country to another, fleeing their home country. In place of that clause, Shacknove just requires a refugee be "so situated that international assistance is possible." Even someone who is stuck in a particular country—perhaps because exiting is expensive or prohibited—can count as a refugee on Shacknove's approach as long as the international community is able to get them out of this situation and provide refuge elsewhere. If the state that person lives under is sufficiently weak it might be possible to, for instance, stage a "rescue mission" sending forces into that country to extract the needy people.

Should the legitimacy approach be accepted? An advantage is that it cleaves more closely than the humanitarian theory to our pre-theoretical notion of a refugee as someone whose problems are in some sense *political*: someone who is not being properly protected by their home state. Shacknove takes that intuitive idea but insists that there are ways of being seriously failed by one's state aside from being outright persecuted.

Let's look at some implications and concerns about Shacknove's view.

One worry about Shacknove's approach concerns his abandonment of the idea that a refugee must be *fleeing* their home country and outside of its borders. As Lister (2013) argues, Shacknove's notion of a person so "situated that international assistance is possible" is significantly more vague than the UNHCR requirement a refugee simply be someone outside of their country of origin. To determine whether an individual is a refugee, on Shacknove's account, we must take into account questions like how feasible it would be to send an external force into that country to help its needy population. Such questions of intervention are notoriously difficult to answer as they require subtle judgments about the military strength of the latter country, the ability of the invading force to act successfully in a relatively unknown territory, and so on. So it may be better to have a definition of a refugee that draws clear lines and doesn't require these kinds of subtle judgment before someone can be counted as a refugee.

Second, perhaps a fundamental appeal to legitimacy can in fact be used to defend a view somewhere between the narrow UNHCR definition and the broad conception that Shacknove favors. Failing to provide members with the basic resources needed to lead a decent life may make a state illegitimate. But some forms of illegitimacy seem graver than others. It is common (though not universal) for the constitutions of liberal democracies to give special place to rights that protect individuals from persecution by the state: The US Constitution, for instance, includes a Bill of Rights that emphasizes the right to a fair trial, to freedom of religion, to due process, and so on, but includes no right to resources. And even in places where economic rights are more central (South Africa, for instance), it is common to insist that the government should not (outside of emergencies) harm or restrict the freedom of particular groups, even for the sake of distributing resources. Likewise, philosophical theories have often emphasized that respect for fundamental liberties and non-discrimination take priority over providing people with resources. So, while a state that fails to provide its members with minimally adequate resources is failing them to the point of illegitimacy, one that actively violates basic freedoms or discriminates against some members creates an especially strong violation of legitimacy. Thus, it may make sense for the international system to prioritize protecting members of the latter group, even if members of the former are also entitled to protection. In sum, we could take, on this approach, refugees to be all people whose basic freedoms are threatened by their state or who are discriminated against. This approach is broader than the UNHCR definition since it does not necessarily require "persecution" on one of the enumerated grounds. But it is narrower than Shacknove's because it does not confer refugee status on all people whose states do not provide them with a basic standard of living.

This route still leaves open protection for members of particular groups that are systematically underserved by the state, even when they are not being directly harmed by the state. Take, for example, victims of domestic violence. US Attorney General Jeff Sessions argued in 2018 that victims of domestic violence should not count as refugees because they have been subjected to "private violence," while "the prototypical refugee flees her home country because the government has persecuted her."

Sessions was relying on a version of the legitimacy theory; because it was husbands and not governments committing the violence, there was no failure of legitimacy. Contrary to Sessions, however, a sophisticated version of the legitimacy theory can count victims of domestic violence as refugees. This is because failures of legitimacy can be generated by *discrimination* against members of targeted groups on the basis of their race, gender, political orientation, and so on. Thus, while general failures of agricultural policy on the part of the state might not count as persecution, an intentional attempt to starve members of a particular race would. Likewise, one could argue that (some) courts have correctly included battered women within the category of refugees, since states have specifically failed to provide members of this gender group with protection from violence and thus discriminated against them.

Take the cases of two women, Shahanna Sadiq Islam and Syeda Khatoon Shah, who applied for asylum in the United Kingdom after fleeing Pakistan (*R. v. Immigration Appeal Tribunal and another, ex parte Shah*, [1999] 2 A.C. 629 (U.K.)). They had been falsely accused of adultery and faced violence and ostracism were they to return. The state of Pakistan refused to provide them with protection (and may even have eventually punished them with stoning). It is clear that their gender played a crucial role in this denial of protection, for a married woman was considered the property of her husband, and since Islam and Shah had been abandoned by their husbands, they were wholly vulnerable to the violence and judgment of the community. Here we can say that Islam and Shah were subject to discrimination and thus an especially strong failure of legitimacy. That failure made them strong candidates for asylum. More generally, states that fail to create or enforce prohibitions on domestic violence are generally doing so out of a lack of regard for the interests and rights of women as a class. This again creates a credible claim of discrimination and thus a failure of legitimacy. Likewise, when states systematically disregard the widespread private violence that LGBTQ people are subject to, those people can claim that they are not living under a legitimate government.

In sum, the legitimacy theory can potentially be used to justify an approach narrower than Shacknove's, but we should be clear that even this relatively narrow definition can still cover *some* cases where the state doesn't directly harm someone but fails to protect them, contrary to common political uses of the theory.

iii. The pragmatic theory

Matthew Lister (2013) argues that one can take on much of the basic outlook of the humanitarian approach or the legitimacy approach (including Shacknove's version) while still ultimately accepting a definition of refugeehood that is close to the UNHCR's. Lister agrees that there is no basic moral difference between people who are very needy because their state threatens them with violence and people who are very needy because their state is unable to provide them with decent sanitation.

We need to remember, though, Lister emphasizes, that granting a person refugee status entitles them to having their needs met in a very specific way: by gaining access to a state outside of their home country (through non-refoulement and, in some cases, "durable solution" remedies). Whether this particular response is required, Lister argues, depends on facts about the person's situation beyond simply the fact that they are in need.

In particular, it matters whether individuals in need "can be helped 'in place,' in their home countries, or by providing a form of temporary protected status to them" (Lister 2013, 645). For instance, perhaps they can be helped by providing greater emergency aid to those countries, or, in the long run, by helping to build stronger political and economic institutions in those countries. Once we see this possibility, Lister argues, we can see that more developed countries do not necessarily have to treat all needy people as refugees, entitled to admission into their territories. Instead, they can discharge their duties to some needy people by helping them "in place" instead. His suggestion also echoes Gibney's (2004, 84) suggestion that "not only are [refugees] in great need, but unlike other immigrants, there is only one conceivable way that their immediate needs can be addressed: through the provision of entrance to a new state."

What does any of this have to do with the UNHCR definition of refugees? Why should we single out people who are being persecuted? Well, Lister claims, persecuted people generally *cannot* be helped in place; whatever aid is provided to their home countries, they will still be at risk of violence and so on at the hands of their own state. So they constitute a special case: More developed countries can only discharge their obligations to these people by admitting them into their territory. Thus, it is appropriate to single these people out as refugees, since they are the group entitled to the special treatment that comes with refugee status. Now, someone might say that there is a way to help these people in their home countries, namely by generating regime change. But Lister insists that the measures one would have to take to generate such change—mainly armed intervention—are typically unjustifiable because they would either put too many people from the intervening country at risk or be counterproductive, making things even worse for vulnerable members of the society.

What about people who aren't being persecuted but are simply, say, hungry? Can they be helped "in their home countries"? Lister proposes that since the relevant countries are not persecuting their populations, it is more feasible to offer aid and development policies that could work to help the needy in those countries. He suggests that such aid is more likely to help the most needy than admission policies because (as we saw in Chapter 1) the very poorest in the world are often unable to make the journey to a new state. He also suggests that by maintaining a narrower conception of refugees that excludes those fleeing poverty we will be able to maintain a refugee regime that is somewhat politically feasible. Here he follows Gibney's findings that increased numbers of asylum seekers have generally triggered strong political backlashes. For example, Britain in the early 2000s saw strong opposition to asylum seekers become a major focus of the tabloid press (Gibney 2004, 126). And British politicians, such as William Hague at the time and more recently Nigel Farage, have attempted to exploit and stoke fears that Britain had reached a "Breaking Point" (in the words of a poster from Farage's United Kingdom Independence Party) in its ability to accommodate refugees. Broadening the definition of a refugee risks raising the political temperature around the issue so much that developed countries become even more hostile to asylum seekers than they would otherwise be.

The pragmatic approach brings in considerations that seem relevant when deciding whether to grant someone asylum. Even if we care about securing someone's ability to lead a decent life or their right to live under a legitimate government, surely we need to consider the different routes for protecting this person, of which asylum is only one. But once we start bringing in pragmatic criteria about which route is best, Lister's focus may seem too narrow. He focuses on the question of whether someone *can* be helped by means other than resettlement in another country. But perhaps we need to also consider whether that person is *likely* to in fact be helped by other means. For example, in a world where the provision of aid is often limited and poorly executed, why should we privilege people who can only be helped through asylum over people who could in principle be helped through substantial and well-administered aid but are in fact very unlikely to be helped in this way? And where there are multiple options for helping someone—including through grants of asylum, the provision of aid, and the application of pressure on a home government to reform—why shouldn't we look more holistically at which of these options is the best given all of the different costs and benefits involved? These might include, for instance, the effects on the global economy of resettlement, and changes in the international political order caused by the application of sanctions on particular countries.

This more holistic approach might well result in a substantial expansion of the class of people who count as refugees. So Lister could defend his approach by falling back once more on considerations of political feasibility; his approach provides a way of shoring up the already beleaguered international refugee system in a politically hostile environment.

Should we take for granted that the populations of developed countries will always be at least somewhat hostile to asylum seekers? Perhaps it is worth comparing political constraints on admitting asylum seekers with political constraints on admitting people considered racially inferior or unacceptable, especially since fears about asylum seekers are often racially or ethnically tinged. (Farage's poster, for instance, was heavily criticized for relying on possibly racist tropes: It depicted a long line of almost entirely people of color.) Many will find those preferences unacceptable and be reluctant to let them feature in policy decisions at all, even as pragmatic constraints. Of course, opposition to granting asylum need not be based on racial or ethnic animus and thus need not be as repugnant; the example of the latter just shows that we aren't always willing to bend policy to accommodate political pressure. And if some people who are fundamentally entitled to refuge aren't being counted within the current international system then it might seem as urgent to resist political pressure against admitting them as it would be to resist political pressure toward racial selection in immigration policies.

In response, Lister could say that ignoring political realities is potentially harmful *to asylum seekers themselves*. Given that the current system is already quite unpopular, broadening the number of people it attempts to serve might create such a backlash that states would admit *fewer* people rather than more. Perhaps there is a trade-off here between risking these immediate costs and creating reforms that in the long run could produce a more inclusive asylum system.

B. Duties to refugees

We have so far considered how refugees should be singled out. We might still ask, though, how much exactly does any given country have to do in order to accommodate refugees? Are there limits on the size of the refugee population that any particular country can be expected to accept?

Various authors suggest that there are important limits on what a given country must do. In this vein, Walzer asserts that admitting large numbers of refugees threatens to thwart the ability of political communities to maintain their distinctive cultures and ways of life: "The distinctiveness of cultures and groups depends upon closure and, without it, cannot be conceived as a stable feature of human life" (Walzer 1983, 39). Walzer argues that admission ultimately brings with it the obligation to make the people admitted full members of the political community. States can resist admitting refugees in order to avoid taking on the obligations that come with making someone a full member of the political community, such as granting them a right to vote and thereby have a say in the legal structure of the country. We looked in Chapter 2 at whether these various reasons for limiting admissions are good ones, but supposing that states have some good reasons for limiting admissions, we can ask how those reasons weigh against those in favor of admitting refugees. To answer this question, we need to look more at the nature of the duties states might have toward refugees.

One obvious source of duties to refugees—one that plausibly applies however we conceive of refugees—is the responsibility some states have for human displacement in other areas of the world (Carens 2013, 195). Take Iraqi people who were recruited during the Iraq War to serve as translators and in other ways facilitate the US-led war. Many of these people became vulnerable to extreme retaliation for this work, and surely this creates an obligation on the part of the United States (and other countries who played major roles in the war, such as the United Kingdom) to allow them to escape Iraq. More controversially, consider people from those countries who have been displaced by the sectarian violence that occurred after the war. Does the United States have a strong responsibility toward these people? This plausibly depends on the extent to which that violence can be traced to the actions of the United States (Carens 2013, 195).

If we think of refugees as primarily a humanitarian concern, then we must consider the general philosophical issues of how much individuals (and, by extension, their states) must do to help the needy. As we saw in Chapter 1, this is a matter of ongoing dispute. Peter Singer's famous principle requires that giving to the needy (or, in this case, admitting the needy) should continue until the point where something of "comparable moral significance" would be at stake. This explains why if you find the victim of a road accident by the side of the road you should surely help them if this would only cost you some bloodstains on your white shirt. Likewise, a fancy dinner is not morally comparable to a human life. So if someone who is about to spend $100 could save a life by giving $90 to an NGO in Rwanda, then they morally must have a $10 dinner instead and put a check in the post. Singer's principle is hard to resist when we think about these individual examples. It becomes more disputable when we think about just how much one has to do for others over the course of a whole life. Perhaps individuals may give some weight to their private projects – beyond what is needed to secure just a morally decent life for themselves – even in the face of great need. For example, maybe it is acceptable for someone to spend time writing their poetry book that could otherwise be spent working for a charity that would save additional lives. And if that is so, then perhaps national projects – cultural goals and so on – can also justify *some* limits on help for refugees. See Chapter 1 (p. 17) for more discussion.

If we think of refugees as not simply needy people but more specifically those who lack a legitimate government, we might think of the obligation to admit them quite differently. Rather than viewing it as a duty to relieve *need*, we might think of it as a duty to satisfy people's *rights*. Specifically, we might think that refugees are denied their right to the protection of a state, as perhaps embodied in the Universal Declaration of Human Rights's (1948) Article 15(1) "right to a nationality." To be persecuted or unprotected, on this account, is not simply to be very badly off but to be denied something you are entitled to.

Where exactly does this right come from? That might depend on how we conceptualize human rights. On one way of thinking about them, human rights are universal rights that each individual has in virtue of being a human being. Nussbaum (2011) offers an account of this kind. We cannot explore the full complexity of her rich view, but here is a very brief overview. Nussbaum considers what it would take for the world to be minimally just and proposes that to discover this we must ask, "What is each person able to do and to be?" In particular, we ask whether they are able to do and to be those things that are worthy of their human dignity. These include, for instance, the ability to be healthy, to exercise one's imagination, and to engage in playful activities. Respect for human dignity, Nussbaum argues, means recognizing that there is a basic *right* to these "capabilities," which entitles people to the resources, education, and so on needed to secure the capabilities.

These rights, Nussbaum argues, have institutional implications. For example, among the important capacities is the ability to have control over one's environment, and that includes having a genuine political voice. More generally, political institutions are to be set up in ways that ensure for each person these basic rights, for instance, by enshrining them in the constitutions of particular states. What do these rights mean globally, though, especially in situations where particular states are failing to protect them? Nussbaum recognizes that this is a more complex question. It means making difficult judgments – requiring a lot of empirical investigation by political scientists and historians – about how to structure the entire world order. For instance, we might consider having a unitary world state. But this would be undesirable, Nussbaum says, for reasons including the difficulty of holding that state accountable and also the importance of national sovereignty or self-determination. Taking seriously national self-determination – the ability of individual nation-states to be self-governing – is important, she says, because it connects to the basic capacity humans have to shape the rules that they are to be governed by.

If we accept this role for national sovereignty, we may be left still with a dilemma of how to balance that sovereignty with the importance of securing various other capabilities for people elsewhere in the world, such as their health and ability to exercise their imagination. Nussbaum's ideal of a world in which all of these capabilities are secured – including those that justify national sovereignty – is very attractive, but it raises questions about what to do in our very imperfect world where it seems we may have to decide which capabilities to prioritize. Should Nussbaum agree with David Miller (2016, 93), for instance, when he writes that "there is a gap between the rights of the vulnerable and the obligations of those who might protect them," given the potential limits on sovereignty that protecting the vulnerable might require? Or should she say that rights to health and so on typically trump any national sovereignty considerations? Whether this is so might depend on what exactly is needed to secure national sovereignty on the capabilities view: Does it require the ability to pursue extensive cultural goals, for instance, or just some basic democratic institutions?

A different approach to human rights takes for granted that we live in, and will live in for the foreseeable future, a world of separate states, and claims that the concept of a human right is needed specifically to help us assess the morality of this world order; we might call this an "institutionalist" approach.[2] Rather than being universal entitlements owed to people as human beings, the concept of a human right is needed to solve a problem that arises in a particular institutional context. In a world composed of separate states, what are the minimal conditions that must be met for that global order to be just? We looked earlier—in our discussion of Shacknove—at what could make it acceptable for one individual state to exercise authority. We are now taking a broader view and looking at what could make a world order as a whole—composed of various states acting individually—acceptable.

Why are there special moral requirements that apply to this global order? In our discussion of Shacknove, we looked at how individual states impose rules upon their populations and how this can give rise to requirements of legitimacy. The individuals who are subject to these rules can ask, "Why should I have to follow them?" And the answer proposed by Shacknove and others is that they should have to follow them when and because the state takes proper responsibility for securing their basic interests. The international order also imposes rules that individuals, as well as their governments, must follow. These rules include a general presumption of respect for state *sovereignty* – the ability of states to make independent decisions about how affairs within their territory are to be organized, including decisions about entry into their territory. For example, there is a presumption that one state may not interfere in another state's economic policies and that states are left free to control their borders, preventing foreign individuals from entering their territories without permission. In effect, the global order leaves most individuals in a situation where they must accept the control of one particular government, only able to escape that control with the permission of some other government. Why should people accept this setup? Why should they be willing to stay within the jurisdiction that they were born in and only move across political boundaries with the consent of other states? Certain basic moral requirements must be met, one might say, if the global order is to be justified to each person. This is where the concept of an international human right comes in: these rights tell us what each person is entitled to for the global order to be justified to each.

What human rights do people have on the institutionalist approach? Institutionalists often say that fundamentally each individual is entitled to live under a legitimate government – a concept we came across earlier in looking at Shacknove – which is to say a government that accepts and carries out a responsibility for serving their basic needs. International human rights are just those rights that guarantee each individual is living under a legitimate government. That includes the Universal Declaration's right to nationality, which ensures for each individual membership in some state or another. And it also includes the various more specific rights – to liberty, to a hearing before an impartial tribunal when accused of a crime, to education, etc. – that constrain how each individual is treated within their state.

Why these rights? Why the focus on securing for each person a life under a legitimate government? The idea could be put like this: What the existing global order secures, in the first instance, is the ability of various states to be self-governing. It assures for them the ability to make their own decisions without interference from foreign states, individuals, or non-governmental organizations. Why should these other states, individuals, and organizations uphold this order? Why should they be prepared to accept the various rules that secure said self-determination for other states? Plausibly, they should accept this when and because the global order secures for them the *same* good: It assures for each state the ability to be self-determining and for each individual a life within a self-determining political community. Individuals who are stateless, for instance – denied the opportunity to be members of any state – are denied the good that the global order is designed to secure for others. They are asked to support the self-determination of various other political communities, even though they are denied the opportunity to be members of any such community themselves. Likewise we might say individuals who live under an illegitimate government are not full members of that political community. It acts on them but not for them. Although they are officially nationals of that place, the government is not taking proper responsibility for their interests, and thus not acting on their behalf. Since the government is not acting on their behalf, not acting as their representative, they can deny that they are a part of any self-determining political organization.

To briefly summarize, let's put all of these parts of an institutionalist view together. The global order, with its various rules that serve to secure state sovereignty or self-determination, stands in need of justification. Why should any individual person or state uphold that order? For it to be justified, it must secure the self-determination of each state and the ability of each individual to live within a self-determining political community. And an individual lives within a self-determining political community only if they live under a legitimate government. International human rights are those conditions needed for each individual to be living under a legitimate government.

Institutionalist approaches have often taken human rights to be the basis for deciding when a state is failing its citizens sufficiently to be subject to censure or intervention by the global community. In Charles Beitz's words, "The central idea of international human rights is that states are responsible for satisfying certain conditions in their treatment of their own people and that failures or prospective failures to do so may justify some form of remedial or preventive action by the world community or those acting as its agents" (Beitz 2009, 13). In other words, these theorists have taken human rights to be standards for when the global community is *allowed* to interfere with a particular state in order to protect the interests of its members. But we might also take human rights to be a measure of what the global community is *required* to do to protect the interests of people whose states are failing them in some important way. As we have seen, where human rights are violated, there are people who have legitimate complaints not just against their particular states but also against the global order as a whole. In these circumstances, it is appropriate for the actors who uphold that global order – including states and other international actors – to take responsibility for remedying defects in it. Requirements of global justice thus give states not just permission to affect the lives of people in other countries, but duties to help secure those people's human rights.

When there is an injustice in that global order—where there is a country that is failing to take proper responsibility for its members' basic needs—it is incumbent on other countries (as well as transnational organizations and other entities) to take remedial steps. For example, to say that there is a human right against persecution on the basis of sexual orientation is to say that if a country persecutes its gay members, then other countries (and transnational actors) ought to work to end this persecution. For example, if

Saudi Arabia is subjecting LGBTQ people to floggings and executions, then pressure should be applied to its government to end this. This pressure might take the form of, for instance, economic sanctions or, in extreme cases, military intervention. In other cases, where a state is trying to protect its citizens' needs but is unable to do so, the appropriate response might be to help that country fulfill its goals. The help might come in the form of, for instance, advice about institution building, offers of more favorable trade agreements, or monetary transfers. Which strategy is suitable will depend a lot on the empirical assessment of what would be effective.

What does any of this have to do with admitting refugees? On one view, associated especially with Matthew Price, admitting refugees is in effect a way of rebuking other states that are violating human rights, and thus trying to move those states in the direction of legitimacy. Compare this with economic sanctions. One function of those sanctions is just to make it more costly for a state to continue persecuting its gay citizens. Another function is to *express* disapproval of the sanctioned state. The hope is that this public condemnation will induce the sanctioned state to reform. Price (2009, 71) makes a similar claim about the admission of refugees: "A decision to grant asylum rests on a judgment that another state has persecuted; such a judgment is by definition critical; granting asylum, thereby, entails the expression of condemnation; and that condemnation aims at reforming the abusive state."

But it is difficult to settle, on this view, just how many people must be resettled in order for sufficient condemnation to be expressed. Nor is it clear that using refugee admission to put pressure on foreign states is at all effective. To be sure, authoritarian states may be very displeased to find high-level dissidents able to operate elsewhere, with the protection of asylum, but the sheer fact of disapproval from abroad may well be shrugged off. Even if the expressive impact is weak, there still seem to be very strong reasons to resettle refugees.

Setting aside expressive functions, admitting refugees can also be a more direct way of protecting people whose human rights are threatened by their home states (Owen 2016). Admission allows them to escape subjection to a government whose rule over them is illegitimate, and instead live under a government that will protect their rights. While a just world order would consist of legitimate self-governing political communities, the fact that some people are denied participation in such communities means that remedial steps must be taken. Ideally, these remedial steps would involve "fixing" these people's home states so that they would be legitimate; however, asylum will be needed, as Lister emphasizes, where these changes are not feasible. In some cases, where their home state is relatively open to outside influence, it might be possible to protect people through economic sanctions or even offers of assistance. But where someone is already displaced from their home country and where returning them would, under foreseeable conditions, lead directly to violations of their human rights, admission may well be the best available option for protecting them, at least until reform in their home country is more feasible. In sum, if we assume that justice in the international order consists of securing legitimate self-governing communities, the existence of illegitimate regimes means that sometimes, as a second-best remedy, individuals must be resettled elsewhere.

The institutionalist account of human rights suggests that there is a relatively *strict* duty to admit refugees, one that cannot be easily overridden by considerations of national sovereignty on the part of host states. The reason is that on the institutionalist approach, protecting the human rights of individuals and ensuring the self-determination of states are not separate goals. A world in which some people's human rights are being violated is a world in which those people are completely excluded from living in a self-determining community. States that insist on being able to exclude refugees in order to promote a particular culture (or other goal) are demanding a global order that secures self-determination for their members at the expense of other people's ability to live in a self-determining political community. Moreover, the threat to self-determination of having to live in a community whose cultural goals are somewhat stymied is surely much lesser than the limit of having to live in a community that threatens your most basic interests.[3]

C. Climate change refugees

To further illustrate the theories we have looked at of refugeehood and responsibilities to refugees, let's look at calls for recognizing a category of "climate change refugees" and what duties states might have toward members of these groups.

There is very broad scientific agreement that, as a UN intergovernmental panel issued in 2014 has put it, "climate change is real and human activities are the main cause" (United Nations, n.d.). Changes have already manifested and are expected to continue: The average global temperature rose by 0.85°C between 1880 and 2012, and the global average sea level climbed by 19 cm between 1901 and 2010 caused by reduced snow and melting ice (United Nations, n.d.). The impact on human beings in vulnerable areas is expected to be substantial as the number of extreme weather events increases. A small sample of these effects includes food insecurity for many with the occurrence of, for instance, failures of crops like maize and wheat in tropical regions, water shortages in rural areas, inland and coastal flooding, and poverty created by reduced economic growth.

Do those who flee climate change–related vulnerabilities count as "genuine" refugees? If we stick very strictly to the UN definition, the answer seems to be straightforwardly, "No" (Lister 2014, 620). These people fleeing natural disasters are not being "persecuted" by their governments and even more clearly not being persecuted because of their race, gender, or other singled-out category.

The more basic theories of refugeehood and responsibility to refugees suggest ways in which at least some victims of climate change should be able to claim refugee status. The humanitarian approach straightforwardly counts these people as refugees once they are, as many will be, in serious need. Thus, victims of famine in tropical regions ought to be able to acquire refugee status. Responsibility to these people seems especially strong for countries that have been major drivers of climate change, such as the United States. As we saw, there is a special duty to help people whom one has put into a situation of need, and given the evidence of human involvement in climate change, there is thus a special duty on the United States to help famine victims in tropical regions.

The legitimacy approach requires a more complicated assessment. One version of the legitimacy approach, discussed earlier, says that we should focus on especially egregious violations of legitimacy, namely those that involve persecution. This version does not seem to straightforwardly count victims of climate change as refugees. However, other versions of the legitimacy approach, such as Shacknove's, can still accommodate a category of climate change victims, since they allow state failures beyond persecution to support claims for asylum if people's basic needs are not being met. Shacknove, you'll recall, points out that the effects of "natural" disasters are often produced in conjunction with institutional factors. As the 2014 UN report emphasizes, it is people in countries with weak institutions that are most likely to suffer the effects of climate change. For example, in places that don't have the ability to build effective dams, flooding is more likely. So Shacknove can claim that many victims of climate change are suffering not simply due to "natural" causes but failures of institutions and thus living under an illegitimate state.

Now, it is not easy to disentangle what to count as (in significant part) an institutional failure and what to count as a "pure" case of climate failure. This might suggest abandoning the legitimacy approach and adopting a simpler humanitarian theory that says all people severely afflicted by climate change are refugees. Alternatively, defenders of a narrower definition of refugees might say here that this vagueness is another reason to avoid expanding the definition of a refugee to include cases where someone suffers through a lack of institutional capacity as opposed to suffering because of a clearer violation of legitimacy, where the government is directly persecuting them.

Clearer cases of responsibility for climate victims, on the legitimacy approach, are those in which an entire territory is threatened by climate change. Take, for example, the state of Tuvalu, which, it is predicted, will become almost wholly submerged over the course of the coming century. Political institutions are geographically based: They require physical locations for their legislatures, courts, etc., and they exercise jurisdiction over a particular portion of the Earth. Without its territory, the entire state of Tuvalu is threatened with non-existence, and thus its members denied the opportunity to live under a legitimate government. Although we don't have persecution or policy failure here, we do have people who are entirely denied a life under a legitimate government, given the total dissolution of their government.

What should happen to these people? We have been focusing on admission to other states as the primary remedy for climate disasters. But some authors, such as Cara Nine (2012), argue that this is not the proper response. Where an entire state collapses, she says, we have not only particular individuals denied a life under a legitimate government, but a whole people suddenly prevented from exercising self-governance. We saw earlier that on the legitimacy approach, responsibilities to refugees are ultimately supported by the value of self-governance and the need for an international order that protects the right of communities to exercise legitimate self-governance and the rights of individuals to live in communities of this kind. Protecting these rights sometimes means, as a second best, taking in people who are not part of legitimate self-governing communities. But where we have a legitimate self-governing community, the duty of the international order is to support this community so that it is able to continue to be self-governing. Destruction of territory plainly undermines that ability entirely, and so, on the legitimacy approach, we might say with Nine that the international order ought to be adjusted so that states like Tuvalu are presented with territory elsewhere so that they can continue to be self-governing political communities.

The pragmatic approach also emphasizes the need to consider not only whether particular people have a basic claim to be helped but also whether admitting them to another country is the appropriate remedy for those claims. The pragmatic approach says that this remedy should only be deployed where someone cannot be helped within their own country, as is the case with someone who is being persecuted by their own government or, as we just saw, in cases of destruction of territory. Can some victims of climate change be helped while remaining in their home countries? Lister (2014, 621) suggests that we need to be sensitive to some subtleties in the situations of these victims. In particular, we need to ask whether the disruption to someone's life caused by climate change is of "expected indefinite duration" and whether "international movement is necessitated." Let's look at these conditions in turn.

Some people displaced by climate change will be affected by acute weather events, such as hurricanes or floods, that devastate a region temporarily but are ultimately compatible with people returning to the area and resuming their lives. This may well require substantial help from other countries, including in the form of temporary access to another territory as well as help in rebuilding infrastructure, but it does not require, Lister says, the full resettlement of people in another country that asylum provides. Thus, on the pragmatic approach, refugee status should not be applied in these cases, because the specific remedies that accompany that status are not required. In other cases, asylum will be necessary, because the effects of climate change will be more long term. The cases of territorial destruction mentioned above are of this kind, but so too are cases where the destruction of access to fresh water makes a country uninhabitable.

In his second condition, Lister emphasizes that the effects of climate change must not only be long term but also require specifically *international* movement—across political boundaries—as opposed to *domestic* movement, across a particular country. The majority of people affected by climate change will not be living in countries that become wholly uninhabitable, even though they may be displaced from specific *regions* of particular countries. This leaves open the possibility of helping these people through means other than granting them asylum in a foreign country, since they could instead be helped through resettlement in their country of origin. This may be preferable both for the foreign countries that would prefer to offer aid than to increase immigration substantially and for the displaced people, who will often prefer to remain in a country whose language, culture, and so on they are attached to. In sum, the pragmatic approach says that only a subset of those harmed by climate change need to be counted as refugees.

D. Global fairness in the accommodation of refugees

We have so far looked at the potential duties states may have to admit refugees, but since more than one state may able to accommodate those refugees, we need to ask *which* states exactly should be admitting more refugees. Even where there are significant constraints on which country (or countries) can admit a group of refugees – for instance because of difficulties in transportation – we can ask whether other states should subsidize those that admit a disproportionate share of refugees.

Before we consider more theoretical issues of fairness, it is worth taking stock of what the existing distribution of refugees in the world looks like. One striking fact is that while discussion in developed countries of refugees focuses on their numbers within *those* countries, the countries that host the largest share refugees are not in fact in, say, Western Europe or Australia. In 2016, the five countries hosting the most refugees were Turkey, Pakistan, Lebanon, Iran, and Ethiopia (UNHCR, n.d.). Most African refugees in recent history have remained within that continent, such as Rwandans and Sudanese who fled to Uganda (Castles, de Haas, and Miller 2014). By May 2017, more than five million Syrians had fled that country to escape the civil war that began in 2011, and the majority of those people – three million – were displaced to Turkey. So while public debate in liberal democracies in the global North often focuses on whether, say, Australians are being asked to accept an excessive number of refugees or how refugees should be fairly distributed across European countries, the fact remains that this is not where most refugees are to be found.

What exactly accounts for this distribution of refugees? One factor is that within the international system, the core legal remedies for refugees are non-refoulement and a durable solution *within the country in which asylum is first sought*. This means that while states may sometimes make arrangements among themselves for how refugees will be distributed, the default is that a refugee is entitled to asylum in the state in which they apply for asylum. Thus, geography plays a substantial role in determining which countries in practice host more refugees than others. For instance, because it is more easily reached from the Middle East, Hungary has received a much greater proportion of asylum applications relative to its population than the United Kingdom and bears the initial responsibility for processing those applications and the default responsibility for giving refuge to those whose applications are successful. The international system as it stands places no obligation on states that receive relatively few asylum applications to assist those that receive many more applications (Gibney 2015, 4). The absence of this obligation means that states in the global North are often able to avoid larger refugee populations.

This feature of the international system – the fact that states generally only have to respect the claims of people who make it to their territory – also helps to explain why many developed countries have adopted non-arrival schemes: "deterrent and preventative measures to reduce the flow of applicants to their frontiers where they could claim asylum" (Gibney 2004, 11). Australia, for instance, has often taken measures to prevent asylum seekers travelling by boat from landing on its shores (Gibney 2004, 177–193). Famously, in 2001, the government refused to allow the Norwegian freighter, MV *Tampa*, to dock in Australia. The boat was carrying several hundred Iraqi and Afghan asylum seekers. Another common measure is the use of "carrier sanctions" (Rodenhäuser 2014). In these cases, states target carriers – entities that transport passengers, such as shipping companies and airlines – that might bring asylum seekers to the territory. These carriers are told that they will be fined unless they verify in advance of arrival that all passengers have valid passports and visas. For many asylum seekers, obtaining these documents is very difficult, especially given that they would have to rely on the very states that may be persecuting them (Rodenhäuser 2014, 224).

Can the current international system be justified? And if not, how should it be changed? An incremental change would be for wealthier countries, in the global North, to stop using non-arrival schemes to prevent asylum seekers from reaching their shores (Gibney 2015). To justify this demand, one might question whether these non-arrival methods are different in any morally significant way from impermissible refoulement at the border. Unlike refoulement, non-arrival schemes involve states acting beyond their territorial boundaries. But they still involve uses of state power designed to keep an asylum seeker out of the territory, so it's quite unclear why it should matter *where* exactly the power is exercised.

A more extensive change would be to allot each country a quota of refugees, ensuring that refugees are distributed more evenly across the world.

There would remain the problem of deciding exactly what criteria to use to judge this distribution. Should quotas be determined by the size of a country? Its per capita income? Its broader institutional capacity to admit more refugees? But in any case, fairness would seem to require a significant shift in responsibilities from less developed to more developed countries.

Now, Wellman stresses that even if there is an obligation to contribute fairly to the protection of refugees, particular states do not have to discharge that duty by admitting refugees into *their* territory. They can instead take steps to help offset the costs to other countries of admitting those refugees, and one way to operationalize this would be to introduce tradable refugee quotas, on the model of tradable carbon quotas in the context of climate change.[4]

Critics object that these schemes spread a demeaning message about refugees: that they are undesirables, perhaps even lower-value human beings. Perhaps what matters here are the apparent motivations for trading away admissions quotas. We saw in the previous chapter how the apparent bases for a selection policy can affect its message. A policy that appears to reflect – or can be reasonably construed as reflecting – racial animus conveys that certain racial groups are inferior. The apparent motivations for monetizing admissions quotas can affect its message. Compare a family that pays for its children to receive day care. If the parents are clearly paying for the day care out of a dislike for their children and a desire to avoid them, then this choice conveys a demeaning message. By contrast, if the choice is clearly made on reasonable financial grounds – the parents need the help so that they can also work outside the home – and made despite a strong desire to be with the children, then no demeaning message is conveyed. Similarly, if a country is plainly trading away its admissions quotas because its members think of refugees as dirty or degraded and thus desire to avoid them, then this conveys a demeaning message. Whereas a country that trades away its quotas out of a reasonable concern that the refugees would be better integrated elsewhere, or out of a reasonable concern that its institutions are less able to accommodate a significant population of migrants, is much less likely to convey a demeaning message about the refugees.

E. Camps and other "temporary" measures

Moral discussion of refugees, as we've seen, generally focuses on their rights to *admission* and *settlement* in other countries. Yet, as Serena Parekh (2017) emphasizes, the proportion of displaced persons who are in fact resettled is exceptionally small. Of the more than 20 million people officially recognized as refugees by the UNHCR, only 1 percent will be given sanctuary in a new country. The remaining populations live in (supposedly) "temporary" situations that in practice often last for many years. For instance, many live in large cities without any legal status, and the UNHCR estimates that 40 percent of the 65.3 million "persons of concern" are living in refugee camps worldwide. The defining feature of these camps is that while they are a way of providing some degree of stability for asylum seekers and refugees, they put significant constraints on the activities of camp members, especially their freedom of movement.

Parekh argues that these camps ought to be subject to much greater moral scrutiny. They are often treated as just a temporary part of the process by which refugees find their way from their home countries to a host country, or at least part of the process by which asylum seekers have their claims processed. Parekh points out that this approach seems at odds with how the camps actually function within the global migration system; the average length of time spent in a camp is 17 years (Parekh 2017, 17). Furthermore, she notes, many members of these camps are not even eligible for resettlement, since they don't meet the official UNHCR definition. Assuming that this feature of the migration system is likely to remain (and perhaps grow), it ought to be subject to ethical scrutiny.

Parekh's work explores what she calls the "ethics of the temporary," focusing especially on refugee camps. Drawing on Hannah Arendt (1951) and Giorgio Agamben (1998), she identifies two central kinds of harm or injustice that might concern us about life in refugee camps. The first is a "political harm," and the second is a distinct "ontological harm." She argues that while the existing literature has somewhat recognized the first kind of harm, it has failed to recognize the second.

The "political harm," according to Parekh, is that stateless people (including, but not confined to, refugees who are not resettled), since they are not admitted into any polity, lack the legal protections that come with membership in a polity. They have no state that takes responsibility for ensuring that their basic rights are protected.

The "ontological harm" occurs because stateless people are not only excluded from the framework of legal protections enjoyed by people who are members of a polity, but they are also excluded from the rest of humanity in a broader range of ways. They are *economically* excluded from participation in the global economy, because refugee camps generally do not allow their members to work. They are excluded *socially* because the physical remoteness of camps, along with restrictions on freedom of movement, prevents stateless people from interacting with the rest of society, and because the stigma of statelessness makes it hard for them to integrate. And they are excluded *politically* because they have no voice in formal political institutions, and because when they do interact with states their opinions and claims are not taken seriously. For instance, asylum seekers are often treated as presumptively untrustworthy and have their testimony given little weight (Parekh 2017, 91).

These economic, social, and political exclusions are harmful in part because of the way they affect the fundamental identity of stateless people. That identity includes a sense of "anonymity": of being treated not as an individual but as just one more member of a "giant, nameless mass." And it also includes a sense of passivity: of being treated purely as a victim, to be taken care of by others, rather than an active person with their own views and capacity to influence their surroundings. The exclusions are also harmful because they create a loss of dignity. A dignified existence requires the ability to meaningfully engage with other members of society and play a part in shaping common economic, social, and political life.

Parekh's approach might be usefully contrasted with another recent discussion of refugee camps: Betts and Collier's *Refuge* (2017a). Betts and Collier also emphasize the denial of "autonomy and dignity" in camps. Likewise, for them, as for Parekh, this denial is problematic both for its psychological impact ("a sense of alienation and hopelessness") and because it is intrinsically problematic for people to be denied the opportunity to act independently and contribute to society.

For Betts and Collier, the key deprivation is economic exclusion: the denial of the right to work.

> If our duty is to restore the lives of displaced people to something as close to normality as possible, reestablishing their autonomy should be high on the agenda. One of the most important components of autonomy is the right to earn a living.
>
> (Betts and Collier 2017b)

They point out that while the right to work is rarely granted, refugees use it effectively where it is. For instance, a study in Uganda "shows that they [refugees] can make a contribution. In Kampala, the nation's capital, 21% of refugees run a business that employs at least one other person; of those they employ, 40% are citizens of the host country" (Betts and Collier 2017b). Where they do not have the right to work, refugees often still engage in economic activity, but under conditions where they are vulnerable to exploitation by people who can take advantage of their limited options.

Betts and Collier propose the creation and use of "Special Economic Zones" (SEZs), with distinctive trade and labor laws, in countries that contain or abut large camps. Jordan, for instance, they argue, could make such zones available to the large population of stateless Syrians present there at the time of writing. These zones would have special rules that allow stateless people to work and engage in entrepreneurship alongside Jordanians, while multinational companies, such as Sony, could make major investments in these areas.

As the example of Jordan illustrates, Betts and Collier recommend that the SEZs be created in developing countries. This is partly because the majority of the world's stateless population already lives in developing countries (which also include Turkey, Lebanon, and so on, as mentioned above). It is also because, Betts and Collier claim, these countries have economies that are more suitable for accommodating a stateless labor force that generally lacks the kind of training needed to participate in the economy of more developed countries.

Comparing Betts and Collier's work with Parekh's, we can ask what exactly is required to respect the autonomy and dignity of stateless people. Betts and Collier's proposals would reduce the *economic* exclusion of stateless people from the global economy: they might quickly become closely integrated into the national industries of host countries and the global supply chains of multinational companies. (However, their economic opportunities would still have limits: A Syrian working in a Jordanian SEZ might be confined to manufacturing and unable to go work as, say, a doctor or nurse elsewhere in Jordan.) Betts and Collier's proposal does little, however, to reduce the *social* and *political* exclusion of stateless people. While they may have some economic interaction with members of the host country in SEZs, they would still be relatively cut off from the rest of that population, given their limited freedom of movement and occupation. Betts and Collier hope that the economic productivity of stateless people in SEZs would change common perceptions of them as victims or as burdens on the host country to a perception of them as a useful economic force. But there is surely a difference between seeing someone as economically useful and treating them as a fellow member of one's community. Furthermore, keeping stateless people somewhat cut off from the rest of society may mean that they remain stigmatized. The use of SEZs would also do little to enhance the political participation of stateless people. It would not give them any formal political rights, and their isolation again may prevent them from engaging in meaningful political discussion with other members of the host society or the world generally.

Parekh might respond to Betts and Collier, then, by insisting that their approach still allows for substantial forms of wrongful exclusion. She does not offer policy proposals as detailed as theirs, but beyond the right to work, she endorses integration into the local population as a whole, rather than just allowing people to work in SEZs.

Should we prefer Betts and Collier's approach to autonomy and dignity or Parekh's? One question to consider is whether the psychological harms that Parekh identifies (and that Betts and Collier also allude to) would be allayed by purely economic integration. Would the sense of anonymity and passivity that many stateless people feel in fact require more extensive engagement with the outside world, and ability to influence it, than just having a job? Another question is what exactly stateless people are owed. To some extent we have explored this question already: We have seen various arguments that (at least some) displaced people are owed full political membership in a new state. If we take those arguments seriously, then Parekh's approach seems closer to the truth: genuine social and political inclusion is required in addition to economic integration. But perhaps even her proposals fall short of what is required by justice, if we endorse some of the arguments given earlier that genuine resettlement is required.

Parekh, as well as Betts and Collier, might make two kinds of response to this claim that really only resettlement is an acceptable solution to displacement.

First, they might say that as long as someone's presence in a camp is genuinely "temporary" it is acceptable. Betts and Collier, for instance, are explicit that their proposals are meant for people who will be able to return to their home countries in due course. This raises the question: Exactly how "temporary" (how short) must someone's stay in a camp be for it to be compatible with justice, especially in a world where the average length of stay is very long? And why does the length of someone's stay in a place make it acceptable to deny them rights that other people in the territory are granted? In the next chapter we will explore some of these questions about how residence and time can change what an individual is owed.

Second, they might point out that given the current state of the world, resettlement for all displaced people is simply not a live policy option (Parekh 2017, 139), and so we are forced to consider what justice requires as a second best. This raises a difficult question about where political time and resources would be best spent: in trying to reduce the number of people in camps and increase resettlement, or in trying to improve conditions for encamped people where they are?

Chapter summary

We began this chapter by looking at the UN Convention definition of a refugee, and saw that it has some key elements, including that a refugee be a. persecuted, b. on the basis of one of the enumerated characteristics, and c. outside of their country of origin. The humanitarian theory proposes a radical expansion of the category of a refugee to all people in serious need. Some (perhaps incipient) version of the legitimacy theory is often used by political actors to defend a narrower definition, requiring something more like the persecution requirement. But the precise implications of that theory are somewhat complicated to work out. It the end it may well entail a definition narrower than they humanitarian theory's, but it can still justify changes in asylum law that have accommodated, for instance, victims of gender-based violence. The pragmatic theory focuses on the final aspect of the Convention definition – the outside of country of origin clause – and uses it to motivate a more general understanding of what the refugee system is for.

We then looked at how these different theories can explain the nature and strength of states' obligations to refugees and considered how a category of climate change refugees might be accommodated under these different views. Finally, we discussed the large number of refugees who spend long stretches of their lives in camps and what, if anything, could make these camps morally acceptable.

Study questions

1   What are the features of the UN Convention definition of a refugee? Is that definition too narrow?
2   What are some potential sources of obligations to refugees? Which do you think are the strongest?

3   Griselda is a transgender asylum seeker from Nicaragua who has been subjected to pervasive and severe harassment and threats of violence.[5] Should she be granted asylum? Is more information needed to decide this question? If so, what information?

4   Should some of the people suffering from the effects of climate change count as refugees? Which people and why?

5   Can refugee camps ever be an acceptable solution to the need to resettle refugees? If so, under what conditions?

Notes

1   More specifically, about half of these refugees agreed to live in camps (the remaining half refused to register with the UNHCR and lived informally in cities).
2   See, e.g., Beitz (2009) for an example of institutionalism.
3   For an alternative approach to sovereignty and the rights of refugees see Risse (2016).
4   For further discussion, see Kuosmanen (2013).
5   The example is drawn from this story, where you can read more details: https://www.azcentral.com/story/news/politics/immigration/2018/05/29/transgender-women-central-american-migrant-caravan-seeking-asylum-now-inside-u-s/639448002/.

References

Agamben, Giorgio. 1998. *Homo Sacer: Sovereign Power and Bare Life.* Translated by Daniel Heller-Roazen. Stanford, CA: Stanford University Press.

Arendt, Hannah. 1951. *The Origins of Totalitarianism.* New York: Harcourt, Brace.

Beitz, Charles R. 2009. *The Idea of Human Rights.* Oxford: Oxford University Press.

Betts, Alexander, and Paul Collier. 2017a. *Refuge: Rethinking Refugee Policy in a Changing World.* New York: Oxford University Press.

Betts, Alexander, and Paul Collier. 2017b. "Why Denying Refugees the Right to Work Is a Catastrophic Error." *Guardian*, March 22, 2017. https://www.theguardian.com/world/2017/mar/22/why-denying-refugees-the-right-to-work-is-a-catastrophic-error.

Carens, Joseph H. 2013. *The Ethics of Immigration.* New York: Oxford University Press.

Castles, Stephen, Hein de Haas, and Mark J. Miller. 2014. *The Age of Migration: International Population Movements in the Modern World.* 5th ed. New York: Guilford Press.

Dummett, Michael. 2001. *On Immigration and Refugees.* New York: Routledge.

Gibney, Matthew J. 2004. *The Ethics and Politics of Asylum: Liberal Democracy and the Response to Refugees.* Cambridge: Cambridge University Press.

Gibney, Matthew J. 2015. "Refugees and Justice between States." *European Journal of Political Theory* 14, no. 4 (October): 448–463.

Kuosmanen, Jaakko. 2013. "What (If Anything) Is Wrong with Trading Refugee Quotas?" *Res Publica* 19, no. 2 (May): 103–119.

Lane, Charles. 2016. "A Lesson for Angela Merkel: Good Intentions Aren't Always Good Politics." *Washington Post*, December 7, 2016. https://www.washingtonpost.com/opinions/a-lesson-for-angela-merkel-good-intentions-arent-always-good-politics/2016/12/07/9fb3a678-bc9d-11e6-ac85-094a21c44abc_story.html.

Lister, Matthew. 2013. "Who Are Refugees?" *Law and Philosophy* 32, no. 5 (September): 645–671.

Lister, Matthew. 2014. "Climate Change Refugees." *Critical Review of International Social and Political Philosophy* 17, no. 5: 618–634.

Miller, David. 2016. *Strangers in Our Midst: The Political Philosophy of Immigration.* Cambridge, MA: Harvard University Press.

Nine, Cara. 2012. *Global Justice and Territory.* Oxford: Oxford University Press.

Nussbaum, Martha C. 2011. *Creating Capabilities: The Human Development Approach.* Cambridge, MA: Belknap Press of Harvard University Press.

Owen, David. 2016. "In Loco Civitatis: On the Normative Basis of the Institution of Refugeehood and Responsibilities for Refugees." In *Migration in Political Theory: The Ethics of Movement and Membership*, edited by Sarah Fine and Lea Ypi, 269–290. Oxford: Oxford University Press.

Parekh, Serena. 2017. *Refugees and the Ethics of Forced Displacement.* New York: Routledge.

Price, Matthew E. 2009. *Rethinking Asylum: History, Purpose, and Limits.* Cambridge: Cambridge University Press.

Risse, Mathias. 2016. "Humanity's Collective Ownership of the Earth and Immigration." *Journal of Practical Ethics* 4, no. 2: 31–66.

Rodenhäuser, Tilman. 2014. "Another Brick in the Wall: Carrier Sanctions and the Privatization of Immigration Control." *International Journal of Refugee Law* 26, no. 2 (June): 223–247.

Shacknove, Andrew E. 1985. "Who Is a Refugee?" *Ethics* 95, no. 2 (January): 274–284.

UNHCR. n.d. "Facts and Figures about Refugees." http://www.unhcr.ie/about-unhcr/facts-and-figures-about-refugees.

UN General Assembly. 1948. Resolution 217 (III), Universal Declaration of Human Rights. *A/RES/217(III)* (Dec. 10).

United Nations. n.d. "Climate Change." http://www.un.org/en/sections/issues-depth/climate-change.

Walzer, Michael. 1983. *Spheres of Justice: A Defense of Pluralism and Equality.* New York: Basic Books.

World Bank. 2018. "Poverty: Overview." World Bank, April 11, 2018. Accessed August 2018. http://www.worldbank.org/en/topic/poverty/overview.

Further reading

Ferracioli, Luara. 2014. "The Appeal and Danger of a New Refugee Convention." *Social Theory and Practice* 40, no. 1:123–144.

Gibney, Matthew J. 2004. *The Ethics and Politics of Asylum: Liberal Democracy and the Response to Refugees.* Cambridge: Cambridge University Press.

Parekh, Serena. 2019. "Beyond the ethics of admission: Stateless people, refugee camps and moral obligations." In Sabeen Ahmed, Lisa Madura, and Kelly Oliver (eds.) *Refugees Now: Rethinking Borders, Hospitality, and Citizenship.* London: Rowman & Littlefield.

Shacknove, Andrew E. 1985. "Who Is a Refugee?" *Ethics* 95, no. 2 (January): 274–284.

Straehle, Christine and David Miller (eds). 2019. *The Political Philosophy of Refuge.* Cambridge: Cambridge University Press. (See papers by the authors cited above for their most current views.)

Part III

Theories of migrant rights

In previous parts of this book, we have looked mainly at the regulation of borders: whether and how states may pick and choose whom to admit into their territory. In this part of the book, we will look at the rights of migrants who are already present in a territory.

If you think about it, there are many different categories of migrants present in receiving countries. Their stays have very different purposes and characters, and they are often granted very different sets of (legal) rights. At one end of the spectrum, receiving countries admit permanent residents, entitled to remain in the country indefinitely, granted many of the rights of citizenship, and often offered a path to eventual naturalization (to becoming full-fledged citizens themselves). At the other end of the spectrum, states often admit tourists on visas that allow them to stay for just a month or two. Some states have even offered "day passes." Colombia gave permits of this kind to Venezuelans who wanted to buy food and medicine from across the border during a heavy shortage. As well as having a limited stay, these migrants also have relatively few of the rights afforded to citizens and are certainly not considered future citizens.

There are also people whose status falls between these extremes. Migrants on student or work visas have rights beyond those of tourists, most obviously, rights to enroll in education or be employed. More controversially, they may or may not have rights to access certain parts of the welfare state, such as state-funded or subsidized health care, and their children may or may not have access to public schools. Unlike permanent residents, they do not have the right to remain in a country indefinitely, and they are often not given a straightforward path to naturalization (indeed states often take aggressive steps to prevent this from happening).

In sum, there is considerable complexity surrounding the legal rights granted to migrants who are present within a territory: States and political actors often make a number of distinctions among different categories of migrant and associate different packages of rights with different categories. (These have been categories of *authorized* migrants. We'll look at *unauthorized* migrants in Chapter 8.)

There remains a huge amount of controversy about exactly which rights different kinds of migrant should be granted, and the purpose of this section of the book is to consider these controversies. Now, some of the reasons states have for granting rights to migrants are purely *pragmatic*. By granting rights to migrants, states can ensure that their own citizens are well treated abroad. And granting rights is also a means of attracting migrants whose tourism brings money or whose work will support local industries. So there are various ways in which the interests of states and the interests of migrants converge, leading to packages of rights being granted that are beneficial to each. But what happens when the goals and interests of migrants and states diverge? What about the visiting student who wants to stay in the country indefinitely or the migrant worker who would like to be more politically active in the receiving country, donating to candidates and voting in at least some elections? In what follows we will look at what *morality* requires of states in these decisions. What legal rights *must* states grant to these migrants? We'll start by considering some general theories of migrant rights, looking mainly at how they can account for some widely agreed upon standards, such as the requirement of extending to permanent residents a growing package of rights over the length of their residence in the host country. We will then see whether these theories can help us solve some important controversies regarding the rights of temporary workers and of unauthorized migrants.

6   General theories of immigrant rights

In this chapter we'll look at some broad theories of immigrant rights. These theories will be illustrated and tested by looking at what they have to say about permanent residents.

A. Human rights

One basis for migrant rights is to ground them in human rights. Few theorists think that these *exhaust* the rights of migrants, but they are often thought, for instance by Carens (2013), to set at least a *floor* of rights that all people present in a territory must be granted. Some rights that are often thought to fall within this category are rights to protection of one's person and property, rights to criminal process, and rights to fundamental liberties of speech and religion. These rights respectively prevent the police from ignoring the plight of an immigrant who is getting assaulted, require the state not to punish an immigrant without a fair trial, and prohibit the state from preventing an immigrant from engaging in artistic expression or practicing their religion. Permanent residents are straightforwardly entitled to these human rights: They are not only present in a territory, but there on an ongoing basis. We'll now look at what might justify granting rights beyond this basic floor.[1]

B. Beyond human rights: Membership rights

The rights we were just discussing accrue to people simply in virtue of their being present in a territory, but other rights are granted, and plausibly should only be granted, to people who are not just in a territory, but in some sense *members* of that society: call these "membership rights" (Carens 2013, 161). They include, for instance, the rights to benefit from social security programs, to access state-subsidized education, to use state-subsidized or directly provided health care, to work, to vote, to serve on juries, to contribute to political campaigns, and to run for office. Why and when must these rights be granted? Can we defend the common thought that *time* – the length of a migrant's stay – matters: either the expectation that they will be present for a significant period or the fact that they have been present in a territory for a significant period? Are there other factors that distinguish migrants with respect to the package of rights that they should be granted?

Thinking about immigrant rights is also difficult because it requires us to *disaggregate* the rights ordinarily associated with citizenship (Cohen 2009).[2] Political philosophers often talk as if people are either citizens or not and entitled to a complete package of membership rights or not. So a theory of immigrant rights must explain which *particular* rights – out of the full package associated with citizenship – different categories of immigrant are entitled to.

C. The contract approach

A first, simple approach notes that governments often announce in advance to immigrants the terms of their stay and that these terms must be honored, just as two parties to a contract must honor the terms of their deal (Motomura 2007, 43). The government might tell students, for instance, that they are entitled to remain for the full duration of a four-year degree course, and that they must continue to satisfy certain requirements during their stay, such as keeping the government updated on any changes of address.

Immigrants often sign documents accepting the terms of their stay – which looks relatively straightforwardly like a contract – and even where there is no formal acceptance of the terms, we might treat the announced conditions of the stay as binding since (a) the immigrant voluntarily enters into the arrangement and (b) the state invites the immigrant to rely on those terms, making plans on the assumption that they will not be changed.

In addition to requiring the government not to "renege" on the terms offered to an immigrant, the contract approach has also been taken to imply that the government must make fully clear in advance what those terms are, since migrants are going to rely on them. Take the case of Sam De George, whose case was decided by the US Supreme Court in 1951 (*Jordan v. De George*, 341 U.S. 223 (1951)). De George had been convicted of two crimes, both involving tax fraud, and the government attempted to deport him under a statute stating that anyone convicted of a crime of "moral turpitude" could be removed. The court rejected this argument: The idea of "moral turpitude" was so vague that De George had not really been given advance warning of the crimes for which he could be deported.

While the contract approach may constrain the government from making *revisions* to the conditions offered to an incoming migrant and must make relatively clear what the conditions of a migrant's stay are, it does not seem to constrain the *terms* that the government may offer. Governments remain free to say, for instance, that a migrant can enter and work but be granted no membership rights whatsoever, even if they work for many years.

Does the contract approach exhaust the rights of immigrants (beyond the floor set by human rights)? Are governments this free to offer whatever terms they wish? Here are two reasons for scepticism: First, few people would agree that all voluntary arrangements are morally acceptable. To take an extreme example, we do not think that governments should enforce a contract where one person agrees to be the other's slave indefinitely. Nor does it seem acceptable for the second person to insist that the first continue to lead a life of subservience just because of their initial agreement. The sheer injustice of slavery means that the contract must be dissolved even if it was entered into voluntarily. Some immigration programs might similarly be thought intrinsically unacceptable (even if they aren't as morally repulsive as slavery), for example, if they offer migrant workers none of the labor and employment protections offered to citizens.

Second, what counts as a genuinely "voluntary" arrangement becomes complicated where there are large imbalances of power between the people making the agreement. Suppose that the only source of clean water is a monopolistic corporation. I can't go without the water, and so the company is free to offer me almost any terms in exchange for it: I'll still agree to the terms. I was not forced at gunpoint to make the agreement, nor did the water company trick me. Yet there still seems to be an important sense in which the agreement was not genuinely voluntary. Even in less extreme cases, the "unconscionability" doctrine in contract law recognizes contracts can be morally problematic when one party is able to set the terms without much influence from the other party. One potential sign of this – again recognized in the law – is whether the contract is one of "adhesion," where, for example, a large corporation offers an individual or a small corporation a take-it-or-leave-it deal. Here the "smaller" entity has no influence at all over the terms of the agreement, and this is a sign of their very limited power in the circumstances. The rights states offer to potential immigrants are typically also offered on take-it-or-leave-it terms, and so we might wonder whether migrants really accept those terms freely.

In sum, while the contract approach has at times been an important route for migrants to claim rights for themselves, it still leaves states fairly free to admit migrants on one-sided terms. Are there other constraints?

D. The affiliation approach

The next few approaches we'll look at all have a similar structure. We might call them "sliding scale" views: They say that the more a migrant is involved with the receiving society in certain ways – we'll come to what those ways might be shortly – the more they are entitled to demand from that society. At the bottom of the scale, the migrant might be entitled to access certain kinds of state welfare, and at the top of the scale, the migrant might be entitled to remain in the country indefinitely, serve on its juries, and vote in its elections.

According to the affiliation approach, the involvement that brings with it more rights is developing social ties to members of that society. As Motomura (2007) puts the view, "the more enmeshed [migrants] become in the fabric of

American life, the more we should treat them like citizens." Carens (2005) similarly argues that "[l]iving in a society on an ongoing basis makes one a member of that society. The longer one stays, the stronger one's *connections and social attachments*. For the same reason, the longer one stays, the stronger one's claim to be treated as a full member. At some point a threshold is reached, after which one simply is a member of society, tout court, and one should be granted all the legal rights that other full members enjoy." (My emphases. Note that Carens, as you'll notice from the quote, speaks about a *threshold* at which someone is entitled to the full rights of citizenship. But we're looking at the affiliation approach as a sliding scale view, since it's worth considering whether it – used alone – has the flexibility to explain why an immigrant might be entitled to certain rights that go beyond human rights but fall short of the full set of citizenship rights. Carens himself supplements an affiliation approach with elements of other views, and so in this and other respects he shouldn't be seen as a straightforward affiliation theorist: we'll see his thinking show up in other views below.)

What exactly do these social ties, these forms of "enmeshment" amount to? Immigrants, once they are a little more settled, join churches, helping to run their fundraisers and participating in their ecclesiastical life, or they get involved with humanist societies. They go to community centers and political party meetings, make friends at the corner shop and in sporting leagues. They become closer to the host society with respect to their "values, lifestyle, language, occupation, family, and so on" (Carens 2013, 164). Applied to permanent residents, we can see that they are generally just as "enmeshed" as citizens, and so the affiliation approach makes a plausible case for granting them much the same rights as citizens.

Why exactly does this enmeshment matter, morally speaking? The basic idea is that other members of the host society must recognize that an immigrant who becomes more enmeshed starts to become (as the pre-existing members could put it) "one of us." Their lives and identities have become more and more linked to those of other members of society. Here's a way to think about it. Suppose that someone joins a new university as a student. As time goes by, let's suppose, they become more involved in the social life of university, helping to plan events, showing up for people's birthdays, and so on. They also begin to identify with the university, wearing its colors and so on. The nickname for members of the university is "the Mallards": it would be natural for more senior members of the student body to think, "That student is a Mallard now." And it would also be natural for them to treat the student's Mallardhood as a reason to look out for them in various ways. Maybe they make sure to invite them to their social gatherings and bring them soup when they're sick.

On the affiliation view, whole societies are also bound together by common projects and activities, and these bonds also determine which people that society should be specially looking out for: who is entitled to its membership rights. Now, historically, this idea that membership rights depend on who is considered "one of us" in a society has been used in an extremely exclusionary manner. In the United States it has often been used to, for instance, deny rights to (and indeed use extreme violence against) Native Americans, who, despite their much longer presence in their territory, were deemed separate from the rest of the nation. In the period leading up to the Civil War, "Native Americans were considered to be members of an alien, uncivilized race, whose values were antithetical to those of the dominant white civilization," and this reasoning was used to justify denying them the ability to naturalize as US citizens (Maltz 2000, 556). Kurds in Turkey have frequently faced cultural suppression, lack of political representation, and violence when they have refused to assimilate by abandoning their language and so on.

Alive to these concerns, Carens suggests that the test for whether someone has developed social ties with a society should be just the amount of time they have spent there. Time is an adequate proxy, Carens says, for how enmeshed they have become, since generally the longer people live in a place, the more they work together with its citizens, participate in its cultural life, and so on. By relying purely on time as the measure of social enmeshment, states can avoid the historical problem of privileging social ties that attach to membership in particular groups, defined by race, religion, gender, and so on. Using time as the primary measurement of social enmeshment also has the attraction of protecting people's privacy – because they don't have to reveal to the state all of their social activities – and removing discretion from individual immigration officers who might otherwise be in a position to pass judgment on the worth of different people's ways of participating in society (judgments that might well again replicate racist or sexist assumptions, at least unconsciously).

Should we ultimately accept the affiliation approach? A potential concern is that in other contexts – outside of immigration – we don't seem to pay attention to someone's social ties when determining the civic rights to which they are entitled. We don't think people should have their citizenship revoked or their entitlements scaled back just because they refuse to take part much in the civil society. Recluses can still be full citizens, even if they don't join churches or clubs, are uncooperative neighbors, stay away from playgroups, etc. These might seem like fanciful examples, but there are certainly groups that are less connected to the rest of society than others: Take the Amish, who live in relatively self-sufficient communities, avoid technology (like phones and the internet) that might otherwise allow them to communicate more with the outside world, and homeschool their children to a significant extent.

Carens offers two kinds of response to these concerns. The first is to suggest that it is in fact a social problem to be addressed, rather than a fact to be accommodated, if an individual is substantially cut off from the rest of society. Given the goods of social involvement, we should worry if someone feels no motivation to join in with others. Society should reach out to that person and help allow them to be involved.

This leads us to Carens's second response, which involves clarifying the requirements for enmeshment. People do not need to mix with the whole body of the nation to count as having social ties; it is sufficient if they mix substantially with some part of society. The Amish certainly have a strong community, and their members are typically well enmeshed into it. But still why should members of other groups care about this? They might deny that the Amish are any more connected to the rest of society than people who are across the border in Canada. The Amish could still be singled out for entitlements if the requirements of social connection are weakened substantially, if very little interaction with the main body of society is needed: ultimately, Carens writes that someone can be substantially enmeshed in a society simply by being present in its territory for long enough: "in the end, simply living in a state over time is sufficient to make one a member of that society and to ground claims to legal rights and ultimately to citizenship" (Carens 2013, 168).

At this point we might wonder whether the affiliation approach has lost a lot of its initial appeal as a way of grounding rights. The intuitive idea was that people who interact and identify a lot with each other come to have more obligations to one another (remember the university community example). But just living in the same geographical space as other people seems quite different. Is that really enough to create mutual moral obligations?

E. The contribution approach

The contribution approach (as we'll call it) is a close cousin of the affiliation approach. It also focuses on certain interactions between people in a society. The relevant interactions, though, are those that involve making contributions to society. The core idea is that people should receive back from a society to the extent that they put something in. This idea is sometimes described as a norm of "reciprocity": People who contribute to a scheme that benefits others ought to also benefit from that scheme themselves, typically in proportion to what they put in. We invoke the idea of reciprocity in a range of contexts. Think of a carpool arrangement. I offer to take some colleagues with me to work in my car a couple of times a week, paying alone for the gasoline used on those days. Reciprocity is satisfied if they in turn drive me to work on other days and pay for the gas on those days.

What counts as a contribution to a whole society? The most obvious suggestion is that people contribute economically, through work, monetary transfers, and so on. By doing work they help to raise living standards; by paying taxes, they fund the government's efforts to promote the common good; by investing in the country, they help to create jobs. This fits with a common way of thinking about the rights of immigrants. People who are trying to defend immigrant rights often emphasize the facts that rates of employment among immigrants are high or that immigrants may do jobs members of the native-born population might shy away from.

These economic contributions may well ground some of the rights that we associate with citizenship (more on these rights later, when we discuss the pluralist approach). An obvious example for why immigrants might be owed access to certain parts of the welfare state is that – if they have been paying taxes for long enough – they have helped to *fund* those programs and so should receive benefits in return. But when it comes to other rights, it seems less likely that they are connected to economic contributions. The right to vote, for instance, is granted to all citizens whatever their economic contributions. Historically there have been attempts to tie the vote to certain kinds of economic status – excluding people without property from the franchise, for instance – but these requirements have been rejected in liberal democracies.

Contribution theorists might try to avoid these problems by adopting a broader notion of what counts as a contribution. Political philosophers have often suggested that there are ways of contributing to a society beyond working or paying into its public finances. Rawls suggests that the existence of shared institutions (what he calls a "basic structure") that citizens support and uphold allows us to think of a society as a "cooperative venture for mutual advantage" (Rawls 1999, 74).[3] And institutions do seem to be very important in promoting the interests of a society's members. Even if we confine ourselves to considering just their economic interests, economists have frequently argued that stable institutions with certain key features – such as enforcement of property rights, which allow individuals to make investments of their time and money without fear that the state will suddenly appropriate all of their property – are essential to shared prosperity (Acemoglu and Robinson 2013). Members of a society can make contributions, we might say, by helping to sustain the existence of these institutions, and working, paying taxes, and so on are just one form of contribution.

But when we expand the notion of a contribution this way, it becomes increasingly hard to get a handle on how much someone has contributed. Suppose that someone in China works hard on technological products that are ultimately shipped to the United States. Meanwhile, someone in the United States is unemployed but upholds the law, votes in elections, and behaves in other ways that keep democratic governance up and running. The low-cost technology produced by the Chinese worker bolsters US institutions by helping to support the public finances that those institutions require, while the actions of the US citizen support those institutions in a very different way. Which of these people contributes more? It seems very hard to tell. Almost all of the accounts that we are looking at require some degree of judgment in figuring out how they apply to particular cases, and this brings with it a degree of vagueness in the precise outputs of those theories. The affiliation approach, for instance, requires us to make some judgments about just how much affiliation is needed before someone is to be counted as a full member of society. But the problem seems more acute for the contribution approach: It's not just vague how much any given person contributes relative to another, it's hard to have any grasp at all on how to compare, for instance, the Chinese worker with the US citizen. Moreover, if we do find a way to assess degree of contribution, the problem mentioned above still arises: When and how exactly does making these contributions generate rights other than economic ones? Why is the US citizen more plausibly entitled to a vote than the Chinese worker? It's not clear how to use the idea of reciprocity to explain these other rights.

F. The autonomy approach

The autonomy approach attempts to avoid some of the problems of the affiliation and contribution approaches in explaining why people who are relatively unaffiliated with others or lesser contributors are often still entitled to the core rights of citizenship. This approach emphasizes the fact that once someone is in a territory, the state exercises jurisdiction over them, forcing them to comply with the rules (laws) that it makes. They must now organize their movements to respect the property laws of that country, arrange their interactions with others in ways that accord with its contract law, pay sales taxes, conform to its marriage strictures, and follow all of the other myriad requirements that the state lays down for people within its domain. If they flout these requirements, they are subject to punishments, from fines to jail time.

This means that states demand of people within their jurisdiction that they relinquish some of their *autonomy* – roughly their ability to exercise and act on their own judgment about how to act – and instead allow the state to exercise control of their lives. (We encountered a version of this idea earlier, in Chapter 1).

Why does this matter? The requirement of relinquishing autonomy to the state is on its face a serious burden (Blake 2001). In other contexts, we would find it very problematic if someone (or some institution) were to demand control over someone else's life on pain of punishment. Just imagine an individual walks into a park and says, "I make the rules now! Obey or else!" Even if the rules are somewhat advantageous to the people in the park, the new regime still seems problematic because of the relationship between the new ruler and their subjects. So what could make the exercise of state power acceptable?

Political philosophers have suggested two main strategies for rendering state control over individuals morally acceptable. The first strategy is to put in place limits on the degree to which the state's authority limits individual liberty. A classic approach is to demand that the state act within the limits of various requirements of the rule of law. These include, especially, ensuring that the state make publicly announced laws, which are made available to people in advance of their decisions about how to act, and which remain reasonably stable over time. The idea is that since people know what is going to be expected of them going forward, they can plan their lives around the rules, still pursuing major projects of their own without fear of punishment. To see why this might matter, imagine a government that flouts the rule of law. It deems a particular stretch of highway off limits to people who are not government officials but refuses to make this prohibition public. Or it suddenly and without warning proclaims certain kinds of profession subject to a high and special tax. These policies would make it impossible for individuals to make long-term plans that take into account the legal environment. People would not be able to organize their driving routes and career choices around the rules.

Even with the first strategy in place, however, there will still be some inevitable infringement of autonomy. For while the first strategy allows people to modify their plans to avoid running afoul of the rules, the fact that they have to make these modifications still means that they cannot pursue just whatever projects they value. They might wish to pursue a particular profession for instance but be unable to do so because of the special tax the state puts on that occupation. This could be so even if they are given clear advance warning of the tax. How can the remaining deprivation of autonomy be justified?

This brings us to the second strategy, according to which the deprivations of autonomy can be justified just in those cases in which the state also takes measures that enhance individual autonomy overall. For example, while taxation puts some limits on individual choice, those taxes might be used to ensure that each person has the medical care needed to be healthy and pursue their personal projects. Deprivations of autonomy can be justified for the sake of enhancing each member of society's autonomy overall.

The autonomy approach gives some degree of guidance about when and why various immigrants should be given certain rights. On the "demand" side – what produces the need for certain membership rights is determined by how much the autonomy of an individual migrant is potentially going to be restricted. And this is affected by the length of time a migrant remains in the country: As time passes, their plans are more and more shaped by the state. On the "supply" side – what has to be done to make these potential restrictions acceptable – what is needed are steps to limit the degree of restriction and to enhance the autonomy of the immigrant overall. For example, it makes sense on the autonomy approach that rights to freedom of speech and religion, essential to autonomy no matter how long a migrant's stay, must be granted immediately upon entry, while rights to, say, state-subsidized university education – autonomy supporting, but not as crucial as freedom of speech – can be granted later.[4]

G. Sliding scales and pluralism

The previous three theories have an important commonality: They emphasize that an immigrant's relationship with the host country tends to evolve over time (whether because their affiliation grows, their contributions stack up, or the degree of control of their life becomes more substantial). This explains why an immigrant's package of rights should grow over time. There is a sliding scale of responsibility toward the immigrant. By when and why should some *particular* rights and not others be granted at particular moments? Why should a foreign student be able to study but not to work or vote? Why do these specific rights seem to come with a longer stay in the country? On the face of it, while the affiliation approach, for example, might tell us that a permanent resident – who is fully enmeshed in a society – is owed all or nearly all the rights of citizenship, it doesn't obviously tell us much about why some rights are owed early in a migrant's stay, while others don't have to be granted until the stay has become substantial.

One way around this might be to supplement these theories with some additional considerations. Here are some initial pointers. A first factor might be the importance of the (migrant) interests that are protected by a particular right. This might be partly a matter of the sheer *strength* of the interest – someone who lacks bodily integrity is much worse off than someone who lacks subsidized education – and it might also be partly a matter of whether that interest is especially important morally speaking. To illustrate the latter, in liberal democracies we tend to think that a person's interests in self-expression should be given special importance because self-expression is central to their dignity.[5]

This factor would help to explain why certain rights should be granted immediately, such as the right to freedom of speech. Some interests might grow stronger with the time spent in a country. For instance, Carens points out that someone's interests in remaining in a country tend to grow over time as they develop stronger roots in that country: It becomes much more painful for them to have to leave a community that they are strongly invested in. This could help explain why the right to remain should be granted only after a sufficiently long period of residence (we'll look at this right in more detail in Chapter 8).

But the sheer weight of an interest does not seem to be sufficient to explain when and why certain rights should be granted. For example, an immigrant might have a fairly strong interest in being able to access means-tested welfare rights, and this interest doesn't seem to grow over time; it's just as valuable to have access to social security on day one as it is to have it in year eight. Indeed, someone altogether outside of the territory might have an equally strong interest of that kind. Yet it is common to think that in this case, too, the right should only be granted to people who are resident for a sufficiently long period. Why should this right come "later," given that the relevant interest is strong from the beginning?

A second set of considerations refers to the *way* in which the state threatens or advances an interest. It seems, for example, worse for the state to directly encroach on someone's autonomy by insisting that they work in a particular job than it is for the state to fail to advance their autonomy by failing to support their projects with additional resources. This might be part of the explanation for why allowing immigrants freedom of occupational choice is a right that takes precedence over granting immigrants access to redistributive programs.

Third, we might consider the countervailing reasons that the state has for not granting certain rights. For example, the state's interest in denying immigrants the right to have a driver's license seems fairly weak, and that might help explain why it seems reasonable for everyone living in a territory to be granted the right to acquire one. By contrast, the state's interest in avoiding fiscal burdens might justify only granting access to means-tested welfare rights to people who have an especially strong affiliation with the state.

If these maneuvers are unsuccessful, an alternative form of the theory, a "pluralist" theory, let's call it, avoids reliance on a sliding scale. Instead, theories of this kind draw on more specific considerations to justify each specific right (often using threads from the various approaches we looked at above). Carens, for example, uses an affiliation argument to justify the right to remain, a contribution argument to justify rights to economic benefits, and an autonomy argument to justify the right to vote. An immigrant's social ties should be matched with a recognition that they are members of society, and that membership should be matched with an ability to remain part of the community. Economic contributions into pension program, taxes paid into general state funds, and so on should be matched with economic benefits from the state. And subjection to laws should be matched (eventually) with an equal say in the formulation of those laws.

One obvious objection to the pluralist approach is that all else being equal, we should prefer a more unified theory. Compare scientific theories. Rather than trying to explain particular events, such as a glass falling and shattering, just by appeal to very specific factors (the shape of the glass, the nature of the floor, etc.) we also try to find *general principles*, such as F=ma (force equals mass times acceleration), that can explain a wide range of phenomena. And when we find ourselves with a plurality of general principles, we try to subsume these too under an even more general principle. A more unified moral theory is likewise more favorable.

A second potential problem is that this lack of unity can make it difficult for a pluralist approach to provide guidance on more disputed issues. In disputes, people might appeal to different, relatively specific, principles for their positions, and these more specific principles might tell in different directions. One person might say that immigrants who make very substantial economic contributions should immediately be granted access to social programs, while another might say that making economic contributions doesn't count as a strong form of affiliation and so access should be withheld until significantly later. Or consider immigrants who have committed crimes. Are they entitled to remain in the country? Can their criminal behavior serve as a basis for denying them various entitlements? For example, if immigrants are generally granted a right to vote after eight years of residence, can committing a misdemeanor of petty theft slow this process down, so that the right is granted only after 12 years (let's assume that citizens who commit misdemeanors are not stripped of the right to vote)? Some of the principles we have looked at might be used to justify limiting political rights for a person who has committed a misdemeanor. For example, it might be said that in committing a crime, they have shown that they are making limited positive contributions to society and can thus be denied (at least for a longer period) the rights of citizenship. On the other side, someone might appeal to an autonomy argument and say that whether or not they have committed a crime, their life is still heavily controlled by the state, to much the same extent as the lives of citizens – indeed the fact that they can be punished for a relatively small infraction *illustrates* this control and should thus have an equal say in the content of the law. By allowing appeal to a variety of considerations, the pluralist approach risks being unable to take a side on which of these considerations should ultimately hold sway, while a more unified approach might be able to settle the issue.

H. The anti-subordination approach

The final approach we'll look at diverges from the others considered so far because instead of focusing in the first instance on an *individual*'s relationship with the state and what they are owed in light of that relationship, it focuses on the relationships among various *groups* within the state. We explored the basic idea earlier in this book that there is something especially problematic with "caste-like" inequalities in a society. We looked at this idea mainly in relation to race and gender groups, but we could also consider immigrants themselves as a class. Historically, states have often mistreated immigrants as an entire class: In addition to laws that targeted specific ethnic immigrant groups, states have made rules limiting the ability of *any* immigrant to access the court system, to participate in a union, and so on. Such laws made it easier for individuals to harm immigrants without consequence and for employers to exploit them. Where a group is persistently disadvantaged relative to others across multiple dimensions, we can plausibly say that the group occupies a caste-like position in society, subordinated to other groups.

Owen Fiss (1999), drawing on his earlier seminal work on subordination, has explicitly applied this principle to the case of immigrant rights (he focuses on unauthorized immigrants, but we can consider his theory as a more general account). Immigrants, he points out, have often been "pariahs," living on the margins of society, systematically disadvantaged, and viewed with suspicion and sometimes hatred. What does it take to avoid this? Fiss focuses especially on rejecting (as he calls them) "social disabilities": "(a) bars on employment, (b) exclusions from public schools, and (c) denials of statutory entitlements, such as food stamps or medical services, that are routinely provided to the poor by the welfare state" (Fiss 1999, 5).

How do these provisions relate to the broader anti-subordination principle? Fiss points out that there are surely relatively clear cases where a denial of rights creates an underclass. Take, for example, *Plyler v. Doe* (457 U.S. 202

(1982)), in which the US Supreme Court reviewed a Texas law denying funding for the childhood education of unauthorized immigrants. The law, the court reasoned, would create a "subclass of illiterates": The children would come of age in society without any of the basic reading, writing, and arithmetic skills needed to function in its economy, civil society, or politics. They would moreover likely be viewed with contempt by other members of their society given their inability to participate. Clearly, Fiss and the court conclude, the Texas law would have produced a subordinated group and a caste-like structure of society as a whole.

Fiss claims that anti-subordination values also rule out the other "social disabilities" noted above: prohibitions on employment and restrictions on access to the welfare state. The combination of these disadvantages forces "illegal immigrants ... to survive by begging or stealing and thus to live at the margins of society – no education, no welfare, no work" (Fiss 1999, 16). People living in a degraded condition of this kind are likely to be viewed as dirty, dangerous, and so on, and hence treated with contempt. Thus, these other "social" rights denials – like the denial of childhood education – would also put immigrants in a position of being unable to participate in ordinary economic, social, and political life in the society and would also render them subject to contempt and stigma.

Does the anti-subordination approach provide the relatively clear guidance on immigrant rights that Fiss claims for it? There are surely some clear examples of rights denials that produce subordination. The childhood education example seems like this. But it can be hard to know beyond these egregious cases what the anti-subordination principle demands. For a society to be caste-like, there has to be not merely some group-based inequalities along some dimensions, but deep and persistent stratification. This suggests that some immigrant rights denials are compatible with anti-subordination values. But which, exactly? While a lack of early childhood education clearly shuts someone out of the main body of society, what about a lack of access to higher education? Or to state-subsidized higher education? How do we determine which rights denials are sufficient to produce subordination and which aren't?

Here Fiss might appeal to the importance of avoiding *stigma*: The rights denials that must be avoided are just those that turn immigrants into a "pariah" class, viewed by others with suspicion or hostility. But while preventing stigma does seem extremely important, it's hard to believe that this should be the *sole* criterion for determining when immigrants should have more rights. Take, for example, denials of the right to vote, which Fiss suggests are generally much more defensible than denials of "social" rights (although he also supports making the ability to naturalize relatively easy for people who have been present for a substantial period). Societies might vary significantly in how the right to vote affects a migrant's social standing. In some places, the lack of a vote, even for relatively temporary migrants, might be taken as a straightforward sign of their being lesser human beings, while in other societies immigrants without that right might still be held in higher esteem: still viewed as foreigners, but not contemptible.

Fiss might respond here that even if migrants are not viewed with contempt it is still not acceptable to view them as foreigners, at least after a certain point. If an immigrant family has been present for multiple generations and yet is still treated as "foreign," then this, Fiss might say, counts as sub-ordination: They ought to be treated as full members of the political com-munity. But what exactly is the point at which they should have full membership? It is hard to see how this question can be answered without drawing on one of the more individualist theories that we looked at earlier: The point at which immigrants must be fully incorporated into the political community is after they have developed sufficient affiliation, or contributed enough, or whatever. Thus, what we are willing to count as subordination –beyond cases of severe marginalization – seems to turn on further questions about what an immigrant is owed by the state, questions that are not answered by the anti-subordination account itself.

In sum, Fiss points out a very serious moral concern that immigrants can become a "pariah" group, living at the margins of society and treated with contempt. But his account does not seem to provide strong guidance about less extreme forms of inequality for immigrants, at least not without supple-mentation from one of the other theories we've reviewed.

Chapter summary

In this chapter we looked at different theories of rights migrants who are present in a territory should be granted. We saw that it is important to dis-aggregate the various rights associated with citizenship (including funda-mental liberties, economic rights, political rights, and the right to remain) and also different categories of migrant (including tourists, foreign students, tem-porary workers, and permanent residents). A fully worked out account should match different categories of migrants to different packages of rights, and we considered various theories of how this might be done. This creates a real challenge for "sliding scale" theories, which say migrants should gain rights as they develop certain kinds of relationship to the host society, because they explain why certain migrants should have *more* rights than others, but have difficulty explaining exactly *which* rights. We looked at potential solutions to this difficulty as well as "pluralist" views, which give up on a unified theory of the source of migrant rights for an approach that gives each individual right a more specific justification, on a case-by-case basis. Finally, we considered a view that looks at rights less from the perspective of what each individual person is owed and more from a perspective of shaping a whole society so that there is no group-based subordination.

Study questions

- Suppose a state tried to strip permanent residents of the right to access social assistance. Would you oppose this? Why or why not?
- Why do different theorists think that the length of time a migrant is present in a territory affects what they are entitled to? Do you agree?
- A theory of migrant rights must explain not only why migrants should have some rights but which *specific* rights they should be granted. Are sliding scale approaches or pluralist approaches best able to account for this specificity?
- What is it for a group of people to be subordinated? If certain migrants are prevented from working in a territory are they necessarily subordinated?
- Is it possible to combine some of the different views we looked at in order to produce a full theory of migrant rights?

Notes

1 Though for a view on which that floor is actually quite high, see Nussbaum (2011).
2 Sarah Song has also emphasized this need for disaggregation (though the discussion here is drawn from my earlier work with Adam Cox). For her current views, see Song (2018) below under 'further reading'. The remainder of this chapter draws heavily on Cox and Hosein (2016).
3 For a theory of distributive justice built around a broad notion of contribution, see Sangiovanni (2007).
4 Cox and Hosein (2016) defend the autonomy approach in more detail.
5 See, for instance, Rawls's (1999) suggestion that when we are considering matters of justice we should give special weight to people's abilities to reflect on matters of justice and what makes for a good life.

References

Acemoglu, Daron, and James A. Robinson. 2013. *Why Nations Fail: The Origins of Power, Prosperity and Poverty*. London: Crown.
Blake, Michael. 2001. "Distributive Justice, State Coercion, and Autonomy." *Philosophy and Public Affairs* 30, no. 3 (July): 257–296.
Carens, Joseph H. 2005. "On Belonging," *Boston Review*, http://bostonreview.net/carens-on-belonging.
Carens, Joseph H. 2013. *The Ethics of Immigration*. New York: Oxford University Press.
Cohen, Elizabeth F. 2009. *Semi-Citizenship in Democratic Politics*. Cambridge: Cambridge University Press.
Cox, Adam B., and Adam Omar Hosein. 2016. "Immigration and Equality." Unpublished manuscript.
Fiss, Owen. 1999. "The Immigrant as Pariah." In *A Community of Equals: The Constitutional Protection of New Americans*, edited by Joshua Cohen and Joel Rogers, 3–21. Boston: Beacon Press.
Maltz, Earl M. 2000. "The Fourteenth Amendment and Native American Citizenship." *Constitutional Commentary* 17, no. 3 (Winter): 555–573.

Motomura, Hiroshi. 2007. *Americans in Waiting: The Lost Story of Immigration and Citizenship in the United States.* New York: Oxford University Press.

Nussbaum, Martha C. 2011. *Creating Capabilities: The Human Development Approach.* Cambridge, MA: Belknap Press of Harvard University Press.

Rawls, John. 1999. *A Theory of Justice.* Rev. ed. Cambridge, MA: Belknap Press of Harvard University Press.

Sangiovanni, Andrea. 2007. "Global Justice, Reciprocity, and the State." *Philosophy and Public Affairs* 35, no. 1 (Winter): 3–39.

Sunstein, Cass R. 1994. "The Anticaste Principle." *Michigan Law Review* 92, no. 8 (August): 2410–2455.

Further reading

Carens, Joseph H. 2013. *The Ethics of Immigration.* New York: Oxford University Press, Part 1, especially chapters 5 and 8.

Fiss, Owen. 1999. "The Immigrant as Pariah." In *A Community of Equals: The Constitutional Protection of New Americans*, edited by Joshua Cohen and Joel Rogers, 3–21. Boston: Beacon Press.

Motomura, Hiroshi. 2007. *Americans in Waiting: The Lost Story of Immigration and Citizenship in the United States.* New York: Oxford University Press.

Song, Sarah. 2018. *Immigration and Democracy.* New York: OUP. Chapter 10.

7 Temporary workers

States often use temporary worker programs (TWPs) to fill labor shortages in their economies.[1] They might bring in additional nurses, computer scientists, or household[2] workers. These programs all have in common that the workers are permitted to stay only for a limited period. This might be for a season of agricultural work or a few years of nursing. Beyond these time limitations, the programs vary substantially in the rights that they grant to the migrants, and in this chapter, we will consider which forms of TWPs (if any) are compatible with justice. While some programs bring highly skilled workers to the host society, those workers are generally granted a fairly extensive package of rights (as a means of enticing them to enter), and so our focus here will be on lower-skilled workers.

To start out, here are a few recent and historical examples of TWPs (all discussed in Castles, de Haas, and Miller 2014):

- From 1945 to 1974, Switzerland relied heavily on a TWP to fill jobs: at its peak, migrant workers were one-third of the total workforce (Castles, de Haas, and Miller 2014, 106).
- In the mid-1950s, the Federal Republic of Germany ("West Germany") used the *Gastarbeiter* (guest worker) program, recruiting workers from, among other places, Morocco, Portugal, and, especially, Turkey. The program was ultimately abolished in 1973.
- From 1942 to 1964, the United States maintained the Bracero Program, bringing large numbers of migrant agricultural and rail laborers, mainly from Mexico. More recently agricultural labor has been performed by workers from Jamaica, on temporary H-2A visas.
- Oil-rich countries in the Middle East have admitted large numbers of workers from, among other places, India, Indonesia, Pakistan, and Sri Lanka (Castles, de Haas, and Miller 2014, 153). These workers made up 87 percent of the population of Qatar in 2010. These migrants have mainly been low-skilled laborers, but in some cases have entered professions, such as law and medicine, and more recently a substantial number of (mainly female) migrants have been recruited to work in the service and household sectors.

- Hong Kong had 285,000 temporary household workers in 2010, about half from each of Indonesia and the Philippines (Castles, de Haas, and Miller 2014, 157).

Aside from their limited duration, these programs vary in the conditions they impose on the workers' stay: conditions that are intended to make the programs to the advantage of the host population.[3] It is very common for programs to limit in various ways the ability of workers to change jobs or at least sectors. These limitations are in place in part to ensure that the workers fulfill labor shortages in particular areas of the economy and do not compete with domestic workers in other sectors. And typically, particular employers apply to the government to sponsor migrant visas, so requirements that workers stay with their initial employers are put in place to ensure that firms have an incentive to bear the time and cost of the visa applications.

TWPs have often limited the ability of workers to bring family members with them to the receiving country, as the Swiss program did until the mid-1960s. Some programs allow the temporary visas to be renewed, and they differ in whether and at what point workers are entitled to apply for more permanent residence. In Hong Kong, for example, household workers are unable to apply for permanent residency no matter how many years they have worked in Hong Kong (while other immigrants are permitted to do so after seven years of work in Hong Kong). This step too is designed to ensure that the TWP does not ultimately produce settled residents. And the same goal is part of the explanation for why temporary workers have sometimes been housed somewhat separately from the rest of the community, so that they would not develop strong social ties. Despite these various efforts, many programs have nonetheless produced a substantial settled immigrant population, either because the workers began to move into unauthorized status once their visas ran out or because, especially after repeated renewals of temporary labor contracts, governments ultimately granted the workers a more permanent right to remain.

The working conditions of temporary workers have also varied. Their contracts with employers have sometimes been poorly enforced, allowing employers to garnish wages and violate other contractual duties. In some programs, temporary workers have been unprotected by the health and safety regulations that states apply to citizens. Ties to particular employers, who are sometimes able to insist on the deportation of a worker no longer deemed necessary, have often led to temporary workers being offered low wages for long hours.

Another set of disputed rights for temporary workers is their ability to participate in social programs. These include contributory programs, such as pensions and social security; programs that distribute goods irrespective of contribution, such as state-funded health care and education; and redistributive programs, which use taxation to make transfers from richer to poorer members of society.

Finally, temporary workers have almost everywhere been excluded from full participation in the political process. While they are now almost always granted, at least within liberal democracies, basic free speech rights to advocate for political candidates, they are typically unable to donate to campaigns or vote in elections.

A. Some potential advantages of TWPs

Why have TWPs seemed attractive? They promise significant benefits both for migrants and for at least some members of the host societies. For migrant workers the appeal of TWPs is simple: they offer jobs, especially jobs with higher wages and sometimes better working conditions. Host societies use TWPs to fill gaps in their labor markets and boost their economies. For example, perhaps the host country has a dearth of nurses or agricultural workers and hence tries to recruit them from elsewhere. That might be because too few domestic workers have the training to be a nurse or because too few domestic workers are willing to do the onerous work of, say, fruit picking. The new supply of low-cost human capital generally benefits employers substantially, and some of those benefits are (at least in the best case) passed on to consumers in the form of better and cheaper products and services.

TWPs are also attractive to host countries because, at least when designed in certain ways, they can potentially minimize some of the costs associated with admitting new permanent residents (costs discussed in much more detail in Chapter 2). By targeting workers with particular skill sets and for periods of time that do not allow for substantial retraining, they can develop a migrant population that works mainly in a non-competitive sector and thus avoid to some extent the problem of crowding out domestic workers. Further protection for domestic workers can be provided by *requiring* the migrant workers to work in a particular sector or for a particular employer although, as discussed below, these steps can potentially bring their own costs for domestic workers by strengthening the bargaining position of employers. Potential fiscal costs of admitting permanent residents, such as their ability to access welfare benefits, can be offset by only allowing migrants access to contributory programs in which any benefits they draw are offset by their payments. Finally, the limited duration of the migrants' stay combined with their limited access to the political process is a way of preventing the migrants from having any significant impact on the national culture of the host state or its ability to be self-governing.

What's not to like, then, about TWPs? As should be clear from the descriptions above, some TWPs have been flatly unacceptable. Surely no worker should be put in a position where their employer can easily garnish their wages without consequences. That's an easy case in part because a program of that kind may well not benefit the workers at all, or at least enough to offset the cost of migrating and working. What happens, though, when the workers are denied certain rights – the ability to stay indefinitely, to access welfare, to vote – but are still better off overall, given their higher wages? Can arrangements of this kind be acceptable, and with which rights restrictions exactly?

B. History, human rights, and contract

While the benefits noted above have created some support for TWPs in liberal democracies, the history of such programs in those countries has been a frequent source of caution. Contemporary discussions of TWPs are highly influenced by the memory of some historical TWPs that now seem very troubling, and it is worth briefly considering these examples, since they may provide guidance for the present. Michael Walzer's important discussion focuses on the "guest worker" programs in Germany and Switzerland in their early 1970s form. Although they were intended to be temporary, these programs repeatedly renewed permits to remain and work, and ultimately produced a settled migrant population. In their initial form, the programs refused the workers the opportunity to bring their families and also insisted on sex-segregated housing. But ultimately the workers produced children, grandchildren, and so on in the host countries: generations of Turkish Germans, for instance. The workers often lived separately from the rest of society, both physically – their housing often on the edges of towns – and socially, with little effort to integrate them beyond their involvement in specific workplaces: "deprived of normal social, sexual, and cultural activities (of political activity, too, if that is possible in their home country) for a fixed period of time" (Walzer 1983, 57). As a result, the workers were stigmatized and often not accepted as Germans even after becoming much more settled. Walzer's reference to "political activity" describes the constraints on naturalization: Germany initially simply made it difficult for Turkish migrants to naturalize at all; when these hurdles were relaxed, Germany prohibited dual nationality, insisting that Turkish citizens renounce all other national affiliations if they were to gain full rights in Germany. The workers were often exploited given their dependence on particular employers who could have them deported, and they were often denied access to the major forms of social assistance in the host countries, such as unemployment insurance.

Where does this leave us? Drawing on the theories that we have examined, what, if anything, was problematic about these programs? Human rights standards can clearly be brought to bear. Workers were often denied not only membership rights, but also had limited abilities to exercise rights – such as freedoms of speech and assembly – that ought to come with sheer territorial presence. Any acceptable contemporary program would have to respect these standards, and many don't. Household workers in the United Arab Emirates, for example, are often abused – a violation of a core human right – because they may not change jobs until the end of their initial contracts without the agreement of their current employers (Human Rights Watch 2014). Like earlier guest workers, they are often exploited, for example by being forced to work up to 21 hours in a day.

What about rights beyond this baseline of human rights protections? One perspective says, drawing on the contract approach, that all other terms are settled by the conditions that were announced to the migrants before they chose to enter. States have to honor their "agreements" with the migrants, but are they required to do more than that?

C. A problem of design?

Let's look now at what the remaining theories of migrant rights have to say about the rights of temporary workers (beyond the floor of human rights protections). One perspective says that there can be permissible TWPs, they just have to be designed appropriately, while another says that no genuinely temporary program can be made compatible with justice: Only a program that puts workers on a track toward full citizenship is acceptable. We'll look at these in turn.

How could a TWP be rendered compatible with justice? The historical cases provide some guidance. Some features of those programs stand out. First, they produced high levels of stigma. The combination of strongly separating workers from the rest of society, having them placed only in jobs with low social status, and so on made for a situation in which they were viewed as inferiors. So one obvious goal for a new program is to avoid stigma-producing conditions.[4] Another important feature of the earlier program is that they ultimately produced a settled population of migrants, through repeated renewals of visas and eventual grants of the right to remain. This too made the programs unacceptable from an anti-subordination perspective. That approach rules out having a permanent class of people who are consistently at the bottom of society. All members of society must stand on basically equal footing. By contrast, a shorter program may be more compatible from an anti-subordination perspective. Suppose that migrants were brought in to work for, say, a single season. In this case, it is more plausible to say that the migrants are not really members of the host society – they remain mainly members of their home countries and operate as brief visitors in the host society. So a more genuinely temporary program at least stands a greater chance of being acceptable from an anti-subordination perspective. (We will look at challenges later, however, to the claim that this would be sufficient to satisfy equality concerns.)

What about economic rights? Carens offers a tripartite categorization. First, there are labor and employment laws. These regulate the relationship between workers and employers in various ways. Labor laws structure the way that workers and employers bargain with each other, setting out rules for union formation (including the right to form a union), striking, and so on.

Employment laws specify minimum standards that must be met in the workplace. For example, they might require that workplaces meet certain health and safety standards: ensuring that workers are not exposed to dangerous chemicals beyond a particular threshold, for instance. And they might stipulate a minimum wage that employers must pay. Second, there are contributory programs in which individuals pay into a fund. These include pension and social security programs. And, third, there are rights to access redistributive programs – often called "welfare" entitlements – which use the taxation system to transfer wealth and income from the better off in society to the less well off.

Carens argues for some moral distinctions between these categories. Specifically, he maintains that the first and second kinds of right must be included in any acceptable TWP, while rights of the third kind may permissibly be denied (this still leaves it open for host countries to grant those rights, they just aren't *required* to). Why these differences? On the first variety of rights – labor and employment rights – Carens argues that they codify what the host society considers the minimum conditions for acceptable work. They are on a continuum with prohibitions on slave contracts – which are grossly unacceptable – also specifying forms of interaction that we think are flatly ruled out. Carens tackles the second category of rights from a contribution approach. Norms of fairness and reciprocity, he points out, require that someone who pays into a fund receive a fair return. If we have settled understandings in a society of what constitutes a fair return within these programs, then we should extend the same understanding to migrants. But redistributive programs are different, according to Carens: They are based on the idea that states have special responsibilities to support the well-being of their citizens. We saw in the previous chapter how the length of time for which a migrant is present can – on views including the affiliation and autonomy approaches – affect what responsibilities a state has to the migrant. Since the stay of temporary workers is somewhat limited, the responsibilities of the state to these workers are also plausibly limited. And so it is permissible for the state to take fewer steps to serve their well-being.

Can Carens's moral distinctions between these categories be maintained? In some important respects, these different types of right in fact serve very similar functions. Labor and employment laws change the bargaining position between employees and employers. Rights to form a union give workers greater power when negotiating with employers. And employment laws give workers a different kind of advantage: They prevent an employer from offering certain kinds of deals such as working hours beyond a certain a limit. The effect of these laws is thus to give workers greater power with respect to employers and make work more favorable for the employee: both the conditions under which the work takes place and the remuneration for that work. Redistributive programs perform similar functions. If workers are able to access various goods irrespective of their employment, then their bargaining position in the labor market is improved (since they have a better fallback position relative to not working). Redistributive programs also in effect improve the remuneration for work by changing the rewards the employers and employees are able to generate for themselves. The minimum wage shifts benefits to the workers prior to the operation of taxes, whereas redistributive steps shift benefits to the worker using the tax system. Each is ultimately a way of affecting how much workers are rewarded for the same work and thus seems morally equivalent at base. Other employment laws might seem quite different from redistributive measures, since they don't involve shifting monetary benefits from employers to employees: They change the hours, forms of labor, risks, and so on associated with the workplace. While these features of work seem on their face importantly distinct from remuneration, they are all ultimately elements that affect workers' well-being. And workers regularly accept trade-offs between these elements and their wage. Working inherently involves giving up free time to some degree, and it often involves running various risks: plainly so in the case of manual labor, and even desk jobs take both a physical and mental toll. Which suggests that improving the lot of workers by altering the conditions of the workplace is not really so morally different from improving their lot through increases in their pre- or post-tax income. It may even be difficult to distinguish redistributive programs entirely from contributory programs: Migrants make economic contributions – not just through paying taxes, but also through simply doing productive work – that ultimately help to prop up the welfare state, and to that extent they are paying into a system from which they do not benefit. We saw in our discussion of the contribution approach that it is difficult to assess what exactly counts as an equivalent return on such contributions, and indeed redistributive states generally eschew the idea of such returns altogether, trying to allocate resources more on the basis of need. So if welfare rights are denied, it isn't for lack of contribution but, again, out of lack of responsibility to the migrants, and we might wonder whether the same argument would apply to contributory programs, setting aside the point made earlier that denying this access seems gratuitous and thus plainly unfair.

Despite these apparently similar functions, are there other ways to distinguish the different kinds of rights? One argument Carens makes is that limiting employment rights has an especially deleterious effect on the political culture of the host state. It tends, he claims, to undermine the sense of equality among members that is essential to a well-functioning democracy, especially a social democracy that maintains a welfare state. This is an empirical claim that needs further investigation. Perhaps limiting labor and employment rights does not have the effect Carens describes. Perhaps members of the host society make a relatively sharp distinction between migrants and members, such that the more limited rights of migrants do not lead them to question the rights of members. Of course, this would also raise concerns about stigma, but perhaps the migrants are viewed as non-members without being viewed with any form of contempt. Or perhaps, on the flip side, limiting migrants' access to redistributive programs would also change the host state's culture, as people come to see welfare generally as a benefit but not a right.

Carens's second argument says that limiting labor/employment rights is especially problematic because it has a more deleterious effect on domestic workers. Employers will have an incentive to hire the temporary workers since, given their more limited rights, this will be cheaper. Which in turn means that domestic workers will either experience higher rates of unemployment or will have to accept lower wages in order to compete with the migrant workers. By contrast, Carens assumes, denying the temporary workers access to redistributive programs will affect only those workers. There are two potential difficulties with this argument. First, there may be ways to limit the labor/employment rights of temporary workers *without* affecting domestic workers. For instance, temporary workers might be required to work in particular industries that employ few workers from the host country. Or it might be that even without these requirements the temporary workers would not be able to compete for the jobs that the local workers are interested in, perhaps because those jobs require strong proficiency in the dominant language in that territory. Second, it may be that denying the temporary workers access to redistributive programs *does* affect local workers. A worker who does not have access to those programs has a worse "fall back" position if they do not accept a particular job, which means that their bargaining position with respect to employers is weakened. And this, in turn, can create an incentive for employers to hire temporary workers over local workers, with the attendant problems of unemployment and decreased wages.

If these observations are correct, then we have to accept *either* that a commitment to equal labor and employment rights for migrants entails a commitment to equal redistributive benefits or that a willingness to limit migrants' access to redistributive programs commits us to limiting their labor and employment rights. Which perspective is correct? The case for more limited rights (of any variety) rests on the thought that host societies have a more limited responsibility to migrants than they have to their members. But even limitations of this kind surely don't justify grossly exploitative arrangements such as those in which migrants work at the very limits of human capacity for wages and entitlements much lower than those available to members. It seems best to start at least with the baseline of offering migrants the full set of rights offered to members and see the extent to which the interests of the host society combined with somewhat more limited responsibilities to the migrants (though still responsibilities that are stronger than those to pure outsiders – the migrants are somewhat affiliated and lead lives somewhat controlled by the state) can justify departures from that baseline. Which rights exactly does that leave us with, do you think?

D. An inherently unacceptable option?

As mentioned earlier, some theorists – most prominently Lenard and Straehle (2012) – argue that *no* TWP, however designed, is compatible with justice.

They focus on two features that all proposed TWPs share: (a) the workers are limited in their ability to remain in the host country, and (b) the workers do not (and will not) have full rights of political participation. TWPs should be replaced with programs that admit a greater number of new permanent residents, with an unlimited right to stay and on track to receive all of the political rights of citizenship.

Lenard and Straehle offer two kinds of argument for this conclusion: an instrumental argument and an intrinsic argument. According to the instrumental argument, admitting workers on a temporary basis *causes* unjust treatment of those workers. According to the intrinsic argument, admitting workers on a temporary basis (and without the right to vote) is *inherently* unjust, irrespective of whatever else it causes.

Lenard and Straehle's instrumental argument says that TWPs enable the exploitation of temporary workers by employers and the host society. This exploitation includes, for example, working under poor conditions, low wages, and denials of economic rights, both contributory and redistributive. They claim that admitting only workers who are on track to citizenship is an important step toward ending this exploitation, first by changing the bargaining positions of workers and second by changing the culture of the host state so that the workers are viewed as "proto-citizens." The bargaining position of the workers is improved since they do not live under the threat of deportation and so cannot be threatened with removal by their employers. And the fact that they will eventually be incorporated into the body politic encourages employers and others to view the workers less as simply financial tools and more as equal members of society who should be fully integrated and supported. Is putting the workers on a track to citizenship really a significant step in ending exploitation? Consider first whether cultural shifts would really have much impact on employer behavior. Perhaps employers will be convinced to treat the workers better by having a different understanding of their broader place in society. But perhaps the employers in the main just respond to economic incentives, hiring and firing in their self-interest, within the constraints of regulation. Turning to those incentives, situations where workers are reliant on a particular employer to avoid deportation will indeed result in exploitation. But host societies could instead allow workers to move between jobs, without granting them a full right to remain. And if this right to move jobs were in place, along with properly enforced workplace regulations, it isn't clear that putting workers on a citizenship track would have much additional impact. The focus might instead be on, for instance, ensuring that the workers have the labor rights, such as the right to unionize, needed to make sure that employers do not exploit them.

Let us now turn to Lenard and Straehle's central argument, which attempts to establish that TWPs are intrinsically incompatible with justice. They draw on both anti-subordination and autonomy approach considerations (subsumed under the idea of "democratic justice"). Temporary worker programs,

Lenard writes, have generally produced a long-settled population of migrants who are denied "the most valuable of political participation opportunities – the vote" (Lenard 2016, 88). This makes them a subordinate class and a set of people who are subject to the state's authority – their autonomy thus circumscribed – without having a sufficient say in how that authority is exercised.

Why not simply limit the length of the migrants' stay? That, defenders of TWPs will say, would make it permissible to deny them rights, perhaps on grounds of their limited affiliation or the limited degree of authority the state exercises over them (and thus relatively limited restriction of their autonomy). Lenard (2016) is skeptical of this strategy. It is difficult, she claims, to ensure that the workers will leave after only a short time. And the steps the state would have to take to ensure that the workers did leave, such as preventing them from bringing their families, would violate human rights.

Empirically, we can ask whether there are any effective mechanisms of assuring that the workers leave at the end of their visas. And we would then have to consider Lenard's second challenge, by looking at whether these steps would inevitably violate human rights. For example, withholding certain benefits from migrants until the end of their stay might incentivize the workers to leave. For example, if they have paid into a pension fund, they might be prevented from having any access to that fund until they leave the country. Even if this is troublingly punitive, is it a human rights violation? And while it is surely a human rights violation to insist that someone live permanently without their family, what if the workers are only asked to leave their families for a few months or a year to do seasonal agricultural work, perhaps with visits from their close family members but not full residence for them? People regularly make such choices: living in different cities, and sometimes different countries, than their spouses for the sake of more preferred work options. Should migrant workers be refused this option on the grounds that it is categorically unacceptable for someone to be separated from their family?

We'll return now to some broader questions about the role of migrant choice.

E. The rights vs. numbers trade-off revisited

We've been looking mainly at some arguments for increasing the rights of temporary workers beyond the minimum floor of human rights and also arguments that TWPs must be replaced with other programs that (ultimately) grant foreign workers the opportunity to remain permanently in the territory and ultimately access the full rights of citizenship. But there's an important perspective that pushes in the other direction. This is the argument that "rights" must be traded off against "numbers": that we should thus limit to some degree the package of rights offered so that a greater number of poor workers will be admitted and the desires of those workers will be respected.[5] Let's call this the "limited rights view."

The argument begins by noting that countries tend to admit a greater number of temporary workers under conditions where the workers will be granted fewer rights. Programs offering fewer rights are less costly to the host state and an easier sell to the host population. Yet given the choice between these programs and not being admitted, many workers will be inclined toward the former. For instance, relatively poor working conditions in the host country may still be better than those in their home country.

This means, the argument goes, that there are two reasons for supporting programs with more limited migrant rights. First, those programs will help a great number of poorer people. Second, those programs are more respectful of the migrants' agency. To reject them is to prevent the migrants from deciding for themselves whether they are willing to accept fewer rights for the sake of higher earnings. Thus, rejecting the program is a form of paternalism, where migrants are told that they are being protected from making potentially bad choices for themselves.

Is the limited rights view compelling? Against the paternalism argument, it could be said that the point of having programs with a more substantial package of rights is not to protect migrants from making bad choices for themselves. Rather, it is to prevent members of the host society from being complicit in unjust treatment of the workers. States, Carens (2013) argues, have special responsibilities to people within their borders and must fulfill those responsibilities to anyone they admit. This means refusing to admit someone under conditions where those responsibilities will not be fulfilled. Likewise (Carens points out), we do not always allow working conditions within liberal democracies to be settled by workers' consent: We refuse to enforce or permit contracts that are highly one-sided to the employer with respect to working conditions, remuneration, and so on, even if workers agree to them.

In response, limited rights theorists might point out that although we often do not allow mere consent to settle working conditions, we often do this in order to enhance the agency of workers. We implement legal limits on the working day, for example, in order to improve their bargaining position: Those limits allow workers to get the results that they ultimately want – a reasonable wage without extremely long days in the factory – by preventing employers from offering a less favorable contract. TWPs are not like this: If we adopt a program with more expansive rights, this will not enable the workers to get more of what they want – it will deny many workers the ability to secure new jobs at all.

Carens may reply here that in addition to agency we also care about justice and equality in the receiving society. Even if migrants would prefer to be admitted to a society in which they will be a subordinate class, it is still a moral scar on that society and its members for it to develop a caste-like structure.

Here defenders of the limited rights view might turn to the importance of poverty alleviation. In addition to respecting migrant agency, they can say, programs with more limited rights will also tend to alleviate more poverty by admitting more workers. Even if justice and equality within a territory are important considerations, surely they have to be at least *weighed* against the importance of poverty alleviation. Why should we assume that creating a just individual society is always more important than helping the global poor? We discussed potential balances of this kind in the first part of this book. Suppose that admitting a greater number of immigrants would be to the detriment of low-skilled workers in the host society and that the resulting inequality would make the host society more unjust. This is a strong reason not to admit the migrants, but if they are sufficiently poor, we might still think there is a balance to be struck between these competing reasons. Of course, some injustices are deeper and more scarring to a society. A degree of economic inequality does not create a severe caste-like hierarchy, for instance, while massive stigma for the migrants does. So we could accept that some forms of unjust TWPs would be categorically ruled out, while others could reasonably be endorsed given the benefits they would bring to the poor.

Two replies have been offered to this argument. The first rejects the claim that TWPs are especially beneficial to the poor. Lenard (2016) argues that even if particular workers benefit from the higher wages created by a TWP, this doesn't mean that members of poor countries generally benefit. If we care about poverty, she argues, our main concern should be promoting broad-based development in poorer countries. This is the best way to create a sustainable solution to global poverty. For while TWPs can benefit particular poorer migrants, the benefits do not necessarily accrue to other members of the sending society, and migration can also create problems for the sending society by destabilizing its institutions (in ways discussed in Chapter 2).

Defenders of the limited rights view might respond by saying that again the real issue is how to best *design* a TWP. Lenard concedes that under certain conditions TWPs are compatible with development (and indeed help to promote it), specifically when the sending countries are places that already have somewhat stable institutions. So host countries might focus on bringing workers from these countries. They might also investigate further steps that support sending countries. For example, direct payments to sending countries, funded out of the gain from TWPs, might be used to compensate them for the loss of workers. And perhaps TWPs are sometimes preferable, from a development perspective, to programs that bring more permanent residents, since they ensure that migrants return to their home countries where they will hopefully use their additional wealth and skills to support institutions in those countries.

A second response to the poverty alleviation argument questions whether there really is a genuine "trade-off" between rights and numbers and thus whether poverty alleviation and justice must really be weighed against each other rather than mutually satisfied. Countries may not *wish* to admit as many migrants with more extensive packages of rights, but that doesn't mean they *shouldn't*. For example, religious minorities have often seen their rights dictated by the willingness of the majority to tolerate their practice. Suppose that a member of the government said, "It would be nice to expand religious freedom for these folks so that they are completely free to practice their religion. But in present circumstances, the best I can do is to push for more limited reforms so that they can practice some of their sacraments and not others. In fact, if I were to press for full religious freedom, this would likely make things *worse* for the minority, since it would stir up resentment and lead them to be treated even worse in society." This speech would surely not make us think that, morally speaking, the right thing for the government to enact is a set of more limited reforms. What the government *ought* to do is allow full religious freedom. The views and behaviors of the majority that make this step difficult are moral failings that ought to be fixed rather than taken for granted.

Carens (2013) and Lenard (2016) reason similarly about TWPs. We shouldn't take for granted the unwillingness of host populations to admit temporary workers with the full package of rights; rather, we should criticize this unwillingness.[6] What the country ought to do is *both* alleviate poverty *and* treat the workers properly. So there isn't really a trade-off here, morally speaking.

In response, defenders of the limited rights view might say that we must distinguish two separate moral questions, each of which is important. First, there is the "ideal theory" question of what the ideally just policy would be. Second, there is a "non-ideal theory" question of what particular political actors ought to do, given the constraints they face. Someone sitting in a cabinet meeting has to decide what to say, and pushing for the most just policy may be completely ineffectual and also, as in the religious freedom case we just looked at, harmful to the very people whose rights it is supposed to serve. So what should *that* person do in *those* circumstances? Surely they must take into account the trade-offs between pushing for strong migrant rights and sacrificing the number of migrants who will be admitted? Knowing the answer to the ideal theory question does not settle for them what to say in the cabinet meeting.

Carens and Lenard might still sound a note of caution about the strong separation between these questions. The cabinet minister's action will not only affect which particular policy is chosen in the meeting. It will also bear on whether, in the longer run, the country moves closer to a situation where the morally best option becomes available: a situation where the population becomes committed both to poverty alleviation and to immigrant rights. Which short-term policies would move the country closer to that ideal – a TWP or a smaller number of migrants admitted as permanent residents? The answer could be the latter, if it encourages members of the host country to become more sympathetic to immigrants and their needs, but this is an empirical question. And even if that empirical claim were established, we would still, morally speaking, have to consider again just how important it is to ensure that temporary workers have the full package of rights – or just how unjust it is to deny them those rights – relative to the relief of poverty in the short run.

Chapter summary

We began this chapter by looking at the potential advantages of temporary worker programs (TWPs) and saw that they can have significant benefits for both migrants and host societies. They can also potentially be more politically feasible than migration schemes that increase the population of fully settled immigrants in a host society and benefit a larger number of migrants. The historical record reveals some serious potential moral pitfalls with TWPs, however, such as producing a stigmatized and exploitable subclass of workers in a society. This raises the question of whether there could be a new TWP that was designed in a way that avoided these problems or whether any TWP will necessarily be unjust. And if they are unjust, is the injustice to migrants serious enough that TWPs can never be justified by their potential benefits to host societies and, especially, migrants themselves?

Discussion questions

- Why are temporary worker programs sometimes attractive to both states and migrants?
- Suppose you are tasked with designing a temporary worker program. What features would it have? Which combinations of rights should the workers be granted?
- Are Lenard and Straehle correct in thinking that any temporary worker program, no matter how well-designed, will never be fully just?
- Is there a genuine trade-off between "numbers" and "rights"? If so, how should that trade-off be resolved?

Notes

1 This is also in response to demographic trends, though we won't focus on that here.
2 In this chapter, to avoid confusion, the term "household worker" will be used exclusively to refer to people who work in employers' households, doing tasks such as cooking, cleaning, and caring for children. In contrast, the term "domestic worker" will be used to refer to workers who are native citizens of a country (as opposed to "guest workers," "migrant workers," or "temporary workers").
3 The survey offered here draws especially on Carens (2013, chap. 6) and Lenard and Straehle (2012).
4 For further discussion of this problem and potential solutions to it, see Cox and Hosein (2016).
5 See, for instance, Ruhs and Martin (2008) for evidence of this trade-off.
6 Indeed, Lenard argues, it is especially important to criticize this unwillingness, since—she claims—members of more developed countries are responsible for much global poverty in the first place. I set aside that argument for now since it would lead us too far afield.

References

Carens, Joseph H. 2013. *The Ethics of Immigration*. New York: Oxford University Press.

Castles, Stephen, Hein de Haas, and Mark J. Miller. 2014. *The Age of Migration: International Population Movements in the Modern World*. 5th ed. New York: Guilford Press.

Cox, Adam B., and Adam Omar Hosein. 2016. "Immigration and Equality." Unpublished manuscript.

Human Rights Watch. 2014. "United Arab Emirates: Trapped, Exploited, Abused; Migrant Domestic Workers Get Scant Protection." Human Rights Watch, October 22, 2014. https://www.hrw.org/news/2014/10/22/united-arab-emirates-trapped-exploited-abused.

Lenard, Patti Tamara. 2012. "Why Temporary Labour Migration Is Not a Satisfactory Alternative to Permanent Migration." *Journal of International Political Theory* 8, no. 1–2 (April): 172–183.

Lenard, Patti Tamara. 2016. "Temporary Labour Migration and Global Inequality." In *The Ethics and Politics of Immigration: Core Issues and Emerging Trends*, edited by Alex Sager, 85–102. London: Rowman and Littlefield.

Lenard, Patti Tamara, and Christine Straehle. 2012. "Temporary Labour Migration, Global Redistribution, and Democratic Justice." *Politics, Philosophy, and Economics* 11, no. 2 (May): 206–230.

Ruhs, Martin, and Philip Martin. 2008. "Numbers vs. Rights: Trade-Offs and Guest Worker Programs." *International Migrant Review* 42, no. 1 (March): 249–265.

Walzer, Michael. 1983. *Spheres of Justice: A Defense of Pluralism and Equality*. New York: Basic Books.

Further reading

Bell, Daniel A. 2001. "Equal Rights for Foreign Resident Workers?: The Case of Filipina Domestic Workers in Hong Kong and Singapore." *Dissent* 48, no. 4 (Fall): 26–34.

Chang, Howard. 2008. "Guest Workers and Justice in a Second-Best World." *University of Dayton Law Review* 34, no. 1: 3–14.

Lenard, Patti Tamara. 2016. "Temporary Labour Migration and Global Inequality." In *The Ethics and Politics of Immigration: Core Issues and Emerging Trends*, edited by Alex Sager, 85–102. London: Rowman and Littlefield.

Walzer, Michael. 1983. *Spheres of Justice: A Defense of Pluralism and Equality*. New York: Basic Books, pp. 56–64.

8   Unauthorized migrants

"Unauthorized migrants" are people who reside in a state without having legal permission to live there. This includes people who entered the country outside of normal legal channels and people who were initially granted permission to enter but have "overstayed" their visas or violated other conditions of their stay, such as working without permission. In recent years, there have been significant unauthorized populations in various liberal democracies: 11 million in the United States and half a million in the United Kingdom, for instance (Gordon et al. 2009, 42; Krogstad and Passel 2015). The issue of how they should be treated – especially whether and when they can be deported – remains a political lightning rod.

We'll start by looking at the human rights of unauthorized migrants and some special difficulties they face in having those rights protected. We'll then discuss membership rights, focusing especially on the "right to remain": to have a protected period of time during which they can remain in a state, perhaps indefinitely.

Before proceeding, let's look briefly at a methodological issue that has been an important topic of political dispute. There are now numerous ways in which people refer to those who are in a country without legal authorization: In addition to "unauthorized," there are also "undocumented," "illegal," and "irregular."

Different sides to the immigration debate push for some terms over others, and "discourse critics" (as we'll call them) analyze the way these terms frame the way we discuss migration. Take "illegal immigrant." Critics say that the term triggers a set of psychological associations between the migrants and criminality, being threatening, and so on. This point is most plausible as applied to the term "illegals," used without the modifier "migrant" at all. The term emphasizes their legal status, and related associations with criminality, as the defining feature of the migrants, to the exclusion of other facts about them. Compare, for example, the choice some newspapers have made to drop the term "prostitutes" for "women who work as prostitutes" or "female sex workers." The former term triggers an assumption that the women are defined mainly by their work as well as the negative character judgment that accompanies the use of "prostitute" as a slur, while the latter terms simply indicate that the women work in a particular area, without triggering any assumptions about the rest of their lives. We should thus favor, according to this perspective, "undocumented" or "irregular."

There are also discourse critics on the other side of debates about migrant rights. According to these critics, framing the question in terms of "undocumented people" itself creates a bias. Using this term, conservative critics say, obscures the fact that these migrants have committed a wrong (they think the migrants have committed a wrong).[1] To call them "undocumented" is like calling someone who stole another person's successful visa application "documented": It describes their physical relation to immigration papers but elides the wrongful nature of having or not having those papers. Still more unacceptable to some conservatives is the term "DREAMer," used to refer to unauthorized migrants who were brought to the United States as children and would have been granted a right to remain by the "DREAM Act." That term, some conservatives claim, draws out a strong set of associations between the migrants and a hard worker in pursuit of the "American Dream."

Where do these arguments about discourse leave us policywise? Which steps should we actually endorse in the end if we agree with the discourse critics? Discourse arguments don't directly produce policy recommendations. Rather they alter how people think and talk about the policies in a way that, it is hoped, will ultimately alter the policy choices that people endorse. For example, some discourse critics typically hope that the less unauthorized migrants are conceived as "illegals" the more inclined people will be to support amnesties. Take, for example, whether unauthorized migrants are understood as members of a society, rather than outsiders. Are they? If we frame the question as, "Are illegals social members?" the natural answer is, "No." To be "an illegal" is to be an outsider – a person who is a threat to society, not a member of it. By contrast, "Are undocumented migrants social members?" is a question that might more naturally be answered, "Yes."

Is there, then, a neutral term that can be used in debate between progressives and conservatives? In this book, our working term has been "unauthorized" – a choice ultimately adopted by, for instance, the Associated Press. But is this neutral? Does it trigger relatively few automatic associations that serve either a more progressive or a more conservative agenda? Carens prefers "irregular." Is this, or any alternative, better? Or is it a mistake to seek neutrality in the first place?

One reason it's hard to find such a term is that all sides to the debate about unauthorized migration are somewhat suspicious of each other. Progressives often assume that anyone arguing against amnesties, for greater border enforcement, etc., is really pursuing (whether consciously or unconsciously) a racist agenda, grounded in demeaning and false stereotypes about unauthorized migrants. And this suspicion surely has some validity given the historical prevalence of racial stereotypes in immigration policymaking. On the conservative side, there is a suspicion that liberal arguments for expanded migrant rights are often made in bad faith: framed as piecemeal changes that would fix particular problems, but really part of a much wider open borders agenda.

Is there a way to get past this? One aspiration for philosophy is to help us find a basis for resolving disagreement by trying to start with commonly held assumptions and looking at their implications. The hope is that by looking directly at arguments, we can avoid having to rely on personal affinity or group affiliations as a basis for agreement, seeking the truth together even without any background bonds of trust. As you consider the following arguments, ask yourself whether this aspiration has been realized, or whether the debate is still being skewed in one direction or another by background framing.

A. Human rights

Human rights standards, we saw earlier, can either be thought of as rights people possess simply by virtue of being human or rights people possess simply by virtue of being present in a territory. Either way, unauthorized migrants clearly have these rights: Their legal status does not in any way affect their humanity or their territorial location (Carens 2013, 130–132). States must thus respect, for example, the rights of these migrants to be protected from physical violence and thus must provide them with adequate police protection. They must also protect the migrants from unjust punishment, by making sure that they receive a fair trial when accused of a crime. Extending some other basic services to migrants, such as fire protection and emergency health care, can also be defended on human rights grounds, since these services are essential to survival.

There is an important problem, however, with ensuring that in practice unauthorized migrants have their human rights fully protected (Bosniak 2006, Carens 2013). Unauthorized migrants are generally trying to avoid deportation. So they have every incentive to avoid interacting with state officials of any kind for fear of having their legal status reported to the immigration authorities. In some cases, these fears are there because there is an official policy of requiring various state officials, such as teachers and local police officers, to investigate people's legal status. In other cases, there is no such formal requirement, but migrants who interact with the officials still risk having their status reported. The incentives migrants have to avoid agents of the state mean that they will not seek help from those officials even when their human rights are under threat. For example, migrants will be less likely to call the police or use the hospital emergency room, even when they are in serious peril. This can have an especially strong impact on groups who are also vulnerable for independent reasons. Transgender unauthorized migrants, for example, face particularly high levels of violence and discrimination.[2] These problems affect not only the human rights of the migrants but also of other members of the society: A migrant will be less likely to report an assault on someone else, for instance.

Can this problem be solved? Linda Bosniak (2006) is skeptical that a state that reserves the right to deport unauthorized migrants will ever be able to properly protect the migrants' human rights. As long as the threat of deportation lurks in the background, the migrants will always fear the state too much to rely on it. Carens responds that there is a way to at least heavily reduce the fears of migrants (even where deportation policies exist). What is needed is a "firewall" between the parts of the state that deal with immigration enforcement and other parts of the state, such as local police (Carens 2013, 130–132). The firewall means that any interaction between these different branches is blocked. Minimally, this means that there should not be any official program of information sharing between these branches. It also requires having outright prohibitions on, for instance, hospitals asking someone about their immigration status. Such measures have become especially controversial recently in the United States because of tensions between federal, state, and local governments. For example, Immigration and Customs Enforcement (ICE) has sought help from local police departments in immigration enforcement, asking those departments to check the immigration status of people who break local laws and to detain those people beyond their release dates if they are unauthorized migrants. In response, so-called sanctuary cities have (among other things) refused to comply with ICE's orders and, in some cases, made regulations prohibiting members of their police forces and other local government agents from sharing information with ICE. Is this unacceptable interference with federal law enforcement priorities, or is it a crucial defense of human rights?

B. Regularization

"Regularization" programs grant unauthorized migrants a legal right to remain in the territory for at least some defined period of time.[3] Straightforward "amnesties" grant an indefinite right to remain, as seen, for instance, in Spain in 2005 and the United States in 1986. Other programs grant a more limited right to remain. US President Barack Obama's proposed Deferred Action for Parents of Americans and Lawful Permanent Residents (DAPA) and expanded Deferred Action for Childhood Arrivals (DACA) programs were intended to secure for unauthorized migrants renewable permits that would allow them to live and work in the United States for two years. For purposes of this section, let's assume that we are considering a program that grants the right to remain for at least a few years – an opportunity to realistically continue living in the host state, rather than simply a chance to organize one's affairs before leaving.

Generally, regularization programs do not grant the right to remain to people who have simply made it across the border: They require that the people have already been present for a reasonable period of time. The 1986 amnesty in the United States, for example, applied to people who had been present since before 1982. So let's assume that we consider a program that grants a right to remain to people who have been present for at least five years: enough time to have already been *living* in a country.

Finally, it's important to note that programs that apply to people who came to a country as children are often less controversial. For example, DACA received broader-based support than DAPA. One good reason for this is that people who came to a country at a young age, and thus grew up there, seem to have especially strong interests in remaining. Another reason is that while people who entered the country as adults may have committed a wrong against the receiving state by entering outside of its legal channels, it is not plausible to say this of people who came at a young age. We do not treat children as possessing the ability to make thought-out decisions for themselves: That's part of why we leave them under the control of their adult caregivers. So it would be inappropriate to hold them responsible for entering without authorization. Let's now turn to some arguments for the right to remain, focusing especially on unauthorized migrants who entered the territory as adults.

i. Humanitarianism

In Chapter 7 we looked at theories of when migrants have *rights* against a host state. It would be *unjust*, according to these theories, for a legal regime to fail to respect these rights. But setting aside issues of justice, there is still a morality of humanitarianism that requires us to care about the needy.

Cervantes's masterpiece, *Don Quixote*, introduces us to a Morisco character named "Ricote." In the early sixteenth century, Muslims – who had been present on the Iberian Peninsula since the eighth century – in all parts of Spain were offered the choice of exile or conversion to Christianity. Some, "Moriscos," chose to be baptized and remained. Yet Christian Spain continued to be suspicious that these people would be loyal to the Turkish and North African Muslim enemy, and they were ultimately expelled in the early seventeenth century.

Ricote says that the Muslims' expulsion was in fact "just and reasonable." After all, he says, even though plenty of Moriscos were "firm and true Christians," you should not risk "nurtur[ing] a snake in your bosom or shelter[ing] enemies in your house." Yet this "reasonable" course, Ricote emphasizes, had an enormous human cost: It was the "most terrible" punishment possible for the Moriscos. "No matter where we are, we weep for Spain, for, after all, we were born here, and it is our native country."

A similar defense can be given of regularization. Even if unauthorized migrants have no claim of justice to remain in the country – perhaps the state is presumptively entitled to remove them as a means of enforcing its borders – there is still a strong humanitarian argument for allowing them to stay. The argument is especially strong in the case of people who grew up there. For them, that country is, as Spain was for the Moriscos, their "native country," the place where they have deep roots and that fostered their basic sense of self. They learned the language of that place, internalized its customs as their basic compass for human interactions, developed foundational connections with teachers, friends, the natural environment, and so on. Carens suggests that while the effect may be weaker, unauthorized migrants who entered as adults and stay for many years generally also develop very deep roots in the host country:

> Connections grow: to spouses and partners, sons and daughters, friends and neighbors and fellow-workers, people we love and people we hate. Experiences accumulate: birthdays and braces, tones of voice and senses of humor, public parks and corner stores, the shape of the streets and the way the sun shines through the leaves, the smell of flowers and the sounds of local accents, the look of the stars and the taste of the air – all that gives life its purpose and texture.
>
> (Carens 2013, 150)

To tear someone away from a people and place that they know and love is extremely inhumane, the argument goes.

Even setting aside the risk of having these roots torn up, many unauthorized migrants in developed countries are in need because they come from countries that may be very poor, politically unstable, and so on. Some proponents of the humanitarian argument emphasize a contrast between these migrants and people who are otherwise quite well off but live unauthorized in a particular country. Michael Blake (2010) suggests that there is an enormous difference between, for instance, a low-skilled unauthorized migrant from Nicaragua working in Arizona and a Canadian citizen who enjoys living in Portland, OR, so much that they overstay their F-1 visa. Blake is surely at least right that the humanitarian argument is *strongest* as applied to people who are disadvantaged across a range of dimensions.

Is this argument successful? Almost everyone agrees that there are *some* humanitarian obligations to help people in serious need, and so the humanitarian argument provides a strong case for granting a right to remain, especially for unauthorized migrants who entered at a young age. There are some limitations to the argument, however. There is significant disagreement about just what counts as serious need and how much any individual or state is required to do for the needy. Certainly where existing law has recognized humanitarian arguments for allowing unauthorized people to remain, the threshold to count as sufficiently needy has typically been very high: For instance, "temporary protected status," giving otherwise deportable migrants some limited permission to stay, has only been granted in conditions where, for instance, the migrants would be returning to a country beset by civil war or a major natural disaster (Motomura 2014, 25).[4] Having to live in a place where you might die because of lava flow is usually a much more extreme burden than having to give up your job and so on and live somewhere very unfamiliar (though I myself think the latter is often a severe burden). So supporters of the humanitarian argument who want to make their case as widely as possible will have to not only point to humanitarian considerations, but also convince those who support the existing regime that our humanitarian obligations are quite demanding (for further discussion of humanitarian duties, see Chapter 1). Limits to those obligations may mean that the humanitarian argument only justifies regularization for migrants who came at a young age and others who can show that removal would create especially strong hardships.

Another potential worry is that the reasons for regularization offered by the humanitarian argument might be outweighed by contrary considerations. Generally speaking, it is easier to override a duty of beneficence than a duty of justice. For example, my obligation to help children in need seems much weaker than my obligation to help specific children that I have promised to take care of. Since the humanitarian argument establishes only a duty of beneficence, rather than a duty of justice, toward unauthorized migrants, that duty can be more easily overridden by other considerations. For example, if regularization has a morally significant effect on the domestic economy or local culture, then the state might be justified in limiting its willingness to regularize unauthorized migrants. So it is worth seeing if there is an alternative argument that can establish a *right* to regularization, which would be more difficult to override with other considerations. Let's now move on to such arguments.

ii. Contract argument

A contract approach to defending regularization appeals to the obligation on states to respect the terms on which they admit a migrant. Now, more or less by definition, unauthorized migrants don't make any kind of formal deal with the government, and nor does the government announce some official terms on which they may enter: They are not permitted to enter at all. So it might seem odd to say that there is any sort of contract between them and the state. The analogy with contractual violations is all the same useful, defenders of this argument claim, because there are values closely associated with contracting that are implicated in the situation of unauthorized migrants (Motomura 2014, 106–111). In particular, they point out that even if I do not formally promise that I will behave in a particular way, I can still lead others to expect that I will behave in certain ways. And it is a plausible moral principle that when I create these expectations intentionally or negligently, I must take reasonable steps to prevent others from suffering losses caused by the frustration of the expectations (Scanlon 1990, 204).

Clearly a large number of unauthorized migrants have acted under the assumption that they would be able to enter, live in, and work in the United

States (and similar claims could be made about, for instance, the UK.). How did they acquire this expectation? One important source is the supply of jobs made available to unauthorized migrants by employers who have taken advantage of the inexpensive labor. These employers in some cases intentionally hired unauthorized workers and in other cases might be considered negligent in failing to take substantial steps to avoid hiring them. Thus, we might hold these employers responsible for the expectations created by their decisions, but this responsibility doesn't seem on its face to be sufficient to justify regularization. It doesn't show that society as a *whole*, which includes many people who were heavily opposed to the employers' behavior, has an obligation to the migrants.

Defenders of the contract argument suggest that responsibility is more broadly shared because the government too has generated expectations in unauthorized migrants. Certainly, the migrants who entered must have assumed not only that they would be able to work on entry but also that they would be able to cross the border in the first place and would be able to work in the territory without getting deported. What expectations has the government created in unauthorized migrants? On the face of it, by formally outlawing their entry, the government has declared a strict policy of preventing them from entering and removing them if they do enter. But proponents of the contract argument point out that governments can create expectations through actions other than making laws. Most importantly for our purposes, governments not only make decisions about what laws to formally enact but also about whether and how to *enforce* those laws, and there can be reasons for and against enforcement beyond those that justified the initial enactment of the law. For instance, many theorists defend an "outlaw and forgive" approach to torture, under which torture is prohibited by statute under any and all circumstances, but in practice, officials who torture under special circumstances – where torture is necessary to prevent an enormous calamity – are acquitted when brought to trial (Gross 2003). This regime is attractive, the theorists claim, because it combines the expressive advantages of a blanket official prohibition on torture with the chance to use torture should it really be necessary. Whatever the merits of this proposal, it illustrates how enforcement decisions can be separated from enactment decisions. Outlaw and forgive is a distinct proposal, with distinct benefits and costs, from (let's call it) "outlaw and uniformly punish."

Proponents of the contract argument claim that whatever its official statutory stance on unauthorized migration, the US government has permitted an enormous amount of it, adopting an enforcement regime that is very limited and highly discretionary (Motomura 2014, 107–110; Rubio-Marín 2000, 83). For instance, in 2009 around 600,000 unauthorized migrants were arrested, which amounts to under 6 percent of the estimated total population of 11.2 million (Motomura 2014, 27). And many migrants who entered without authorization were ultimately able to gain, via the discretion of immigration officials, legal permission to remain (Motomura 2014, 22–25).

Furthermore, there are other steps the government can take – but the US government has in the past not really taken – to reduce unauthorized migration beyond simply enforcing immigration laws. In particular, it can try to alter the strong economic incentives behind unauthorized migration by preventing employers from hiring unauthorized migrants. There are programs intended to regulate employers in this way, but again enforcement has been quite limited: In 1998 only about 3 percent of employers of unauthorized migrants were investigated, and most of those investigations did not result in penalties (Andreas 2009, 101). Another way to change the economic incentives driving unauthorized migration would be to offer alternative, more closely regulated, routes for migrants to work in the United States, such as temporary worker programs, so that entering without authorization becomes less attractive. But legal entry has been all but impossible for the vast majority of unauthorized migrants (Motomura 2014, 42).

Has this limited enforcement, and the expectations it has created, been intentional or negligent on the part of the government (as would be required to assign responsibility to the government)? Here the empirics become rather less clear. Certainly there were strong incentives for the government and various interest groups to maintain a system of limited and discretionary enforcement rather than a policy of tightly regulated borders and mass deportations. Unauthorized migrants provide a supply of cheap labor that benefits employers and consumers, and they impose very little fiscal burden, given that they have no access to the welfare state. A system of highly discretionary enforcement can be also advantageous because it allows the government to engage in "*ex post* screening" – in choosing whom to ultimately allow to settle in the United States, the government can observe the behavior of people who have already been present in the territory for some period, including whether they have worked, committed crimes, and so on (Cox and Posner 2007, 835–844). This allows the government to make decisions with more information than it typically has about prospective immigrants who apply from outside of the territory, whose records with respect to work and criminality may be hard to acquire.

On the other hand, there are also some significant constraints – of both capacity and of morality – on the government's ability to act. In terms of capacity, enforcement is extremely expensive. The border between the United States and Mexico is 1,989 miles long, making it extremely difficult to patrol in its entirety. And huge sums have been devoted to enforcement, as discussed in Chapter 3. Moral constraints on the government's ability to act here include the importance of respecting anti-discrimination norms. For instance, even the limited attempts at enforcement against employers who hired unauthorized migrants were seen to create increased levels of discrimination against Latinx Americans and others, as employers racially profiled applicants in their attempt to avoid getting caught with unauthorized workers (Motomura 2014, 47). Avoiding such discrimination was surely a strong reason not to pursue any more extensive policing of employers. In sum, the government did face significant limitations, and, insofar as these dictated the government's enforcement priorities, it cannot be said that it intentionally or negligently encouraged unauthorized migrants to enter the territory or expect that they would be able to live and work there.

What is hard to say is whether overall the government made enforcement decisions mainly to reap the advantages of an unauthorized workforce or mainly because it deemed the costs, both financial and moral, to be excessive. It thus seems at least somewhat inconclusive whether the government acted deliberately or negligently in creating expectations in unauthorized migrants. And this means that the contract argument in its standard formulation is somewhat inconclusive: It remains somewhat unclear to what extent the government has incurred obligations to unauthorized migrants by inducing various expectations in them. We will see shortly, however, that there may be a way to salvage the argument by merging it with some elements of the contribution approach.

iii. The affiliation argument

The affiliation approach, you'll recall, seeks to base immigrant rights on the social ties that migrants develop to the host society. Picking up on this idea, some argue that unauthorized migrants ought to be granted the right to stay in the United States because they are, in some important sense, *already Americans*, their lives integrated with the nation despite being legally treated as non-members. In her book, *Just Like Us* (2009), Helen Thorpe follows the lives of three high school students who came into the United States without authorization. These teenagers, she emphasizes, grow up in a manner that should be familiar to any family in the United States: They study the same textbooks, have similar discussions about dating, attend the same churches, and so on. The differences between the lives of Thorpe's young women and those of other teenagers are largely because of their uncertain legal status – which means they must avoid certain kinds of interactions with the authorities, face different fees for college, and so on – not because of fundamentally different values or behaviors.

Carens (2013) uses connections of this kind to leverage an argument in favor of regularization. Given their *social membership* – their ties to American society – unauthorized migrants must also be granted full *political membership*, including all the rights of citizenship, especially the right to remain. Again, the case is especially strong in the case of unauthorized migrants who came to the territory as children and are likely to have developed especially strong ties to the only country they really know. But it also extends to people who came into unauthorized status as adults. The key (for reasons explained in Chapter 7) is the length of *time* the migrant has been in the country, since this is a good proxy, Carens claims, for how enmeshed in a society they have become.

But what if being unauthorized itself affects someone's degree of enmeshment in society? Given their vulnerable position, it is likely that unauthorized migrants are more tentative about involving themselves fully in social and associational life: They must avoid getting reported to the immigration authorities at all costs. This is plausible even if we accept Carens's important observation that if we are to avoid discriminating, "integration" must be understood in a capacious way that doesn't exclude ways of behaving that are outside of a (presumed) white, English-speaking norm: attending a Spanish-language church, playing mahjong, etc., must all count as ways of integrating. The point is that the precarious situation of unauthorized migrants gives them some reasons to avoid associating with *any* other people in *any* manner, given that just leaving the house and driving on the road might lead to arrest. In sum, just as time is likely a proxy for greater enmeshment, so too unauthorized status is likely a proxy for lesser.

Defenders of regularization will likely be disturbed by this possibility. There is something troubling about the implication that the difficult and uncertain conditions unauthorized migrants live in might be a basis for denying them certain rights: If anything, the fact that they often live under these conditions seems to be a reason to *grant* them rights. Later we will look at an argument, the autonomy argument, that tries to make good on this idea and emphasizes the instability unauthorized migrants must live with as a basis for regularization.

iv. The contribution argument

Unauthorized migrants typically make substantial contributions to the receiving society. They bolster the economy through their labor and support the government through their tax payments (including property, sales, and, often, income taxes). They also contribute in more informal ways to the culture, civil society, and so on of the country. And contributions – we saw in Chapter 6 – plausibly trigger requirements of *reciprocity*. As people who contribute to the host society, unauthorized migrants are, plausibly, owed something in return, perhaps including, as Williams (2009) argues, regularization.

We saw in Chapter 6 that the contribution approach has a general problem of explaining entitlements other than economic entitlements. This problem seems especially acute when we consider regularization. Why should paying taxes, or making any other kind of contribution, specifically entitle someone to *remain* in the country?

Suppose that a contractor has done extensive work for a club on its clubhouse. Justice requires that the contractor be properly remunerated for their work, but this obligation can be met by simply paying them the market value of their labor. The club is not required to *admit* them as a member. Similarly, someone might object that unauthorized migrants are owed only suitable compensation for their labor, not admission into the political community or a right to remain.

Here, defenders of regularization programs might usefully combine elements of the contract argument and the contribution argument. The contract argument, as we've seen, emphasizes the expectations that unauthorized migrants developed, but seems to flounder on the question of whether the state is *responsible* for those expectations. The contribution argument emphasizes how much the sacrifices of unauthorized migrants have *benefitted* receiving countries but seems to flounder on the question of whether those sacrifices must be compensated by a right to remain. In a combined approach, these benefits to, for example, the United States might be relied on to assign responsibility to the United States for the expectations of unauthorized workers. The United States has benefitted enormously not just from the work of migrants, but also from migrants developing the relevant expectations and planning their lives around those expectations. This plausibly is sufficient to make the United States responsible for the development of those expectations.

To see the force of this combination argument, consider the following example. Suppose that a country needs inexpensive low-skilled workers and to fill those jobs creates a new immigration program to bring in migrant laborers. The laborers fulfill the economic needs of the host country, providing work, taxes, and so on. After a time, though, the program becomes politically unpopular and is officially discontinued, despite still being highly advantageous to the receiving country. All the same, migrants continue to cross the border, work, and benefit the host state. This new state of affairs remains in place for many years, and successive generations of migrants continue to develop the expectation that they will be able to live and work in the host society.[5] Surely the host country ought not to ignore the fact that current migrants are playing the very same economic role previously occupied by people admitted under an official program. Specifically, it seems that the host country must accept some responsibility for the continued expectations of these migrants. And unauthorized migration in the United States is relevantly similar to that described in my example: It "operates … as a shadow guest-worker program in which millions of migrant workers enter and live in the country without formal permission" (Cox 2012, 57).

Now, some theorists, such as Pevnick (2011), will object that the contributions of unauthorized migrants are not morally relevant because the host country has not *consented* to the receipt of those benefits. I cannot, for instance, foist a cake on you that I have baked and then demand that you pay me for it. There are at least two replies to this objection. First, even as a matter of private law, it is sometimes possible for people to recover for benefits they bestow on others without those others formally accepting those benefits. The doctrine of unjust enrichment allows plaintiffs to sue for compensation (Birks 2005). This, assuming that said doctrine is well founded, means we might reject Pevnick's claim that in these private contexts involuntarily bestowed benefits cannot be a basis for entitlement. Second, and more importantly, it is not clear how relevant our intuitions about private contexts are to the question at hand. It is true that the host society does not formally consent to receiving any benefits from unauthorized migrants. But it is also true that many of the contributions individual citizens make to their broader society are not formally asked for or accepted by that society. The work that these citizens do, and the contributions that they thereby make to the economy, seem to form a basis for entitlement, even if they are not specifically asked to do it. Parity of treatment suggests that the contributions of unauthorized migrants should also be given moral weight.

v. The autonomy argument

The autonomy argument (Hosein 2014) takes a very different approach than the others that we have looked at. Rather than emphasizing things that migrants themselves have done to earn or become entitled to regularization – such as forming social bonds or making contributions – it instead emphasizes what the receiving society does *to the migrants*: exercising authority over them. As we saw in Chapter 6, the exercise of authority can be reconciled with respect for someone's autonomy – their ability to make and carry out plans for themselves – only if that authority is *cabined* in ways that leave space for someone to plan their lives around it and exercised in a manner that *supports* someone's autonomy by, for instance, providing them with the resources needed to carry out their plans.

How do these requirements relate to the right to remain? Consider someone who lives their entire life in a territory. First, the right to remain seems essential if authority is to be cabined in a manner that ensures individuals can plan around potential state sanctions, thus avoiding having the state suddenly interfere in their lives. Someone who lacks the right to remain has no protection from such state intervention. Being removed from the territory would be a very large change in the direction of one's life, and without the right to remain one cannot make plans that are secure from this potentially very large disruption.

Second, we can use the law to create for individuals a sphere in which they can act independently, secure from the interference of others. The right to remain is also essential if the law is to play this role. Consider again rights to resources, which enable individuals to commit certain objects to uses that will serve their long-term plans. Rights to resources are only able to play this role if individuals possess the right to remain. The plans people have for their property are typically territorially bound. For instance, suppose that I decide to build a temple for my community. My plans include both building the physical structure and helping to integrate it into the broader community. I will only be able to follow through on these plans if I am able to remain within the territory. If I am forced to leave, then I will be severely hindered in my ability to carry out these plans since it will be very difficult for me to oversee or participate in the building of the temple. And it will make it impossible for me to attend temple functions, ensure that they are run successfully, and so on. Many other plans that form part of ordinary lives are also territorially bound, as the example we just looked at suggests.

A right to remain seems essential for someone to exercise autonomy in a society, at least if they are there for a sufficiently long period of time. Someone who lacks that right, and is thus potentially deportable, is much more limited than others in their ability to make and carry out stable plans for their life: Uncertainty about where they will be in the future makes it very difficult to predict the conditions under which they will be pursuing any particular plan. And their ability to plan is also limited by the fact that they must always consider which courses of action might make deportation more likely.

Now, perhaps someone can live autonomously for a shorter period of time in a country without certainty about when they will have to leave. This person can be cautious about investing too much in long-term plans. But they can still make decisions about how to live and carry them out. They can make plans that are more short-term or "hedge their bets," making some plans contingent on their continued stay and others not. But to have to live like this for a long period of time – for ten years, say – seems incompatible with autonomy. Moreover, on the Autonomy View, the longer someone is in a territory, the more their life is shaped by the state's directives and thus the greater the responsibility the state has to support their autonomy. So, again, the length of time someone is present in a territory seems to matter.

Putting these pieces together, the autonomy argument says that since unauthorized migrants are subject to the state's authority, that authority must be exercised in a manner that respects their autonomy, and that includes granting them the right to remain.

vi. The anti-subordination argument

The anti-subordination approach says that a society of equals must reject the creation of *underclasses* in a society. Unauthorized migrants have often formed just such a class: viewed with widespread contempt, confined to poor-paying jobs or shut out of the workforce entirely, and often mistreated by state officials and by private individuals.

This means, anti-subordination theorists have argued, that unauthorized migrants must have certain rights, even if they are not entitled to be in the country. To deny them access to food stamps, for example, is to scar the nation with a significant group of people who live on the verge of starvation. As we saw earlier, the *Plyler* Supreme Court decision insisted that unauthorized children must have access to public education. To act otherwise is to create a "subclass of illiterates" who will become social pariahs, incapable of the most basic participation in society. A commitment to social equality constrains these policies.

How does this relate to the right to remain? The threat of deportation heavily affects the behavior of unauthorized migrants and how others treat them. We looked earlier at how it can result in the under-protection of the migrants' human rights. It also creates other social disabilities that are associated with underclass status. For example, the ability of other citizens to report the migrants to immigration authorities means that those citizens can mistreat the migrants with more limited repercussions (including forms of mistreatment that fall short of being human rights violations). For example, it means that people who hire the migrants are in a much stronger bargaining position and can thus exploit the migrants, garnishing their wages, paying them subsistence amounts, making them work under dangerous conditions, and so on. The threat of deportation also allows other citizens to look down at the migrants, who are always living in the shadows and must beg others for assistance. Thus, regularization can be used as a means of ensuring that the migrants do not continue to form an underclass.

One potential problem for this approach is how it deals with *responsibility*. Migrants who come into unauthorized status as children cannot be held responsible for this. And that point was a core part of the Court's reasoning in *Plyler*. It is clearly wrong to turn them into members of a pariah class for something they had no control over. But what about people who became unauthorized as adults? Can regularizing them be justified? This is harder to do. For instance, punishing criminals certainly disadvantages them relative to non-criminals, both in material terms and by stigmatizing them, but that *alone* doesn't seem to make them a morally problematic underclass. "Look," someone might say, "criminals are certainly a systematically disadvantaged group, but this doesn't give rise to a complaint of unjust treatment. Given that they have done wrong, it is fair for the state to deny benefits to them (and even inflict harms on them)."

Similarly, someone might say that (some) unauthorized migrants committed a wrong in violating immigration law. As such, the state may fairly treat them differently from citizens and other migrants, including by denying them a right to remain. And so denials of the right to remain would not be subordinating because they would not be unjust.

Fiss, in fact, accepts this suggestion. He agrees that unauthorized migrants have acted wrongly and that this means the state can fairly deny various rights to them. All the same, he says, their disadvantage sustains an objectionable form of society: a society of superiors and inferiors. And that can be troubling for reasons other than the migrants' own complaints of injustice: "We ought not to subjugate immigrants, not because we owe them anything, but to preserve our society as a community of equals." A society can be *bad* ("disfigure[d]"), Fiss suggests, even if it is not unfair and no individual is wronged (Fiss 1999, 17).

Is this position coherent? To subordinate a group is not simply to put them in a disadvantaged (or even systematically disadvantaged) position, but to do so *unjustly*. Mass killers who are given long prison sentences are thereby severely disadvantaged relative to other groups in society, but they are not thereby subordinated. So to accept that no injustice is done to unauthorized migrants by denying them the right to remain is, it seems, to also accept that they are not subordinated.

What if, as some of his remarks suggest, Fiss were to simply drop the claim that unauthorized immigrants are genuinely *subordinated* and say that there is all the same something unattractive about a society in which they are denied the right to remain. This way of thinking about regularization seems to imply that it would be a *good* policy to have, but all the same *optional* in some important sense. For instance, someone might say that a society in which there are relatively strong norms of politeness or courage is a *better* society, but the state would not do anyone an *injustice* by failing to substantially promote these norms and could set them aside for any number of other goals. So if we interpret Fiss's argument this way, then the values he appeals to can be overridden relatively easily by other considerations.

Here are three remaining paths that Fiss could take. First, consider the example of felons: While they have done wrong, we might still deny that this failing is sufficiently great to justify denying to them certain fundamental rights that they are owed as citizens. For instance, we might say that voting is a sufficiently strong entitlement that it would be unfair, because disproportionate, to deny that right to someone who has committed a felony. A parallel argument could be made that the right to remain is so important that its denial is far out of proportion to the wrong done by unauthorized migrants. But to make this argument more would need to be said about why exactly the right to remain is a very fundamental right, perhaps drawing on some of the arguments above, by emphasizing its costs for the immigrant's sense of self or their autonomy.

A second path for Fiss can also be seen by exploring the example of people who have committed crimes. Let's agree that since they have done a wrong against the state, the state has fewer obligations to these people than it does to other members of society and may thus fairly deny them certain benefits that it extends to others. There might still be a concern of justice about how these denials affect their relations with other individual members of society (and non-state institutions). For instance, these denials might leave them open to exploitation, abuse, or domination. Take, say, the stigma that follows former prison inmates who are trying to find work after being released. This puts them at a major disadvantage relative to other job seekers, and unscrupulous employers might decide to exploit this by offering them very one-sided conditions of employment.

The denial of certain rights to migrants may have a similar effect of enabling unjust relationships between individual members of society. For instance, the denial of an elementary education, as discussed in *Plyler*, surely puts someone in a very vulnerable position in society, their illiteracy and limited knowledge relative to others making them easy targets for fraud and so on. These interactions are not merely *unattractive*, but *unjust* and thus something a society is morally *required* to prevent. In the same vein, Fiss could argue that the right to remain is also crucial in protecting individuals from unjust treatment at the hands of other members of society. For example, as mentioned earlier, unauthorized migrants are frequently exploited in the labor market. Perhaps there are also more subtle and basic ways in which lacking a right to remain affects people's relationships with others. As the autonomy argument points out, lacking that right means someone must live constantly in a state of uncertainty, never able to fully commit to any particular plan or project. And maybe this instability is itself enough to severely disadvantage unauthorized migrants relative to other members of society and thus make them (all else being equal) the inferior partners in any relationship. Every time an unauthorized migrant attempts to pursue some project or other – whether it be work, or further study, or within an association – they must ensure themselves against the possibility that they won't be able to complete that project, and this means that they are inevitably disadvantaged and disempowered relative to others.

A third path for Fiss maintains that deportation is connected not only to the subordination of unauthorized immigrants but also of other members of society (including citizens, permanent residents, and so on) who share racial or ethnic commonalities with the immigrants. We saw earlier, in Chapter 3, how enforcement mechanisms have often involved racial profiling, especially of Latinx people, and how this can place burdens on members of that group. Amy Reed-Sandoval argues that in general "the problem of illegals" is in the popular consciousness often code for "the problem of Latinos," and that results in subordination of the latter group within US society. Given this association, Latinx people have to deal with suspicion that they may be unauthorized migrants and thus not entitled to work, education, and so on. And they also have to face the stigma that comes with being associated with unauthorized status and thus undesirability to the nation.

Now, it would be politically infeasible, and also produce unfairness, Reed-Sandoval suggests, for the state to cease all deportation of Latinx people (while still having some deportation of other groups). Instead, she proposes periodic amnesties. Would this be enough to solve the problems of Latinx stigma? We need to know how exactly the narrative of Latinx criminality interacts with the reality of deportation policy. Can we end the former with minimal changes in the latter? Or is having amnesties a necessary (though perhaps insufficient) step in changing the narrative?

C. Arguments against regularization

We have looked at various specific objections to the particular arguments for regularization offered above. We'll now turn to the most basic reasons critics of regularization reject it.

One way of defending deportation treats it as rectifying an injustice. A helpful metaphor here might be trespass. First, suppose that my car rolls onto your lawn. The proper response is for me to remove the car. You have a right that my car not be there, and so I should rectify the situation by making sure that my car is no longer there in violation of your rights. Similarly, suppose that I am on your lawn without your permission. Again, you have a right that I not be there. And to rectify this situation, I must remove myself. Finally, on this argument, deportation is to be thought of along similar lines. Removing someone from a territory is not (or not only) an attempt to punish them. The goal is to remove someone from a place where they are not supposed to be, just as we might move the car. Moreover, defenders of deportation often say, to fail to deport is to violate the "rule of law." One aspect of the rule of law is that legal rules ought to be consistently and impartially enforced, and according to these authors, such as Kobach (2007), failing to remove unauthorized migrants makes an unjustified exception for them while other people in society who commit infractions are made to bear the costs of restitution.

How might those who endorse regularization respond to this argument? Let's look at a few options. First, those who rely on the humanitarian argument might emphasize that even where an infraction is committed that doesn't mean restitution of some particular kind should always be required, especially where less harmful options are available. For example, suppose that someone fraudulently gains admission to a hospital (perhaps he lies about his medical insurance) and is now receiving crucial medical care. Even though he is not supposed to be there, it seems problematic for the hospital to immediately cease care and put him out on the street if it is going to leave him in serious jeopardy. It seems especially problematic to do this if there is another way for the hospital to recover its costs later (perhaps the person's son will later be able to help pay for most of the treatment received). Similarly, it might be said, the cost of removal is very great for unauthorized migrants who have been present for a substantial period of time, especially those who entered as minors, and so it would be wrong to remove them, even if they have no moral right to remain. Just as the hospital could try to recover its costs later, so too, it might be said, there are ways for the state to seek restitution that don't require inflicting the damage of deportation. For example, it could ask migrants to pay a fine before being regularized. In response, it might be argued that the costs of unauthorized migration cannot be properly offset through cash payments, since they involve effects on culture or self-governance. Here, then, we need to think about what exactly counts as a morally significant form of cost to the host state and the extent to which unauthorized migrants in fact create costs of this kind.

Affiliation theorists can respond to the critics of regularization in a different way. On their approach, one can say that as time goes by the relationship between migrants, on the one hand, and the receiving society and state, on the other, evolves in a manner that makes the migrant no longer "in the wrong place."

"The moral right of states to apprehend and deport irregular [unauthorized] migrants erodes with the passage of time," Carens writes. "As irregular migrants become more and more settled, their membership in society grows in moral importance, and the fact that they have settled without authorization becomes correspondingly less relevant" (Carens 2013, 150). To compare, suppose that someone enters a community of some kind – a club, a society, a neighborhood group – under somewhat false presences. Perhaps, for example, they misrepresent their previous experience of running a group in order to gain admission. What should happen if, after a few years, the person's initial misrepresentation is discovered? Some will say that it doesn't really matter that much – if the person has developed important relationships with the other members – becoming friendly with them, sharing responsibilities in their group, and so on – then they have become full-fledged members of the community, and it would be wrong to expel them. Perhaps the initial lie is a cause for upset, but the more time goes by the less relevant it is. If that's right, then perhaps similar reasoning applies to unauthorized migrants.

But maybe for some people the analogy cuts the other way. For example, suppose we are talking about a writers' society, whose goal is to bring together people who already have a significant publication record. If it turns out that someone's purported work was largely plagiarized, then the society may well think it is acceptable to expel this person, even if they have been a member for a long time.

We might wonder, then, whether there is anything special about the state that prohibits expulsion even though other organizations may have a broader right to expel. The autonomy view proposes such a difference: The state distinctively exercises authority, and thus control, over people. This means that however the person entered the territory it is important for the state to be able to render that control compatible with respect for individual autonomy. And, for the reasons given above, this means making sure that person is able, in the long run, to plan their life around the law and have it work to support their autonomy. This view can provide an especially strong response to Kobach's objection to regularization: that it violates the rule of law. For on the autonomy view regularization is itself demanded by one of the central values that the rule of law is there to project: the ability of people to plan their lives around the law (see the discussion of the rule of law in Chapter 6). Rather than violating the rule of law, regularization is supported by some of the very reasons we care about the rule of law in the first place.

Anti-subordination theorists will take a different tack. On that approach, what matters is not fundamentally whether a particular migrant is entitled or not to be in the country, but whether the use of deportation to remove unauthorized migrants will create a substantial underclass in society as a whole. Inequality is still a scar on a society, even if the state violates no individual rights in creating it. Now, those who favor deportation sometimes say that in fact it is a good way to *block* the existence of a migrant underclass, since the fewer unauthorized migrants there are, the fewer people there are that are vulnerable to exploitation because of their unauthorized status. In response, it can be said that while deportation may remove some unauthorized migrants, those who remain will be especially vulnerable, and it can also be pointed out that (as mentioned above) the treatment of unauthorized migrants often has repercussions for other members of society who are ethnically similar to the migrants.

Chapter summary

In this chapter, we looked at the rights of unauthorized migrants. We began by looking at some methodological issues around whether there is a "neutral" terminology within which to discuss these migrants. We then considered their human rights and saw that there are special difficulties with making sure that those rights are protected, given the precarious position of unauthorized migrants. In the remainder of the chapter, we focused on the right to remain and how different theories of migrant rights might support a regularization program. Lastly, we looked at how those theories might respond to the objection that regularization programs violate the rule of law.

Notes

1 "Progressive" and "conservative" are of course very crude labels here. Historically, there have been many "progressive"-identifying people who have resisted immigration on grounds of its effects on domestic workers, and many "conservative"-identifying people who have pushed for much expanded immigration, as well as amnesties, such as the libertarians discussed in Chapter 1.

2 See p. 4 of the following report: https://transequality.org/sites/default/files/docs/usts/USTS-Executive-Summary-Dec17.pdf.

3 For a survey of different varieties of program, see Levinson (2005).

4 It might be that some of the actions mentioned here are justified not (just) by humanitarian duties, but also by duties of justice, such as the *non-refoulement* requirement discussed in Chapter 5. If so, then there is all the more reason to distinguish these commonly accepted duties from those of humanitarianism.

5 This stylized example is in fact quite similar to the actual history of the United States, in which the workers initially supplied through the official Bracero program ultimately came to be replaced by unauthorized migrants (Ngai 2004, 127–167).

References

Andreas, Peter. 2009. *Border Games: Policing the US-Mexico Divide*. 2nd ed. Ithaca, NY: Cornell University Press.

Birks, Peter. 2005. *Unjust Enrichment*. 2nd ed. New York: Oxford University Press.

Blake, Michael. 2001. "Distributive Justice, State Coercion, and Autonomy." *Philosophy and Public Affairs* 30, no. 3 (July): 257–296.

Blake, Michael. 2010. "Equality without Documents: Political Justice and the Right to Amnesty." In "*Justice and Equality*" (Supplementary Volume 36). Supplement, *Canadian Journal of Philosophy* 40, no. S1: 99–122.

Bosniak, Linda. 2006. *The Citizen and the Alien: Dilemmas of Contemporary Membership*. Princeton, NJ: Princeton University Press.

Carens, Joseph H. 2013. *The Ethics of Immigration*. New York: Oxford University Press.

Cox, Adam B. 2012. "Enforcement Redundancy and the Future of Immigration Law." *Supreme Court Review*, 31–65.

Cox, Adam B., and Eric A. Posner. 2007. "The Second-Order Structure of Immigration Law." *Stanford Law Review* 59, no. 4 (February): 809–856.

Fiss, Owen. 1999. "The Immigrant as Pariah." In *A Community of Equals: The Constitutional Protection of New Americans*, edited by Joshua Cohen and Joel Rogers, 3–21. Boston: Beacon Press.

Gordon, Ian, Kathleen Scanlon, Tony Travers, and Christine Whitehead. 2009. "Economic Impact on the London and UK Economy of an Earned Regularisation of Irregular Migrants to the UK." GLA Economics, Greater London Authority, May. http://www.lse. ac.uk/geographyAndEnvironment/research/london/pdf/irregular%20migrants%20full% 20report.pdf.

Gross, Oren. 2003. "Chaos and Rules: Should Responses to Violent Crises Always Be Constitutional?" *Yale Law Journal* 112, no. 5 (March): 1011–1134.

Hosein, Adam Omar. 2014. "Immigration: The Argument for Legalization." *Social Theory and Practice* 40, no. 4 (October): 609–630.

Kobach, Kris W. 2007. "Reinforcing the Rule of Law: What States Can and Should Do to Reduce Illegal Immigration." *Georgetown Immigration Law Journal* 22, no. 3 (Spring): 459–483.

Krogstad, Jens Manuel, and Jeffrey S. Passel. 2015. "5 Facts about Illegal Immigration in the U.S." *Fact Tank* (blog), Pew Research, November 19, 2015. http://www.pewresearch. org/fact-tank/2015/11/19/5-facts-about-illegal-immigration-in-the-u-s.

Levinson, Amanda. 2005. "The Regularisation of Unauthorized Migrants: Literature Survey and Country Case Studies." Centre on Migration, Policy and Society (COMPAS), Oxford University. https://www.compas.ox.ac.uk/media/ER-2005-Regularisa tion_Unauthorized_Literature.pdf.

Motomura, Hiroshi. 2006. *Americans in Waiting: The Lost Story of Immigration and Citizenship in the United States*. New York: Oxford University Press.

Motomura, Hiroshi. 2014. *Immigration Outside the Law*. New York: Oxford University Press.

Ngai, Mae M. 2004. *Impossible Subjects: Illegal Aliens and the Making of Modern America*. Princeton, NJ: Princeton University Press.

Pevnick, Ryan. 2011. *Immigration and the Constraints of Justice: Between Open Borders and Absolute Sovereignty*. New York: Cambridge University Press.

Pevnick, Ryan. 2014. "The Ethics of Immigration Symposium: The Theory of Social Membership." *Crooked Timber* (blog), May 27, 2014. http://crookedtimber.org/2014/05/ 27/the-ethics-of-immigration-symposium-the-theory-of-social-membership.

Rawls, John. 1999. *A Theory of Justice*. Rev. ed. Cambridge, MA: Belknap Press of Harvard University Press.

Reed-Sandoval, Amy. 2015. "Deportations as Theaters of Inequality." *Public Affairs Quarterly* 29, no. 2 (April): 201–215.

Rubio-Marín, Ruth. 2000. *Immigration as a Democratic Challenge: Citizenship and Inclusion in Germany and the United States*. New York: Cambridge University Press.

Scanlon, T. M. 1990. "Promises and Practices." *Philosophy and Public Affairs* 19, no. 3 (Summer): 199–226.

Sunstein, Cass R. 1994. "The Anticaste Principle." *Michigan Law Review* 92, no. 8 (August): 2410–2455.

Thorpe, Helen. 2009. *Just Like Us: The True Story of Four Mexican Girls Coming of Age in America*. New York: Scribner.

US Department of Homeland Security. 2016. "Fiscal Year 2016: Budget-in-Brief." http://
www.dhs.gov/sites/default/files/publications/FY_2016_DHS_Budget_in_Brief.pdf.

Valdez, Inés. 2016. "Punishment, Race, and the Organization of U.S. Immigration Exclusion." *Political Research Quarterly* 69, no. 4 (December): 640–654.

Williams, Reginald. 2009. "Illegal Immigration: A Case for Residency." *Public Affairs
Quarterly* 23, no. 4 (October): 309–323.

Further reading

Carens, Joseph H. 2013. *The Ethics of Immigration*. New York: Oxford University Press,
Chapt.7.

Cohen, Elizabeth F. 2015. "The Political Economy of Immigrant Time: Rights, Citizenship
and Temporariness in the post-1965 Era." Polity 47. no. 3: 337–351.

Hosein, Adam Omar. 2014. "Immigration: The Argument for Legalization." *Social Theory
and Practice* 40, no. 4 (October): 609–630.

Motomura, Hiroshi. 2014. *Immigration Outside the Law*. New York: Oxford University
Press, especially Chapter 6.

Reed-Sandoval, Amy. 2015. "Deportations as Theaters of Inequality." *Public Affairs Quarterly* 29, no. 2 (April): 201–215.

Index

Abizadeh, Arash 15
affiliation approach 149–152, 152–160 *passim*, 168, 172, 187–188, 195
Afghanistan 136
Africa 9, 41, 135; North Africa 103, 182; sub-Saharan 17; *see also* Organization for African Unity (OAU); *see also specific countries*
African American people 28, 55n4, 76, 98, 100; *see also* black people
Agamben, Giorgio 138
agricultural workers *see* workers, agricultural
Algeria 30
Aliverti, Ana 61, 69
"anchor babies" 96
anti-subordination approach 158–160, 167, 171–173, 191–194, 196–197
apartheid (South Africa) 85
Appiah, Kwame Anthony 41, 83–84
Arendt, Hannah 138
Arizona 66
Armenia 119
Asian immigrants 74, 83–84, 95–96
asylum: camps for seekers of 138; climate change and 133–135; country responsible for 136; determination of status 68, 125, 131, 138; dissidents and 131; domestic violence and 123; in Germany 117; interviews 61; laws on 141; need for 66, 131–132; non-arrival schemes and 136; political backlash and 124, 125–126; refugee status and 117–118; Syrian applicants for 117; transgender applicants for 142n5; in the United Kingdom 123, 124
Australia 4, 70, 83–85, 106, 135, 136; White Australia 83–85
autonomy approach 154–155, 156–160 *passim*, 161n4, 168, 171–172, 188, 190–191, 193, 194, 196

Barbados 88, 93
Beitz, Charles 130, 142n2
Betts, Alexander 139–141
Bhagwati tax 53–54
biology and race 83–84, 86–87, 88, 100
black people 74–75, 85–86, 95; *see also* African American people
Blake, Michael 32n3, 49–54, 55n5, 63, 69, 85–87, 91, 154, 183
border guards 5, 9, 15, 58–61, 66–67, 73–74, 77
Border Industrialization Project (BIP) 25–27
border zones 77
Bosniak, Linda 180–181
Bracero Program 163, 197n5
brain drain 10, 30, 52–54
Brazil 4
Brignoni-Ponce, United States v. (1975) 73–74
Brock, Gillian 52–54
Burundi 41, 93
Bush, George W. 74

California 40, 74, 95–96
camps *see* refugee camps
Canada 5, 105; Quebec 103–104; Supreme Court 109
capabilities approach 127–128
Carens, Joseph: on border enforcement 15; on duties to residents 173; on economic rights 167–168; on employment rights 169–170, 173; on fairness 12, 14, 173; on family ties 22, 183; on freedom of contract 23; on freedom of movement 18–19, 21; on human rights 147, 180, 181; on membership and enmeshment 147, 150, 151–152, 156, 157, 183, 187, 188, 195–196; on poverty 16; on refugees 126; on sovereignty 36; on temporary worker programs 175, 176n3; on terminology 179
Caribbean 88

Fortuyn, Pim 102
Foster, Bill 71
France 19, 30–31, 102, 106
freedom of association 51, 65, 71; as argument
  for closed borders 44–49
freedom of contract: as argument for open
  borders 23–25
freedom of movement: as argument for open
  borders 18–23; refugees and 137–141
freedom of religion *see* religion, freedom of
French language 103

genocide 119
Germany: Alternative for Germany (AfD)
  117; Aussiedlung 86–88, 103; Basic Law
  101; Bundestag 117; family ties 106;
  federalism in 37; guest workers
  (Gastarbeiter) 163, 166; identity 101;
  selection for admission 83, 86–88, 103;
  speech rights in 36; as subject of this
  book 4; Syrian refugees 117; Turkish
  immigrants 166
Ghana 52
Gibney, Matthew 3, 118, 124, 136
global North 117, 135–136
global South 23
Gove, Michael 37
guards *see* border guards
guest workers *see* workers, guest

Habermas, Jürgen 100
Hague, William 124
Haiti 31, 101, 104
Hansen, Randall 37, 44
Harvard University 87
Hawaii, Trump v. (2018) 90–93
health care workers *see* workers, health care
Hing, Bill Ong 74
"Hispanic countries" 86
HIV (Human Immunodeficiency Virus) 99
Holocaust 36, 87, 117, 120
home countries *see* sending countries
homogeneity 41–42, 44, 84, 86
Hong Kong 70, 164
Honohan, Iseult 107, 109–112
household workers *see* workers, household
humanitarian approach 15–18, 119–120,
  121, 123, 133, 141, 182–184, 195,
  197n4
human rights 61–63, 180–181; capabilities
  approach and 127–128; concept of
  127–132; family and 106, 112, 172;
  institutionalist approach and 128–132; as
  limits on enforcement 61–63, 172, 181;
  migrant rights based on 147, 148, 150,

172; protections for residents and 49;
  refugees and 131–132; right to nationality
  and 127; temporary worker programs and
  166–167, 172; unauthorized migrants and
  178, 180–181, 192, 197
Human Rights Watch 62, 166–167
Hungary 136
hunger *see* food insecurity

Immigration Act of 1990 (IMMACT) 97
INS, Nguyen v. (2001) 94
*Immigration Appeal Tribunal and another, ex
  parte Shah, R. v.* (1999) 123
India 88, 101, 163
indigenous peoples 5, 91, 103, 151; First
  Nations 5; Kurdish 151; Maori 103; Native
  American 151
Indonesia 163, 164
inequality: caste-like systems and 28, 76, 78n7,
  158–159, 173–174; economic 14, 28, 32,
  174; fairness and 12–14, 32n4, 74–75,
  158–160, 196; global 5, 27, 29; race
  and 28, 74–75, 158–160; redressing of
  14, 55
inferiority and superiority *see* subordination
institutionalist approach 128–132, 142n2
International Covenant on Civil and Political
  Rights 62
International Refugee Organization (IRO) 120
intersectionality 95–99
intranational movement 18–21, 135
investment: foreign investment 22, 25–30, 139;
  personal investment 152, 153; public
  investment 24, 44
Iran 90, 135
Iraq 92, 117, 126, 136
Ireland 40–43
Islam 90–93; *see also* Muslims
Islamic State 92
Islam, Shahanna Sadiq 123
Israel 87, 89
Italy 83

Jamaica 10, 163
Jewish people 18, 20, 87, 89, 117
Jim Crow era 28
Johnson-Reed Act 84–85
Joppke, Christian 83, 86
Jordan 10, 117, 139–140
Jordan v. De George (1951) 148
Juarez 60, 74

Kennedy, John F. 14
Khatoon, Syeda 123
Kurdish people 151